The Egypt Code

For Michele . . .

Also by Robert Bauval

Secret Chamber
The Orion Mystery (with Adrian Gilbert)
Keeper of Genesis (with Graham Hancock)
The Mars Mystery (with Graham Hancock and John Grigsby)
Talisman (with Graham Hancock)

The Egypt Code

Robert Bauval

Century · London

Published by Century in 2006

1 3 5 7 9 10 8 6 4 2

Copyright © Robert Bauval 2006

First published in the United Kingdom in 2006 by Century
The Random House Group Limited
20 Vauxhall Bridge Road, London, SW1V 2SA

Random House Australia (Pty) Limited
20 Alfred Street, Milsons Point, Sydney
New South Wales 2061, Australia

Random House New Zealand Limited
18 Poland Road, Glenfield
Auckland 10, New Zealand

Random House South Africa (Pty) Limited
Isle of Houghton, Corner of Boundary Road & Carse O'Gowrie
Houghton 2198, South Africa

Random House Publishers India Private Limited
301 World Trade Tower, Hotel Intercontinental Grand Complex
Barakhamba Lane, New Delhi 110 001, India

The Random House Group Limited Reg. No. 954009

www.randomhouse.co.uk

A CIP catalogue record for this book is available from the British Library

Papers used by Random House are
natural, recyclable products made from wood grown in
sustainable forests. The manufacturing processes conform to
the environmental regulations of the country of origin

ISBN 0712619518
ISBN-13 9780712619516

Typeset by SX Composing DTP, Rayleigh, Essex
Printed and bound in Great Britain by
William Clowes Ltd, Beccles, Suffolk

Academic Praise for *The Orion Correlation Theory*

'The theory known as "The Orion correlation theory" was first proposed by Robert Bauval in his bestseller *The Orion Mystery*. According to this theory the disposition of the three Giza pyramids was inspired by the disposition in the sky of the three stars of Orion's belt, a constellation connected to Osiris (and therefore to the after-world) which was extremely important to the Egyptians as attested in the Pyramid Texts. And although the validity of this theory is still disputed, it is at present the most convincing hypothesis aimed to explain the enigmatic and clearly not due to the simple chance disposition of the Giza pyramids.'
Dr Giulio Magli, Professor of Applied Mathematics at Milano Politecnico

'I am very much in agreement with your (Bauval's) contention that the stars in Orion's belt were an important element in the orientation of the Great Pyramid. I think you (Bauval) have made out a very convincing case that the two other pyramids were also influenced by it.'
Sir I.E.S. Edwards, CMG, CBE, FBA, Curator of the Egyptian Antiquities Department (1947–74), British Museum

'Mr Bauval has performed an important service in giving it (the Orion Correlation Theory) an airing. I've no doubt it will be criticised. It's bound to be. Such things are when they start.'
Sir I.E.S. Edwards, CMG, CBE, FBA, Curator of the Egyptian Antiquities Department (1947–74), British Museum

'I have known Mr Bauval for many years and I have taken an interest in his astronomical studies insofar as they are related to the Giza pyramids. In my opinion he has made a number of interesting discoveries and I believe more are likely to come.'
Sir I.E.S. Edwards, CMG, CBE, FBA, Curator of the Egyptian Antiquities Department (1947–74), British Museum

'I was deeply interested in your recent presentations on astronomy in relation to the Pyramid Texts. You have shown the important role the three stars of Orion's belt have had to the ancient Egyptians, especially attested in the south shafts in the King's Chamber (of the Great Pyramid) as well as the important deliberate alignment of the three pyramids of Giza.'

Jean Kerisel, Professeur Honoraire à l'Ecole Nationale des Ponts et Chaussées, President des Ingénieurs et Scientifiques de France

Contents

All reasonable effort has been made to obtain official permissions to
reproduce some of the above illustrations. Credit and thanks go to:
Anne-Sophie Bomhard (Illus. 4); reproduced with the kind
permission of David Jeffreys (Illus. 6); reproduced with the kind
permission of IFAO (Illus. 7 & 8); reproduced with the kind
permission of SFE and Sylvie Cauville (Illus. 9); Ron Wells (Illus. 10
& 11); EES (Illus. 12).

Acknowledgements

During the last 25 years my quest has been to bring to life again the old sky religion of Egypt and to show how it inspired the Egyptians to turn their land into an 'image of heaven'. I published the initial results of my findings in 1994 in *The Orion Mystery* which received the backing of the BBC 2 Everyman documentary *The Great Pyramid: Gateway to the Stars*. In the course of the next few years three other books on the sky-religion of Egypt were to follow. *The Egypt Code* is the culmination of my quarter-century of research, and I therefore decided to write it on location. In February 2005 I moved into a rented apartment in the leafy suburb of Hadayek El Ahram, less than a kilometre from the Giza Pyramids. Armed with a good desktop computer with DSL Internet connection, and also a wide selection of Egyptological books and articles, I spent the next eight months putting into book form the research material that I had compiled over the many years while in the UK. Writing this genre of non-fiction is not an easy task, but thankfully I was constantly inspired by the sight of the Great Pyramid from my office window. I am not sure how one can thank an inert mass of stone that stares implacably at you all day and all night. But somehow I feel a strange sense of gratitude towards it.

I would like to also thank the many colleagues and friends who have helped me throughout my quest. My foremost thanks go to my wife, Michele, for her enduring patience, her tolerance and her unflinching support. It is not easy to live with a man whose mind is partly in ancient Egypt. Thanks also to my two wonderful children, Candice and Jonathan, and to the former for making me in the course of researching this book a proud grandfather. I am grateful, too, to my brother Jean-Paul, my twin sister Thérèse, and my mother Yvonne for always being there when I needed them. I also thank the astronomers Mary Brück (Edinburgh), Archie Roy (Glasgow), John Brown (Astronomer Royal for Scotland), Chandra Wickramasinghe (Cardiff), Percy Seymour (Plymouth) and Giulio Magli (Milan), for their collegial interest and their constructive criticism. The authors Graham Hancock (Bath), Colin Wilson (Devon), Ahmed Osman (London), John Gordon (Surrey), Michael Baigent (Bath), Robert Lomas (Bradford), Yuri Stoyanov (Jerusalem), Timothy Freke (Glastonbury) and John West (New York), for their friendship and helpful advice. My friends Mohamad Nazmy (Giza), Hoda Hakim (Cairo), Roger Bilboul (London), Chafik and Racha Kotry (Alexandria), Mohamad and Nayra Ezzat (Alexandria), John and Josette Orphanidis (Athens), Gouda Fayed (Giza, Nazlet El Salman), Javier and Eva Sierra (Malaga), Adriano Forgione (Rome), Arianna Mendo (Torino), Sandro Mainardi (Florence), Roel Oostra (Hilversum), Andrea and Patrizia Vitussi (Trieste), Deborah Signoretti (Rome), Marilena Lancetti (Bologna), Linda and Max Bauval (Hawaii), Robert Berube (Quebec), Mark Scurry (Melbourne), and also Ihab, Methat, Hattem, Emile, Inas, Alia, Ahmed, Fathi, Shereen, Sameh and all the other people of Quest Travel, for their love, their much appreciated Egyptian warmth and their good humour. I want to express my deep debt of gratitude to my literary agents Bill Hamilton and Sara Fisher of A.M. Heath & Co. Ltd., who have always been there to encourage and advise me, and to listen to my enthusiastic rambles without revealing the dolorous feeling that I surely must often cause them. The same gratitude also goes to my editor and friend Mark Booth and Timothy Andrews at Century Books, Random House, for their patience and invaluable help. Finally I give thanks to all my readers, old and new, and hope that *The Egypt Code* will be as rewarding for them to read as it was for me to write.

Robert G. Bauval
Cairo, The Pyramids, October 2005

Introduction

What are the pyramids for?!!

Emma Freud, BBC 2 Everyman documentary *The Great Pyramid: Gateway to the Stars*, December 1993

This king is Osiris, this pyramid of this king is Osiris, this construction of his is Osiris . . .

Pyramid Texts, 1,657

Behold, he has come as Orion, Osiris has come as Orion . . .

Pyramid Texts, 820

Cosmic Ambience

What are Egypt's Old Kingdom pyramids for? What possible purpose could they have had? Why do they have low tunnels, long, narrow shafts leading nowhere, and corridors, galleries and chambers that are stark and empty? Why were they astronomically aligned to the stars? Why are they scattered in clusters along a 40-kilometre strip of desert? And, more intriguingly, why are some devoid of texts while others have their walls fully covered with texts that speak of the cycles of the sun and the stars? Until very recently the standard theory dished out by Egyptologists was that the pyramids were tombs, large sepulchres principally meant to house the bodies of dead kings. As for their elaborate internal systems of tunnels, shafts, corridors and chambers, these were intended mainly to confuse and outsmart tomb-robbers, while their astronomical alignments were either meaningless or just a fluke. Amazingly, such views went mostly unchallenged for nearly two centuries, this in spite of the maddening detail that no body of a king (not a skeleton or skull or even a bone splinter) was ever found inside a pyramid, or, for that matter, outside it. And more maddening still, no one had an explanation for why, if they were tombs, these pyramids were not placed in a single well-defined cemetery instead of being scattered over small clusters in a vast desert plain west of the River Nile like strange volcanic islands in a sea of sand. Yet, oddly enough, the clues that suggested a much higher purpose than just tombs were plentiful and always there for all to see and evaluate. And these clues screamed of a connection with the stars. For example:

1. The base of each pyramid was aligned to the astronomical directions using star alignments.
2. The largest of the pyramids contained air shafts oriented towards important star systems such as Orion, Sirius and the circumpolar constellations (namely the pyramid of Khufu at Giza).
3. Pyramids were given 'star' names or names implicit of stars ('The Pyramid of Djedefre is a sehedu star'; 'Nebka is a star'; 'Horus is the Star at the Head of the Sky' and so forth).
4. Pyramids had chamber ceilings decorated with five-pointed stars (namely the Step Pyramid and Fifth and Sixth Dynasty pyramids at Saqqara).
5. Pyramids contained writings carved on the inside walls that spoke of a star religion and the destiny of kings in a starry world called Duat which contained Orion and other constellations (namely the Fifth and Sixth Dynasty pyramids at Saqqara).

It is therefore somewhat odd, not to say perverse, that with so many 'stellar' connections there has not been a single Egyptologist who was sufficiently compelled to consider a stellar function for the pyramids. And because this important matter was left uninvestigated for so long, it is not surprising that untrained researchers, dilettantes, cranks and charlatans have dished out theories that range from the derisory to the completely insane. The pyramids were built by the lost civilisation of Atlantis; they were built by a lost technology using levitation; they were power plants; they were electromagnetic receivers for interstellar communications; they were built by aliens; they were built by the Jews while in captivity in Egypt; the Great Pyramid was designed to contain detailed information of the world's history and future in every inch of its plan; it was a Bible in stone. So when I burst on the scene in 1994 with my first book, *The Orion Mystery*, showing that the pattern of the three Giza pyramids and their relative position to the Nile mirrors the pattern of the three stars of Orion's belt and their relative position to the Milky Way, the subject was so much soiled and degraded that any new theory that mentioned the stars or astronomy was immediately met with a barrage of academic indifference (at best) or vociferous opposition. The reaction was even more violent because my theory had received the backing – albeit cautious – of one of the world's most eminent and respected Egyptologists, Sir I.E.S. Edwards, who had gallantly and boldly stuck his neck out on my behalf by appearing on a BBC documentary in support of some of my ideas. This brought him the wrath of his peers but it nonetheless twisted their arms and forced some to grudgingly review my theory. But in the years that followed, and especially after Edwards's death in 1996, I was derided and pilloried by a cabal of Egyptologists and other 'experts' seemingly determined to debunk the Orion Correlation Theory, as my hypothesis was now being called (see Appendix 3). All this academic onslaught was most daunting and distressing, but I held my ground, for I knew that not only had I generated massive interest and support among the general public and the international media, but that the theory I had proposed neatly dovetailed into the context of Egypt's Pyramid Age and provided the 'missing link' to an otherwise baffling mystery. Even the most entrenched sceptic could not easily dismiss the Orion–Giza Correlation as 'coincidence'.

Twelve long years have now passed since the publication of *The Orion Mystery*. In the meantime the book has been published in more than twenty languages and there have been dozens of television documentaries fully or partially based on the Orion Correlation

Theory (on Britain's BBC 2 and Channel 4; America's ABC, NBC and FOX TV; Europe and America's Discovery Channel and History Channel; Italy's RAI 3; Germany's ZDF and ARD; France's ARTE and TF3; South Africa's SABC and M-net TV; Holland's AVRO TV; Australia's Channel 7; Egypt's NILE-TV and many other channels in the Far East and Middle East). Two more documentaries are forthcoming, one with National Geographic Television titled *Unsolved Mysteries of the Pyramids*[1] (where my theory will be critically reviewed), and another made for Italy's RAI 2 and Holland's AVRO fully based on *The Egypt Code*.[2] Slowly but surely the Orion Correlation Theory has crept, like a thief in the night, into mainstream Egyptology and the new discipline of archaeoastronomy. And even though it is given much criticism, it is very obvious that it has touched the proverbial nerve of academia.

To be fair, not all academics were prone to dismiss *The Orion Mystery*. Some very eminent Egyptologists, such as Dr Jaromir Malek of the Griffith Institute and the American Egyptologist Dr Ed Meltzer, kept an open mind in the same fashion as the late Sir I.E.S. Edwards had done. More refreshingly, the theory received cautious support from the astronomical community, particularly from Professor Archie Roy of Glasgow University, Professor Mary Brück of Edinburgh University, Professor Giulo Magli of Milan Politecnico, Professor Percy Seymour of Plymouth University and Professor Chandra Wickramasinghe of Cardiff University. Even though these high-ranking astronomers maintained a healthy scepticism, they nonetheless found the theory intriguing and deserving of careful consideration and further research. Also in the course of the years a crack began to appear in the Egyptological academic armour when Dr Jaromir Malek (who had reviewed my theory in 1994 in the Oxford journal *Discussions in Egyptology*)[3] declared himself favourable to the possibility that the apparently illogical scattering of pyramids in the Memphite necropolis (a 40-kilometre-long desert strip west of the Nile near Cairo) might, after all, have had more to do with 'religious, astronomical or similar' considerations than with purely practical considerations such as the topography and geology of the land. Similar views began to be heard throughout Egyptology, especially by the

American Mark Lehner, the Czech Miroslav Verner and David Jeffreys in Britain (see Chapter 3). It was, however, the archaeo-astronomer Anthony Aveni, a professor of astronomy and anthropology at Colgate University, who, in my view, would come closest to providing an overall picture of what might have been in the minds of the ancient architects who designed and planned such mysterious structures (not only in Egypt but in other parts of the ancient world) when he wrote that

> In order to understand what ancient people thought about the world around them, we must begin by witnessing phenomena through their eyes. A knowledge of each particular culture is necessary, but learning what the sky contains and how each entity moves is also indispensable . . . strange but true: whole cities, kingdoms and empires were founded based on observations and interpretations of natural events that pass undetected under our noses and above our heads.[4]

Dr Aveni was referring to the Maya and Inca civilisations when he made the above statement. But he may as well have been talking about Egypt's Old Kingdom, for I am now even more convinced that such a statement holds true for the sacred cities, pyramids and temples built by the ancient Egyptians all along the 1,000-kilometre-long Nile Valley during their 3,000 years of civilisation. And this, in a nutshell, is what I set out to prove in *The Egypt Code*.

By the year 2000 I was ready to put the findings of my investigations into book form. To this end I presented a synopsis to my editor at Random House in London, who promptly commissioned the project. By early 2004 I had a first draft ready. The final draft, however, was completed in Egypt. Being there gave me the unique opportunity to refine the book with a hands-on approach to the pyramids in Lower Egypt and the great temples of Upper Egypt, and to verify and test the various ideas of my thesis. Imbued with the enchantment and magic of these ancient sites, I have, I believe, succeeded in more ways than one in bringing the sky–ground correlation theory I started two decades ago to its natural conclusion.

In *The Egypt Code* I have made use of primary sources whenever available, and relied only on scholarly research published in peer-reviewed journals or in textbooks by renowned Egyptologists and other scholars. Culling my data from all these sources, I have come to this conclusion: the ancient Egyptian theocracy was regulated by a cosmic order called Maat, which was none other than the order of the sky, that is, the observable, precise and predictable cycles of the sun, the moon and the stars. I have also concluded that this cosmic order was fervently believed to influence the material world below, especially the all-important annual flooding of the Nile, for nothing fascinated, awed and frightened the ancient Egyptians more than the Nile's flood, which began in late June and ended in late September. This was the annual miracle that rejuvenated the crops and all other life in Egypt. But too low a rise in the waters in June would bring famine and pestilence. This double-edged sword that hung perpetually over Egypt compelled the Nile-dwellers to seek magical means to ensure a good flood. Early in their development they came to observe that the stars of Orion and Sirius would disappear beneath the western horizon after sunset in late March and remain for a protracted period (about three months) in the 'underworld' before re-emerging in the eastern horizon at dawn in late June, *just when the waters of the Nile began to rise*. During this crucial period of the stars' sojourn in the 'underworld', the astronomer-priests also noted that the sun travelled from a point on the ecliptic just below the bright cluster of the Pleiades (marking the vernal point) to a spot further along the ecliptic just below the chest of the celestial lion, Leo (marking the summer solstice), which bracketed the constellation of Orion and Sirius. The idea began to enter their minds that when the sun-god journeyed through that special part of the sky – the Duat, as it was called – he performed a magical ritual, a sort of Stations of the Cross, that would bring about the rebirth of the stars as well as the rebirth of the Nile when, in late June, Sirius would reappear at dawn in the eastern horizon. This also happened to fall on the day of the summer solstice, when the sun would reach its maximal northerly declination, and was for good reason taken as New Year's Day and called, among other things, 'the Birth of Ra', the sun-god.

A mythology and sky-religion developed around this cosmic and

Nilotic theme, and more intriguingly, in around 2800 BC an ambitious plan was gradually hatched to 'bring down', in the literal sense, the cosmic order so that the pharaoh, the son of Ra on earth, could undertake the same magical journey in an earthly Duat and thus secure for Egypt a 'good' flood. To use the Hermetic dictum: *as above, so below*. To this end a massive pan-generation project was put into action that would involve building clusters of 'star' pyramids at predetermined sites to represent Orion and the Pleiades, as well as great 'sun' temples set on both sides of the Nile to define the part of the ecliptic along which the sun god travelled through the Duat from vernal equinox to summer solstice.

My new theory does not stop here, for I will also demonstrate in *The Egypt Code* that the slow cyclical changes witnessed in the sky landscape, caused by precession and by the peculiarity of the Egyptian civil calendar over the 3,000 years of the pharaonic civilisation, are reflected in the changes witnessed on the ground all along the 1,000-kilometre-long Nile Valley in the evolution of temples throughout the same 3,000 years. In other words *The Egypt Code* proposes, no less, to prove that there existed a sort of 'cosmic Egypt' ghosted in the geography of the Nile Valley, stretching from north to south, that was once literally regulated and administered by astronomer-priests headed by a sun-king, that lasted for over three millennia, and that can still be discerned in the layout of pyramids and temples that remains today.

The Egypt Code, contrary to what Egyptologists will surely be quick to claim, is not a New Age book that regurgitates wild speculations and theories that cannot be verified or tested. My thesis is entirely verifiable, testable and ultimately falsifiable if need be. Indeed, I welcome Egyptologists and other scholars in the field of Egyptian archaeology and history who wish to step up and challenge it. Let them not be fooled or be put off by the easy-to-read style of presentation and concise arguments. This is for the benefit of the general public, who, when all is said and done, are the true judge-and-jury of all new ideas.

In closing I would like to add that while I was writing the last version of *The Egypt Code* in Cairo I would often take short breaks from my long hours at the computer and go up on the roof of our building to look at the pyramids. From that vantage point I had an unobstructed view over the Giza pyramids hardly a kilometre away. It sometimes felt as if I could reach out and touch them. But my gaze would always wander beyond Giza to a place on the southern horizon where I could see the outline of the first pyramid built in Egypt, the Step Pyramid at Saqqara, with its distinctive staggered profile gleaming through the thin veil of haze. The quest for *The Egypt Code* began there, while casually standing one day next to the figure of the king who built this strange monument and whose seated effigy, very mysteriously, was made to stare eternally at the circumpolar stars. So I now would invite you to join me at that same spot to retrace my quest for the holy grail of the pyramid- and temple-builders of ancient Egypt.

Please come and meet the pharaoh who began all this . . .

CHAPTER ONE

The Star at the Head of the Sky

God who rules alone, the Fabricator of the universe, bestowed on the earth for a little time your great father Osiris and the great goddess Isis . . . It was they that established upon earth rites of worship which correspond exactly to the holy powers of heaven. It was they that consecrated the temples . . .

Walter Scott (ed.) *Hermetica*

And God arranged the Zodiac in accord with the cycles of nature . . . (and) . . . devised a secret engine (viz. the system of the stars) linked to unerring and inevitable fate, to which all things in men's lives, from their birth to their final destruction shall of necessity be brought into subjection; and all other things on earth likewise shall be controlled by the working of this engine . . .

Walter Scott (ed.) *Hermetica*

Saqqara

All discoveries begin with the question why. Indeed, the urge to know why is what distinguishes us from other creatures on this planet and, more importantly, it is the root of all knowledge. To ask why triggers the intellectual process and launches an investigation which, if all goes well, will lead to a breakthrough. A bathtub overflows, the sun rises and sets, an apple falls, two imaginary bicycles collide; some gifted people asked why and the next thing you know man has walked on the moon. Asking why will, in fact, take us beyond the moon, beyond our solar system, beyond our galaxy, beyond our wildest dreams and, who knows, perhaps one day to God. My own 'why' and the investigation that I launched because of it began 25 years ago. And my falling apple was, quite literally, in the sky, with its counterpart in the desert west of the city of Cairo in Egypt. In 1994 I presented the discovery (known as the Orion Correlation Theory or OCT) that was reaped from this investigation in a book that became an international bestseller.[1] It was not, however, to be the end of this strange intellectual adventure. Another apple still hung precariously in my mind waiting patiently for the right moment to fall. It did so eight years later, when I visited the world's oldest pyramid complex at Saqqara for the umpteenth time. There, and also for the umpteenth time, I examined the seated statue of the pyramid's owner gazing upwards at the northern sky. Yet for reasons that only the gods know, this was the first time that I was prompted to ask *why*. Why was the king made to look at the northern sky? Finding no explanation that quite satisfied me in the many Egyptological textbooks I owned, I decided to seek the answer for myself. My story, then, starts here, at Saqqara, with the question why.

The site of Saqqara lies some 20 kilometres south of modern Cairo. Five kilometres long and two kilometres wide, it stretches like a surreal abandoned moon station in the western desert where the Sahara meets the green Nile Valley. It is by a long shot ancient Egypt's largest royal cemetery. Here, 5,000 years ago, on this dusty and often windswept promontory, a powerful idea fired a people, launching them into a building frenzy the likes of which the world would never experience again, in a breakneck momentum that was to last for nearly 500 years. The result of this seemingly irrational enterprise can still be seen today: giant pyramids strewn like stony atolls along a 40-kilometre archipelago of sand. Egyptologists call this mysterious region the Memphite Necropolis on account of its proximity to the now-lost city of Memphis. An estimated 50 million tons of stone was quarried, transported, hauled, cut, shaped and lifted by armies of workers toiling like ants across several generations. And all this high-tech engineering without the help of iron tools, without wheeled vehicles or lifting machines, without even the assistance of a single pulley. This was, to quote a phrase from the late Sir I.E.S. Edwards, the Pyramid Age *par excellence*.

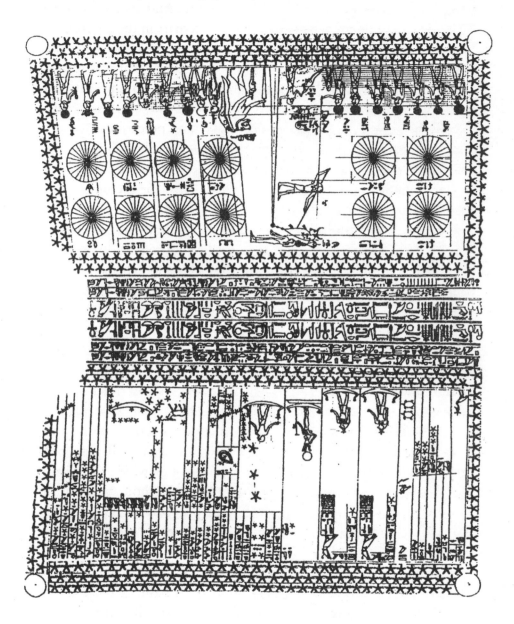

Astronomical ceiling of the Tomb of Senmut

The first pyramid to be raised in the Memphite Necropolis was not a smooth-faced structure as one sees with the famous triad at Giza, but a six-tiered edifice known to Egyptologists as the Step Pyramid of Saqqara. According to accepted chronology, the Step Pyramid was built in 2650 BC and belonged to a Third Dynasty king called Djoser. But it is believed to have been the brainchild of a genius called Imhotep, an architect-cum-astronomer who was high priest at the sun-temple at Heliopolis, the principal religious and intellectual centre at that time. Imhotep, who was vizier to King Djoser, named his pyramidal architectural masterpiece 'Horus is the Star at the Head of the Sky'.[2] Why this cryptic name? What strange cosmic function could the Step Pyramid have had? *What function at all?*

The orthodox view goes something like this: the Step Pyramid is just a tomb, admittedly a very large and elaborate tomb, but a tomb nonetheless. And as for the reason why it was built at Saqqara, this was simply because the king wanted it within sight of his palace at Memphis. But this tomb-only theory (and it is only a theory) did not quite stick with me. It never did. For one, it did not explain why no mummified body – not a single bone or even mummy linen, nothing – was found, either here at Saqqara or at any of the other pyramid sites in the Memphite Necropolis. But for me it also did not explain why the Step Pyramid bore the name 'Horus is the Star at the Head of the Sky'. It didn't sound like your typical epitaph to me. So as far as I was concerned, there had to be some other explanation for all this that fitted the scale and context of what I saw there.

Let's begin at the beginning. Scientific research started at Saqqara in the early 1920s with the arrival on site of two British archaeologists, Cecil M. Firth and James E. Quibell. They were later joined by a Frenchman, Jean-Philippe Lauer. Lauer had the rare quality of being both an architect and an archaeologist, and so smitten was he by the magic and mystery of this site that he spent the next 60 years of his life lovingly restoring it as best as he could to its former glory. The thing that first strikes you when you reach the Step Pyramid complex is its imposing entrance façade. This façade is an integral part of the huge 10-metre-high boundary wall that once enclosed the whole complex. Running 550 metres in length and 220 metres in breadth, the boundary wall alone is a brilliant masterpiece of intricate architecture that would tax even our contractors today. I shall return to this extraordinary wall later on, for it represents much more than a mere boundary to the whole complex. Meanwhile, as you go past the entrance and through the roofed corridor flanked by columns, you will emerge into a vast open courtyard that will take your breath away. For at its northern end looms the 60-metre-high Step Pyramid like some giant tsunami of stone. At such proximity it boggles the imagination and fires up the senses. The Step Pyramid was, in fact, built in several phases that finally resulted in the six tiers or 'steps' that one sees today. It was originally encased in polished white limestone slabs which, except for a few weather-beaten ones on the first two tiers, were completely stripped off by Arabs in medieval times to built mosques and villas in Cairo.

To enter the Step Pyramid you must descend a sloping shaft cut into the bedrock on its north face. At the bottom of the shaft, some 20 metres below ground level, is an elaborate and very bizarre system of tunnels, corridors, chambers and pits. The ceiling of one of the underground chambers is engraved with an exquisite motif of five-pointed stars, a reminder that this tenebrous place was once considered a cosmic environment interfacing with the starry world of the gods. On the walls of what is prosaically known as the King's Apartments are carved depictions showing the king performing rituals related to his jubilees, which, presumably, were to be celebrated in his afterlife ad infinitum. In here one gets a curious and very unsettling feeling of the *presence* of the king – still lingering unseen, unheard, but most definitely felt. But if you want to *see* a tangible representation of the king's alter ego then you have to go outside the pyramid to a strange little room that looks very much like the control cabin of a tower crane and that has long baffled Egyptologists and other researchers with its meaning or function.

The Serdab

Imagine a powerful laser beam shooting up from the King's Apartments to emerge on the north face of the Step Pyramid. Then imagine this beam passing through the head and then the eyes of a statue of the king seated in a small stone cubicle. Known as a *serdab* (meaning 'cellar' in old Arabic), this bizarre cubicle was for me the black box of the Step Pyramid complex.

The *serdab* was discovered when Firth and Quibell were clearing the debris around the north side of the Step Pyramid in 1925. They were intrigued by its design, which, for some curious reason, was not level but was tilted against the lower step of the pyramid. This quite clearly was not due to settlement or subsidence, since the *serdab* was built into the stone masonry of the Step Pyramid as one builds a skylight window into a sloping roof. In other words, the tilt was deliberate. Even more intriguing was the presence of two round holes that had been drilled in the north face of the *serdab* at eye level. And when Firth and Quibell took their first peep through them, they were astounded to find staring back at them the placated eyes of a seated life-size statue of the king (which has now been moved to the main hall of the Cairo museum and replaced with a replica). Now, seeing it again myself, I could not shake off the feeling that the king was not simply gazing at something just outside the *serdab*, but at something far beyond, in the lower part of the northern sky.[3] From my knowledge of astronomy, I knew that it could not have been the sun or the moon because these can never occupy this region of the sky. There was thus only one other candidate left to consider: a star. This conclusion certainly fits with the Step Pyramid's name 'Horus is the Star at the Head of the Sky'. As for the identity of 'Horus', according to the American Egyptologist Mark Lehner, 'Djoser is the name given to this king by New Kingdom visitors to this site a thousand years later. But the only royal name found on the walls of the complex is the Horus name, *Netjerykhet*.'[4] The same is confirmed by Egyptologists Ian Shaw and Paul Nicholson of the British Museum, who wrote that 'Only the Horus name *Netjerikhet* was found in 3rd dynasty inscriptions associated with the pyramid, and it is only through New Kingdom graffiti that an association has been made between this name and Djoser.'[5]

Horus was an ancient sky-god who had a very 'close association to the king'.[6] Indeed, so close was this association that the king was given not only a Horus name but also a Golden-Horus title at his

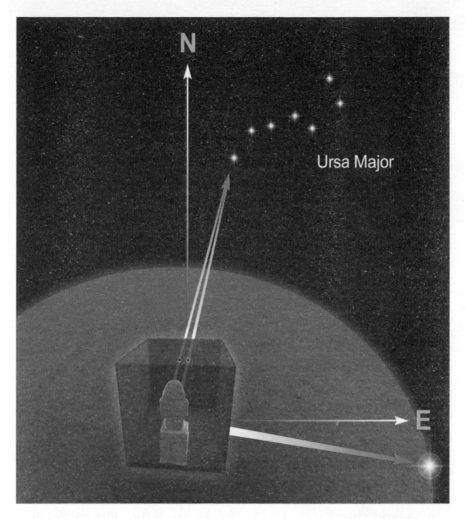

The statue of the pharaoh Djoser in the serdab oriented 4 deg. 35' east-of-north towards the star Al Kaid in the Big Dipper (in Ursa Major) marking the rising of Sirius in the east.

coronation. To put it more bluntly, the king was seen as the incarnation of Horus on earth. The god Horus was always depicted either as a falcon or as a man with a falcon's head. According to the British Museum's *Dictionary of Ancient Egypt*, his 'eyes were interpreted as the sun and the moon, and he was frequently described in the Old Kingdom (2686–2181 BC) as a god of the east, and hence of the sunrise. In this guise he became known as Horemakhet ("Horus in the Horizon") and he was also merged with Ra (the sun-god) to become Ra-Horakhty (Horus of the Horizon).'[7] Egyptologists will tell you that there are numerous forms of Horus, such as 'Horus the Child', 'Horus the Elder', 'Horus of Edfu', 'Horus of Behdet', 'Horus Son of Osiris' and so on.[8] But this is like saying that there were numerous forms of Jesus because we read of 'Jesus the child', 'Jesus the man', 'Jesus the son of God', 'Jesus the son of Joseph', 'Jesus the Lamb of God', 'Jesus the Messiah', 'Jesus of Nazareth', 'Jesus of Bethlehem' and so on. Recently the American Egyptologist Edmund Meltzer has put an end to this modern confusion by cogently arguing that there was only one Horus, with 'different aspects, or facets, of the same divine persona'.[9] I have to agree with Meltzer that this makes a lot more sense. At any rate, all Egyptologists nonetheless agree that the most common aspect of Horus throughout the whole history of ancient Egypt was 'Horus son of Osiris'. And as Meltzer further explains: 'The living king was identified as an earthly Horus and the dead king (his father/predecessor) as Osiris. When the king died, he became Osiris . . . Horus is the royal heir/successor par excellence, the epitome of legitimate succession.'[10]

The other problem is that most Egyptologists insist that the god Osiris was not known until the Fifth Dynasty, long after the building of the Step Pyramid. But this stance, too, has been seriously challenged in recent years, with the growing acceptance that Osiris was known in early dynastic times under the title Khentiamentiu: 'Foremost of the Westerners' (i.e. 'the dead').[11] At any rate, there is another aspect of Horus which we have to contend with when it comes to the Step Pyramid. For as we have already seen, Horus was a sky-god closely associated with the sun-god Ra and even sometimes merged with him. Why, then, would the Step Pyramid be identified with a star and not the sun? Osiris was a stellar god identified with Orion, and his wife was a stellar goddess identified with Canis Major (Orion's dog in Greek mythology). They were the parents of Horus, and it would thus be in total conformity with the astral context that he, too, would have astral attributes. Indeed, according to British Egyptologist Aidan Dodson, 'A pyramid was intended as the burial place of the pharaoh, but the complex also served as a temple to the god Horus, with whom the pharaoh was identified in his life, and to Osiris, with whom he would be identified in the next.'[12] Yet there is a problem: neither Orion nor Canis Major can be seen in the lower northern sky. Not now, not then, not ever. They are southern constellations and can only be seen rising in the eastern horizon then sailing across the southern sky to the west. In ancient Egyptian the word *akhet* means 'horizon', and more specifically the eastern horizon where the sun and stars rise. The word *netjer*, on the other hand, means 'divine' or 'god'. The 'khet' in the Horus-name of Djoser, Netjerykhet, apparently stands for a 'corporation' of very ancient gods.[13] So Netjerykhet could mean 'the Divine Corporation', which, at least to me, does not make any sense. Could the 'khet' in Netjerykhet be a phonetic (rather than a cryptogram) to evoke the idea of 'horizon', i.e. *akhet*? Could the Horus name Netjerykhet mean 'the divine Horus in the Horizon'? Was Horus a star that was seen being born from Osiris–Orion and Isis–Canis Major? But then why was the statue of Netjerykhet in the *serdab* looking north and not east? Could the statue also be doing something else other than only looking at the lower northern sky? What else? Sitting with such an air of authority and with his eyes transfixed towards the northern sky, this statue of the Horus king Netjerykhet gives the strong impression that it is somehow controlling something in the northern sky from its position on earth. And as odd as this idea may seem to us today, the belief that the king could actually control the cosmic order from a chamber within or attached to his pyramid complex was as valid to the ancient Egyptians as the present-day belief that the president of the United States can control the world from the Oval Office in the White House. But how did the Egyptians imagine that the cosmic order could be controlled? What else was known about this *serdab* or perhaps others like it that might tell us more about this cosmic function? As far as I could make out, however, there were no *serdabs* at other pyramid complexes in the Memphite Necropolis or elsewhere. Djoser's *serdab*, it seems, was unique. There were, however, many *serdabs* attached to various *mastaba* tombs, a sort of flat-roofed bunker-like structure that is thought by many Egyptologists to be the precursors of the step pyramids. But I found out that none of these were inclined towards the sky or had rounded peepholes cut on their north face like Djoser's *serdab*. Still, and in spite of these differences, there were features that were common to all, such as having a statue of their owner inside and their alignment, if not inclined, towards the north.

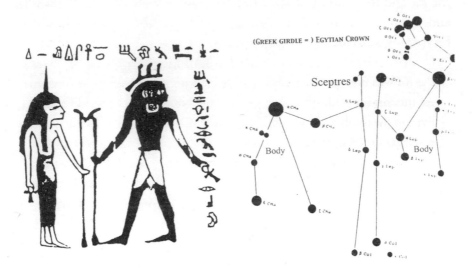

Representation of Sirius and Orion during the Middle Kingdom

In 1912 the German archaeologist Hermann Junker, while excavating south of the Sphinx's Causeway at Giza, discovered a *serdab* attached to a *mastaba* belonging to a Fifth Dynasty official called Rawer. Most fortuitously the *serdab* had inscriptions on it. Judging from the important location and also the size of the *mastaba*, Junker concluded that Rawer had been a very important official and even perhaps a member of the royal family. Although Rawer's *serdab* did not have rounded peepholes, it did have a long squint cut in the north face that had probably served the same purpose. Indeed, according to British Egyptologist A. M. Blackman, who studied Rawer's *serdab*, the squint symbolised the 'eyes' of the *serdab*. And most revealing, above the 'eyes' were inscribed the words *house of the ka*.[14]

The Egyptians believed that a human being was made of various unseen entities, in much the same way as we think of a person having a spirit, a soul, an ego and so on. An important entity was the *ka*, which is generally defined by Egyptologists as the 'double' or 'essence' of a person, a sort of alter ego that was an integral part of that person's life and, after death, his afterlife. Another important entity was the *ba*, generally defined as the 'soul' of the person, which was imagined to become a star after the person's death. We shall return to the *ba* and its relation to stars later on. Meanwhile, a more elaborate and even more revealing definition of the *ka* is given by the Egyptologist Manchip-White:

> the *Ka* was born with a person and remained earthbound on his death. At the instant of death a man's *Ka* and his body were united. The *Ka* lived in the tomb with the mummy, feeding upon the daily offerings and *dwelling in the statue* enclosed in the serdab[15] . . . The idea that the *Ka* 'dwelled' in the statue of the dead person is made evident in this passage from the ancient funerary texts, where the dead person declares: '*Let my Ka be remembered after my life; let my statue abide and my name endure* . . .'[16]

The *ka* statue in the *serdab* also had to be nurtured in the same manner the person it belonged to had been nurtured during his lifetime. Food offerings to the statue were, of course, symbolic and were depicted in drawings on the walls of the tomb, although real food was often part of the funerary items. On such drawings the most prominent depiction was the thigh of a bull or calf. The thigh – or rather its plough-like shape, as we shall see later – was called *meskhetiu*. The *meskhetiu* was generally carried by a priest, who solemnly presented it to the *ka* of the deceased. Curiously, the same word, *meskhetiu,* described a small metal cutting tool, a sort of carpenter's adze, used on the mummy in a ceremony known as 'the opening of the mouth'. In this ceremony the mouth of the mummy was symbolically sliced open with the cutting tool to allow the 'breath of life' to enter the corpse of the deceased. The word *meskhetiu*, oddly enough, was used also to describe a constellation of stars which today we call the Plough (or the Big Dipper in the US). It was often drawn on the ceilings of tombs and on the lids of sarcophagi in the form of a bull's thigh sometimes surrounded by seven stars. The common denominator between these three types of *meskhetiu* – the bull's thigh, the carpenter's adze and the Plough – was clearly their adze- or plough-like shapes. From my astronomy I knew that the Plough constellation had always been seen in the northern sky (it still is today), and that once a day it would have passed into the line of sight of the *ka* statue in the *serdab*.

Scanning through the Pyramid Texts – those sacred writings that were found engraved on the walls of Fifth and Sixth Dynasty royal pyramids at Saqqara[17] – I found a particular passage that gave a rather vivid picture of the dead king sharing his pyramid with his *ka*. What grabbed my attention, however, was the curious way the pyramid had been described: 'A boon . . . that this pyramid and temple be installed for me and my *ka* . . . Anyone who shall lay a finger on this pyramid and this temple which belong to me and my *ka*, he will have laid his finger on the Mansion of Horus in the sky . . .'[18] The enigmatic description of 'the Mansion of Horus in the sky' given to the pyramid had, as one can imagine, a familiar ring to it. It was, of course, uncannily similar to the name given to the Step Pyramid' 'Horus is the Star at the Head of the Sky'. It was obvious that both these names strongly indicated that the pyramids were imagined to have their counterparts in the sky in the form of stars. Or, to put it inversely, that certain stars (in this case one associated with Horus) were symbolised on the ground by certain pyramids. As early as 1977 the Egyptologist Alexander Badawy had drawn attention to precisely this pyramids–stars connection when he wrote that 'the names of the Pyramids of Snefreru, Khufu, Dededfret, Nebre indicate clearly stellar connotations while those of Sahure, Neferirkare and Neferefre describe the stellar destiny of the Ba (soul).'[19]

Later, in 1981, the distinguished British Egyptologist I.E.S. Edwards looked into this mysterious correlation between stars and pyramids and pointed out that the names of two pyramids belonging to the Fourth Dynasty kings Djedefra and Nebka, 'Djedefra is a *sehed* star' and 'Nebka is a star', 'clearly associate their owner with an astral after-life.'[20] And more recently the Egyptologist Stephen Quirke brought this matter up again by noting that, 'The (names of the) Step Pyramid of *Netjerkhet* (Djoser) and the Abu Ruwash complex of Djedefra are explicitly stellar, in the one case using the word *seba* "star", in the other case using the word *sehdu* "firmament" or "starry sky". By contrast, there is not a single instance where the name of a pyramid refers explicitly to the sun.'[21]

These 'explicitly stellar' names given to pyramids carry a clear and straightforward message: pyramids on the ground are to be regarded as 'stars'. If this was true, then the implications were astounding, and a whole new rethink of what motivated the ancient Egyptians to build pyramids was required. This was precisely what I had done, starting in 1983, at the Giza pyramids. I knew that now I was about to do the same again for the Step Pyramid complex at Saqqara. For I very much suspected that the 'star' that the Step Pyramid represented on earth was no ordinary star, but one that was deemed vital to the welfare of Egypt; a star, no less, that was imagined to completely control, as the Hermetic texts said, 'all things on earth'.

Plough, Dipper or Thigh: It's all in the Bear

The Plough is not, strictly speaking, a constellation. Some astronomers will insist on calling it an asterism because its seven bright stars are part of the larger constellation we call the Great Bear or Ursa Major. But to any casual observer it is only those seven stars and not the whole of the Great Bear constellation which stand out, with their distinct pattern of a plough or dipper. This often causes many people to erroneously use the name Great Bear when they in fact really mean Plough. This, most annoyingly, is especially true of Egyptologists, which has caused much confusion all round. At any rate the ancient Egyptians, like most people, perceived only the pattern of the seven bright stars, which they likened not to a plough but to a bull's thigh. This is the constellation they called *meskhetiu*, and it figured prominently in their religious texts and funerary drawings in connection with the afterlife destiny of kings and nobles. It was one of three distinct constellations, along with Ursa Minor (the Little Bear) and Draconis (the Dragon), that, in ancient times, revolved perpetually around the north pole of the sky like a wheel. The stars in these constellations were known as the *ikhemu-set*, which means 'the Imperishable Ones' or 'the Indestructible Ones,'[22] and are known to modern astronomers as the circumpolar stars because they perpetually circumnavigate the north celestial pole, making them the perfect metaphor for 'eternal life', due to the fact that they never set but are always visible in the night sky. As early as 1912 the influential American Egyptologist James H. Breasted was to write that, 'it is especially those (stars) which are called "the Imperishable Ones" in which the Egyptians saw the host of the dead. These are said to be in the north of the sky, and the suggestion that the circumpolar stars, which never set or disappear, are the ones which are meant is a very probable one.'[23]

Today Breasted's views are universally accepted. Indeed, the British Egyptologist R.T. Rundle Clark drove the same point even further by asserting that 'no other ancient people were so deeply affected by the eternal circuit of the stars around a point in the northern sky. Here must be the node of the universe, the centre of regulation.'[24] In the same vein, the archaeoastronomer E.C. Krupp, an accredited specialist in this field, also pointed out that the Egyptians associated the Plough 'with eternal life because its stars are circumpolar. They were the undying, imperishable stars. In death the king ascended to their circumpolar realm, and there he preserved the cosmic order.'[25] The idea that the king preserved the 'cosmic order' or harmony of the universe by making use of the circumpolar stars as 'the centre of regulation' is most intriguing, because it may indeed explain the cosmic function of the *ka* statue in the *serdab* and why its gaze is eternally locked on these stars. Actually, the cosmic order that Krupp was alluding to was called Maat by the ancient Egyptians. Maat was their most fundamental and important religious tenet, and was portrayed as a seated goddess wearing an ostrich feather – the 'feather of truth' – on her head. The pharaohs were often shown presenting a small figure of Maat to the gods, the supreme gesture of piety and respect, and they often adopted the epithet 'Beloved of Maat'. The goddess Maat figured prominently in the so-called Judgement Scene where the souls of the dead were weighed against the feather of truth. Indeed, it would not be an exaggeration to say that the whole religious edifice upon which the pharaonic theocracy rested was Maat.

Although Egyptologists generally define it as 'truth, justice and balance', a closer examination shows that Maat was also intrinsically linked to the harmony and order of the cosmos, which principally entailed the stately motion of stars and their relation to the cycle of nature. As Egyptologists Ian Shaw and Paul Nicholson further explain:

> On a cosmic scale, Maat also represented the divine order of the universe as originally brought into being at the moment of Creation. It was the power of Maat that was believed to regulate the seasons, the movement of the stars and the relation between men and god. The concept was therefore central both to the Egyptians' ideas about the universe and to their code of ethics.[26]

> Kingship belonged much more with the overall role of the king in imposing order and preventing chaos. The function of the king as the representative of the gods was to preserve the original harmony of the universe, therefore a great deal of the iconography in Egyptian temples, tombs and palaces was concerned much more with this overall aim than with the individual circumstances of the ruler at any particular point in time.[27]

From these definitions it is self-evident that the Egyptians believed in a heavenly force or power that regulated the movements of the constellations in the sky and the changing of the seasons on earth, and that somehow the king could control this power. Attached to this belief was also the notion that there had been a time when sky and earth were one and in perfect harmony. In the so-called Heliopolitan creation myth, the sky-goddess Nut and the earth-god Geb were at first locked in a tight embrace and the fruit of their amorous union were the twin souls and archetypal lovers Osiris and Isis, who became the first divine king and queen of Egypt and bore the first Horus-king. But then Nut 'swallowed' her children to make them 'stars' in her body. Because of this act of infanticide she suffered the eternal punishment of being separated from her husband by the hand of her father Shu, the air-god.[28] But now sky and earth were out of synch. No more did the cycle of the stars in the sky perfectly match that of nature on earth. For the Egyptians, whose very survival relied entirely on the regularity of the Nile's flood, this presented a serious problem. As we shall see in the next chapter, the annual flood had to be predictable and 'good', otherwise calamity befell the land and its people. And so from this constant fear was spawned the belief that the cosmic order of the sky, which was perfect and could be relied on to the nearest minute, could be brought down to earth through the magical power of rituals. Only by the stringent adherence to Maat could the pharaoh ensure the welfare of Egypt and the regulated and orderly flooding of the Nile.

The goddess Nut (the sky)

There exist ancient Egyptian teachings dating from the first century known as the *Corpus Hermeticum*, which, as we have briefly mentioned earlier, express the fundamentals of this belief system which saw a connection or 'influence' between the cycle of the stars and that of men and all things on earth:

> *God arranged the Zodiac [the twelve seasonal constellations] in accord with the cycles of nature . . . (and) . . . devised a secret engine ('viz. the system of the stars') linked to unerring and inevitable fate, to which all things in men's lives, from their birth to their final destruction shall of necessity be brought into subjection; and all other things on earth likewise shall be controlled by the working of this engine . . .*[29]

Mulling over this archaic perception of the visible world, I knew that I was trying to somehow get into the mindset of the ancient Egyptians.

I had to stop thinking as scientific man and begin thinking like cosmic man. I had to bring myself to believe, like they did, that the constellations were the wheel of a cosmic engine that could influence events on earth. I had to believe, like they did, that the king and his *ka* could control the working of this cosmic engine. Finally I had to believe, like they did, that the Step Pyramid complex was not a cemetery as such but a 'centre of regulation' from which the king could control the cosmos. It was, I knew, the only way to truly understand the ancient Egyptians and their legacy of pyramids and temples.

Another inscription from Rawer's *serdab* provided a further missing piece from this strange and elaborate puzzle. According to Blackman there was, just above the squint on the north face of the *serdab*, a line of hieroglyphs that simply stated: 'the eyes of the *ka*-house'.[30] But the term '*ka*-house', according to Egyptologists, referred not to the *serdab* alone but to the whole *mastaba* complex to which it was attached. This, of course, implied that the two peepholes on the north face of Djoser's *serdab* were also regarded as the 'eyes' of the whole Step Pyramid complex. From my previous studies I was aware that pyramids were not only thought of as stars on earth but also as *being* the pharaoh himself. In the Pyramid Texts there are numerous claims that the soul, or *ba*, of a dead king became a 'star'.[31] Also, as Richard Wilkinson further pointed out, 'Nut (the sky-goddess) also became inextricably associated with the concept of resurrection in Egyptian funerary beliefs, and the dead were believed to become stars in the body of the goddess.'[32]

This intriguing stellar connection of the king and his pyramid is made even more evident by a series of inscriptions and engravings found on the capstone (pyramidion) of a royal pyramid from Dashour that belonged to a Twelfth Dynasty pharaoh, Amenemhet III. On the east side of the pyramidion are engraved two large 'eyes' and a line of hieroglyphs that read: 'May the face of the king be opened so that he may see the Lord of the Horizon when he crosses the sky; may he cause the king to shine as a god, lord of eternity and indestructible.'[33] The name of the pyramid that bore this capstone was 'Amenemhet is beautiful', which, not surprisingly, meant to Egyptologist Mark

Lehner that 'Like the names of the pyramids . . . the eyes (on the pyramidion) tells us that the pyramids were personifications of the dead kings who were buried within them.'[34] The American Egyptologist Alexander Piankoff, well known for his translation of the Pyramid Texts of Unas (a Fifth Dynasty king who built a pyramid at Saqqara), also wrote that 'the embalmed body of the king lay in or under the pyramid, which together with its entire compound, was considered his body. The pyramids were personified . . .' In addition Piankoff also showed the personification of the king's pyramid with the title that queens of the Sixth Dynasty adopted. As an example he gives the title of King Unas's daughter as being 'the royal daughter of the body of "Perfect are the places of Unas"', the latter epithet being the name of Unas's pyramid. According to Piankoff, the dead king rested in or under his pyramid 'as Osiris in the Netherworld, and received his sustenance through an elaborate ritual'.[35]

There are several pyramids, as we have already seen, that bore unequivocal stellar names, such as 'Djedefre is a *sehedu* star', 'Horus is the Star at the Head of the Sky' and 'Nebka is a Star'. We have also seen how Alexander Badawy argued that other pyramids which were identified with the king's *ba*, or soul, must be taken as stellar since the *ba* becomes a star in the firmament. By simple transposition, if A equals B, and B equals C, then A must equal C. In other words, if the king becomes a star in the sky and he also becomes his pyramid in the Memphite necropolis, it must follow that his star is also to be regarded as his pyramid and vice versa. This would certainly indicate that certain clusters of pyramids such as those of Giza and Abusir may represent clusters of stars, i.e. constellations. Let us leave this intriguing possibility for a moment, however, and return to the two peepholes of Djoser's *serdab*.

Looking deeper into this issue of Djoser's *serdab*, I was pleased to find that there were many eminent scholars who had also independently arrived at more or less the same conclusion as I had regarding the stellar function of the two peepholes. For example, the French Egyptologist Christiane Ziegler concluded that 'through the two peep-holes the king would gaze towards the "imperishable" stars near the North Pole'.[36] Although Ziegler did not venture why this was a necessary feature of the complex, she nonetheless recognised that the peepholes had a stellar function. She was echoed by Mark Lehner, who wrote that

> On the northern side of his Saqqara Step Pyramid Djoser emerges from his tomb in statue form, into a statue-box, or *Serdab*, which has just such a pair of peepholes to allow him to see out[37] . . . with eyes once inlaid with rock crystal, Djoser's statue gazes out through peepholes in the serdab box, tilted upwards 13° to the northern sky where the king joined the circumpolar stars . . .[38]

To support such a conclusion, Lehner quoted a passage from the *Book of the Dead* in which the dead person is made to say: 'Open for me are the double doors of the sky, open for me are the double doors of the earth. Open for me are the bolts of Geb, exposed for me are the roof . . . and the Twin Peepholes.' In addition to Ziegler's and Lehner's conclusions renowned Russian astronomer Professor Alexander Gurshtein wrote that 'On the north side of Imhotep's Step Pyramid there is a small stone cubicle canted towards the north, with a pair of tiny holes in its façade likely for astronomical observations by the dead pharaoh.'[39]

In my experience with such things, it is an excellent sign when several researchers come to the same conclusion on the same issue, because the likelihood is that they are on the right track. Indeed, it had to be admitted that the evidence for a stellar function for the *serdab* was overwhelming, textually, astronomically and architecturally. It now remained to work out which specific star in the northern sky was targeted by the peepholes.

And why.

X Marks the Spot

To see Djoser's *serdab* one has to walk past the east side of the Step Pyramid and then turn left at the far corner. From here one can already get a side view of the *serdab* and even a glimpse at the *ka* statue through a small glassed window on the upper part of its side. Once you stand in front of the *serdab*, you will immediately see the peepholes.

By leaning back against the north wall and fixing your eyes at the place in the sky where the peepholes are directed, you can mentally project an 'X' to mark the spot. And even though it will be broad daylight, it is not too hard to imagine how the Plough constellation would sweep over the X during its diurnal cycle. Now if the angle of inclination of the *serdab* and its azimuth could be known with a good degree of accuracy, it would be a relatively easy excercise to calculate which one of the Plough's seven bright stars would superimpose on the X at the time the *serdab* was built, *c.* 2650 BC. Normally such data should be relatively easy to obtain in Egyptological manuals or publications. As it turned out, however, it proved to be a far more complicated matter than I had anticipated.

Finding the azimuth or orientation of the *serdab*'s north face was the least troublesome task. All I needed was the azimuth of the north face of the Step Pyramid to which the *serdab* was attached. I was aware that the latest study undertaken on the astronomical orientation of Egyptian pyramids was by the German Egyptologist Josef Dorner in the early 1980s. Unfortunately Dorner did not publish his data but simply lodged it in thesis format at the University of Innsbruck. Fortuitously, the Italian astronomer Giulio Magli, of the Politecnico di Milano, whom I know very well, had managed to obtain a copy of Dorner's thesis and was happy to pass me the data on the Step Pyramid that I needed. I found out that, according to Dorner, the sides of the Step Pyramid *'do not exactly face the cardinal points, the northern front being 4°35' east of true north'*.[40] Dorner – and other Egyptologists – tend to attribute this rather large deviation from true north to either carelessness or inefficiency on the part of the ancient surveyors. On closer scrutiny, however, this explanation does not hold water. It was well known, for example, that the Egyptians of the Pyramid Age were more than capable of orienting pyramids to much higher levels of accuracy than this. The Giza pyramids are, of course, a prime example of this, with alignments within the 20 arc minute level of accuracy. The Great Pyramid, in point of fact, is accurate within an astounding 3 arc minutes from true north (0.05°), which is almost 100 times more accurate than the 275 arc minutes (4° 35′) for the Step Pyramid! Yet there is no good reason to suppose that the surveyors of the Step Pyramid were either less efficient or did not have the same sighting devices and methodologies that their immediate successors had. Indeed, *mastabas* that were built *before* the Step Pyramid were aligned well within the 1° level of accuracy. Furthermore, any practising surveyor will confirm that an error might be considered if the deviation was no more than 1°, but a deviation of 4° 35′ is far too large to be assumed a mere mistake. Even the most inexperienced surveyor using the most rudimentary of sighting instruments would not make such a slip-up, unless he deliberately wanted to. There are only two realistic explanations for this large deviation: either the surveyors were not interested in true north, or, more likely in my view, *they were aiming at something else in the sky that was at 4° 35′ east from true north*. My gut feeling was that the second explanation was probably the right one. Experience had shown time and time again that nothing the pyramid builders did was left to chance.

It was at this point that I could have kicked myself for not remembering earlier a very important and very ancient ceremony related to the astronomical orientation of pyramids and temples. With mounting excitement I realised that the missing piece of this puzzle might well be in the hands of a very unusual and very well-groomed lady surveyor.

The Lady of the Stars

Since the beginning of their recorded history the ancient Egyptians had performed a religious ceremony known as 'the stretching of the cord' to align the axis of their sacred monuments. This ceremony involved the king and a rather fetching priestess who personified the goddess Seshat. Seshat was the erudite one among the many goddesses of ancient Egypt. Some even think of her as the archetype of female librarians and civil engineers. Tall, slender and very becoming, she was adored and venerated by the royal scribes in the 'House of Life' (temple library), for she was among other things the patroness of sacred writing, and also the keeper of the royal annals relating to the coronations and jubilees of kings.[41] She also had another, more technical role, which involved assisting the king in fixing the four corners of his future temples and pyramids and aligning them towards the stars. Oddly, however, you won't find much written about the goddess Seshat in Egyptological textbooks. For example, Mark Lehner pays no attention to her in his recent book *The Complete Pyramids*, and Richard H. Wilkinson hardly mentions her in his latest book *The Complete Gods and Goddesses of Ancient Egypt*.[42] Other Egyptologists either choose to ignore Seshat like Lehner did,[43] or mention her in the most scant of ways, as if she is but a footnote in Egyptian mythology. And even on those rare occasions when she is discussed at greater length, she is generally presented as a pretty bimbo who accompanies the king in the 'stretching of the cord' ritual only to give decorum and piquancy to the act. This, of course, is unfortunate; for if the truth be told about Seshat, as one Egyptologist did in the 1940s, this elusive goddess comes across not just as a pretty face in the Egyptian pantheon, by as a high-powered woman who decided on the length of the king's reign and, according to at least one eminent Egyptologist, probably his life.[44]

At any rate, the goddess Seshat is always shown dressed in a leopardskin that clings to her slender body. In conformity with the fashion of the time, her dress is cut low to expose her well-rounded breasts. The yellow spots on the leopardskin are sometimes shown as stars, apparently symbolising the leopard's and Seshat's ability to see in the dark.[45] On her head she wears a golden tiara with an antenna-like stem that has a seven-pointed star or rosette at the top. In the pantheon she is presented as the wife of Thoth, god of wisdom and inventor of the sacred hieroglyphs and of the sciences, especially astronomy. Not surprisingly, she was given an array of impressive epithets befitting this privileged relationship: 'Foremost in the Library', 'Mistress of Writing in the House of Life', 'Keeper of the Royal Annals' and so forth.[46] Very often Seshat and Thoth are seen together recording the jubilees or coronations of kings on notched palm branches. In this capacity they are to be seen as the divine time-keepers or astronomers *par excellence* who recorded the annual cycle of the sky and the calendar. The French scholar Anne-Sophie

Bomhard, an acclaimed authority on the ancient Egyptian calendar, expanded on this issue by saying that

> The recognition of the annual cycle and its definition, the linking of celestial phenomena to terrestrial happenings, are essential pre-liminaries to establishing any kind of calendar. This enterprise requires long prior observations of the sky and the stars, as well as the recording, in writing, of these observations, in order to verify them over long periods of time. It is quite natural, therefore, that the divine tutors of Time and Calendar should be Thoth, God of Science, and Seshat, Goddess of Writings and Annals.[47]

As one of the divine 'tutors of Time and Calendar' as well as the recorder of the king's annals, Seshat was directly responsible for computing the long-range jubilees. British Egyptologist Sir Wallis Budge thus pointed to a relief from the New Kingdom where the goddess is seen

> . . . standing before a column of hieroglyphics meaning 'life' and 'power' and 'thirty-year festivals' which rest upon a seated figure who holds in each hand 'life' and who typifies 'millions of years'. In connection with this must be noted a passage in a text in which she declares to a king that she has inscribed on her register on his behalf a period of life which shall be 'hundreds of thousands of Thirty-Years periods' and has ordained that his years shall be upon the earth like the years of *Ra* (the sun-god) i.e. that he shall live forever.[48]

It is generally agreed by Egyptologists that the king's first jubilee (or *heb-sed* festival, as it called by the ancients) was celebrated in the thirtieth year of his reign. But some others are of the opinion that the 30-year period was calendrical, i.e. that it fell in cycles of 30 years irrespective of the number of years the king had reigned. At any rate, it is evident from the text quoted by Budge that the term 'thirty-year festivals' is a euphemism for royal jubilees. Also the mention of the 'Thirty-Years periods' alongside the term 'years of *Ra*' should affirm to us that the computations of this period had something to do with the sun or rather its yearly cycle, and thus, by extension, the solar calendar. Such an association with the sky and Seshat's royal duties is also evident in the 'stretching of the cord' ceremony, since, as we shall see, this entailed observing the motion and position of the circumpolar stars. Indeed, because of this last role Seshat was also called 'Lady of Builders', 'Goddess of Construction', 'Founder of Architecture' and, perhaps more aptly, 'Lady of the Stars'. To be concise, we can think of Seshat as the royal librarian, the royal scribe, the royal astronomer, the royal architect, the royal engineer, the royal herald and perhaps even the royal adviser all rolled into one[49] – a sort of Condoleeza Rice to the pharaohs.

It is well established that the 'stretching of the cord' ceremony was practised from at least the Second Dynasty (c. 2900 BC). As Egyptologist George Hart further explains: 'As early as Dynasty II she (Seshat) assisted the monarch . . . in hammering boundary poles into the ground for the ceremony of "stretching the cord". This is a crucial part of a temple foundation ritual.'[50] To be precise, it is fair to say that much of the knowledge we have about the 'stretching of the cord' ceremony comes from very late inscriptions, mostly from the temples at Edfu and Dendera. Earlier evidence of the ceremony is found only in drawing form, without any explanatory captions. Nonetheless, as I.E.S. Edwards correctly argued:

> In spite of the relative late date of the inscriptions referring to the episodes of the foundation ceremonies, there is no reason to doubt that they preserved an ancient tradition. Some indication that similar ceremonies were already current in the Pyramid Age is provided by a fragmentary relief found in the Vth Dynasty sun-temple of Niuserre, which shows the king and a priestess impersonating Seshat, each holding a mallet and a stake to which a measuring cord is attached. The scene is in complete agreement with the text in the temple at Edfu which represents the king saying: 'I take the stake and I hold the handle of the mallet. I hold the cord with Seshat' . . .[51]

In the many depictions of the ceremony found all over Egypt, Seshat always faces the king and each is seen carrying a peg in one hand

and a mallet in the other. A short cord is looped between the two pegs, and it is evident from this scene that the protagonists are aligning the axis of a temple or pyramid by stretching cord and aiming it at a distant object, and then fixing the alignment by hammering the two pegs into the ground. Here are some of the inscriptions from the temples at Edfu and Dendera which describe the scene:

[The king says:] *I hold the peg. I grasp the handle of the mallet and grip the measuring-cord with Seshat. I turn my eyes to the movements of the stars. I direct my gaze towards the bull's thigh* [meskhetiu; *Plough*] . . . *I make firm the corners of the temple* . . .[52]

[A priest says:] *The king stretches joyously the cord, having turned his head towards the bull's thigh and establishes the temple in the manner of ancient times.*[53]

[The king says:] *I grasp the peg and the mallet; I stretch the cord with Seshat; I observed the trajectory of the stars with my eye which is fixed on the bull's thigh; I have been the god who indicates Time with the Merkhet instrument. I have established the four corners of the temple.*[54]

[A priest says:] *The king . . . while observing the sky and the stars, turns his sight towards the bull's thigh* . . .[55]

Recently, the British Egyptologist Kate Spence of Cambridge University proposed a method other than the 'stretching of the cord' that could have been used by the ancient pyramid builders and which she dubbed 'the simultaneous transit method'.[56] Her theory caused huge interest in the international press, partly because it first appeared as a feature article in the prestigious scientific journal *Nature*, and partly because of the solid backing Spence immediately received from eminent scholars such as the Harvard astronomer Owen Gingerich and the Egyptologist Betsy Bryan of Johns Hopkins University.[57]

According to Kate Spence, the ancient Egyptian surveyors had aligned the axes of the pyramids not to one star, but to the 'simultaneous transit' of two circumpolar stars using a simple plumb line attached to a rudimentary wooden frame and a candle for sighting at night. I have previously commented on Spence's theory in great detail, so I do not wish to repeat the exercise here.[58] But briefly, I was opposed to her 'simultaneous transit' for the simple reason that it required the Egyptians to aim at the stars when they were in perfect vertical alignment, which, at the most, would only be for 20 seconds or so twice a day (before their slow diurnal motion pushed them out of vertical alignment). Considering that the ancients had no optical instruments and that the operation had to be made in total darkness, in my opinion the Egyptian astronomers could not have achieved with this method the incredibly high accuracy that we see in the orientation of the Great Pyramid. In other words, Spence's method works in theory but not in practice. At any rate, here I simply want to draw attention to one of the two stars that she claimed was targeted by the ancient surveyors: Mizar, in the Plough (the other was Kochab in the Little Bear, or Ursa Minor). Notwithstanding the validity of her proposed method, Spence *did* have the right constellation. It did not occur to her to question the validity of her main assumption: that the main intention of the pyramid-builders had always been to try to align their pyramids to true north as accurately as they could. To be fair to Spence, no one else questioned this assumption either. So any axis that was misaligned from true north was claimed by Spence to be due to one thing and one thing only: the slow drift of the stars caused by precession, which, she endeavoured to show with mathematical graphs, more or less matched the misalignments of the pyramids. So convinced was Spence of her theory that she, as well as many of her supporters, touted it as incontrovertible proof that the ancient Egyptians were poor astronomers because they allegedly had not noticed the effect of precession as the Greeks did many centuries later. Consequently she claimed that the high accurary of the astronomical alignment of the Great Pyramid was simply because 'Khufu was just lucky'.[59]

This sort of mental gymnastics by an Egyptologist to make the facts fit a pet theory never ceases to amaze me. Anyone who has studied the Great Pyramid and has marvelled at this pristine example of ancient high-tech engineering cannot possibly conclude that luck had anything to do with the precision of its alignment. It is self-evident that the Great Pyramid was accurately aligned because its builders wanted it to be so. But there was something in Spence's conclusion that made me ponder on the target at which the ancient surveyors had really wanted to aim their pyramid. Was it really true north that was their target, or rather the stars? Perhaps there was luck at play here, but not for Khufu. Perhaps it was true north that had been lucky because the stars happened to be there when the surveyors took their sighting. Looking at it this way, it occurred to me that, as far as I could make out, there was absolutely nothing in the Pyramid Texts or elsewhere to suggest that the direction of true north had any particular meaning to the Egyptians. On the other hand, there were an overwhelming number of statements in the Pyramid Texts confirming that the circumpolar stars were of paramount importance to the afterlife of the king. It was the stars in the north, not north itself, that were of interest to them. And even though we can agree with Spence that circumpolar stars transit true north twice each day, this only lasts for a few seconds. For the rest of the 24 hours these stars would either be seen east or west of true north. Could this be the reason, then, why most pyramids were aligned a fraction east or west of true north with the exception of the Great Pyramid? But if so, then what determined the exact time of sighting – and consequently the position of the targeted star? A clue to this last question was inadvertently given by Egyptologists Ian Shaw and Paul Nicholson, who pointed out that the sightings made during the 'stretching of the cord' ceremony were not only towards the stars of the Plough in the north but also sometimes towards the stars of Orion in the south.[60] Naturally this statement immediately caught my attention, for I, of all people, am aware that Orion had a very special role in the sky-religion of the pyramid-builders.[61] Suddenly I realised that the answer had been staring me in the face. I knew why the Great Pyramid was so perfectly oriented towards true north, and what was more, I had a strong feeling that the same reason ought also to apply to the significant 'misalignment' of the Step Pyramid.[62]

Orion and Me

To say that I have had a special interest in Orion and the Great Pyramid would surely be a gross understatement. But also, to be perfectly truthful, I only developed this interest rather late in life, when I was in my mid-thirties. When I left my native Egypt and headed for England in 1967, I was only 19 years old. Not even in my wildest dreams could I have imagined that one day I would write a bestseller about Orion and the Great Pyramid. Indeed, after qualifying in 1973 at the University of the South Bank in London, I pursued a career in building contracting in the Middle East and Africa, oblivious of any studies on astronomy and the Great Pyramid. It was while working in Saudi Arabia that I made a startling and unexpected connection between Orion and the Giza Pyramids that was to change the course of my life. One night, while looking at the three stars of Orion's belt in the clear desert night sky, it struck me that these stars had exactly the same layout and positioning to the Milky Way as the layout of the three pyramids of Giza and their positioning relative to the Nile.

I became intrigued by this uncanny correlation, the more so because I found out that the kings of the Pyramid Age saw the region of Orion as being part of the celestial afterworld they called the Duat.[63] I also discovered that in 1964 two academics at UCLA had worked out that a shaft within the Great Pyramid had pointed towards Orion's belt in c. 2500 BC, when this pyramid was built. It took me 12 years to compile my research in a book, which was published in London in 1994. Backed by a BBC documentary, the book took off and shot to number 1 in the bestseller lists.[64] One particular point that I made in 1994 relevant to the present discussion was this: with the use of two illustrations showing the Plough and Orion, I demonstrated how the lower meridian transit of the Plough took place in the north at exactly the same time as the rising of Orion's belt in the east. My conclusion was that the ancient surveyors had aimed the Great Pyramid at a star in the Plough not because it was at true north (although it did happen to be there at the time) but because it could be used as a time-marker to tell them precisely when Orion's belt would be rising in the east.

Their true focus of interest was not the northern sky per se, but the mechanism of the circumpolar stars as indicators of the rising of Orion's belt in the east. In other words, it was Orion's belt rising in the east that was their ultimate objective in aiming the pyramid at the star Kochab or Mizar (or both, as Spence has theorised) during their transit in the north. Thus the tiny misalignment that is registered in the orientation of the Great Pyramid was not, as Spence believed, due to the vertical misalignment of these two northern stars at 'simultaneous transit' but rather due to the fact that this was the orientation the priests wanted the structure to have in order for it be locked for ever in a time-frame (*c.* 2500 BC) when Orion's belt was rising (i.e. being 'reborn') in the east. In this way the Great Pyramid was tied ad infinitum to the date of Khufu's 'rebirth', i.e. as an Osiris–Orion entity, by means of the mechanism of the stars. I now had a strong feeling that this reasoning would also prove correct for the 'misalignment' of the Step Pyramid at Saqqara. In other words, was the rising of a star in the east the reason for the 4° 35′ 'misalignment' of the Step Pyramid at the attached *serdab*?

The Step Pyramid, as we have already seen, is generally dated to *c.* 2650 BC, although most researchers will allow for a margin of uncertainty of 150 years either way. I had the orientation of the Step Pyramid from Dorner's data. What I now needed was the exact angle of inclination of the *serdab*, and with this data I could work out which star in the Plough it was aimed at. In his latest book on the pyramids, Mark Lehner had stated that the *serdab* was tilted upwards by 13° towards the northern sky.[65] Normally I would accept such a statement at face value, but I soon discovered that there was much confusion regarding the angle of tilt of the *serdab*. Jean-Philippe Lauer, deemed by many to be the supreme authority on the Step Pyramid, gives a much higher value than Lehner. In Lauer's own words: 'Two round holes drilled in the north face of the serdab, whose sides are inclined parallel to that of the Pyramid, allowed the statue to communicate with the outside world . . .'[66] The slope of its faces is near 16° to the vertical . . .'[67] This same value of nearly 16° is given by Sir I.E.S. Edwards, another renowned expert on the pyramids. To complicate things further, the eminent French Egyptologist Jacques Vandier gives a value of 17°.68 I realised that the only way to be sure was to measure the angle of tilt myself. The opportunity came along in July 2002. After several trials using a simple inclinometer with a plumb line and also a spirit level with a large protractor, I concluded that the angle of tilt was, in fact, very near 16°, as Lauer and Edwards had affirmed.[69]

Reconstruction

Using the powerful astronomy programme StarryNight Pro v.4 (and Skymap Pro7 as a back-up) I punched in the latitude of the Step Pyramid: 29° 49' N and 31° 15' E. I then entered the date of 2650 BC. Within a few seconds I was looking at the ancient sky above the 'newly built' Step Pyramid. I then looked at the northern part of the sky and placed the cursor at azimuth 4° 35' and then at 16° above the horizon line. I was now looking at the spot at which the *ka* statue in the *serdab* was gazing so intently. I then activated the sky at ×300 speed and waited. After several observations of the lower transits of the Plough, I was fairly sure that the star in question was Al Kaid, the 'hoof' star of *meskhetiu*, the bull's thigh.[70] Trying a variety of dates within the +/- 150 years ranges, I was also relatively certain that the observation had been made near the date of 2800 BC. I now 'froze' the sky at this date and the precise moment Al Kaid aligned with the *serdab*, and directed my screen view to the east. There it was, shining brighter than anything else in the horizon: the star of Horus was Sirius!

I suddenly remembered that the architect Imhotep, who had been responsible for the design of the Step Pyramid complex and, presumably, its astronomical alignments, had also been a high priest of Heliopolis. It was well known that Heliopolis was where regular observations of Sirius had been made since the beginning of Egyptian civilisation and that it was because of the timely rising of this star that the calendar had been invented at Heliopolis in around 2800 BC – the same date that was now highlighted on my computer screen. And although Heliopolis, it is true, was dedicated to the sun-god Ra, nonetheless, according to Professor I.E.S. Edwards:

Imhotep's title 'Chief of the Observers', which became the regular title of the high priest of Heliopolis, may itself suggest an occupation connected with astral, rather than solar, observation . . . It is significant that the high priest of the centre of the sun-cult at Heliopolis bore the title 'Chief of the Astronomers' and was represented wearing a mantle adorned with stars.[71]

Did Imhotep study the various cycles of Sirius, 'the star at the head' of all the other stars in the sky? And did he incorporate these cycles into the overall design of the Step Pyramid complex?

To what end?

CHAPTER TWO

The Quest for Eternity

The Nile and its flooding were dominant factors in the newly formed Egyptian state . . .

Jaromir Malek and John Baines, *The Cultural Atlas of the World: Ancient Egypt*

The importance of Sirius for the Egyptians lay in the fact that the star's annual appearance on the eastern horizon at dawn heralded the approximate beginning of the Nile's annual inundation which marked the beginning of the agricultural year . . .

R.H. Wilkinson, *The Complete Gods and Goddesses of Ancient Egypt*

The Egyptian year was considered to begin on 19 July (according to the later Julian calendar) which was the date of the heliacal rising of the dog star Sirius . . .

Ian Shaw and Paul Nicholson, *The British Museum Dictionary of Ancient Egypt*

The Egyptians . . . were the first to discover the solar year, and to portion out its course into twelve parts. They obtained this knowledge from the stars.

Herodotus, *The Histories*, Book II

A Sense of Eternity

'The quest for Eternity,' wrote the French scholar Anne-Sophie Bomhard, 'was the most essential preoccupation of the Egyptian civilisation.'[1] This is a bit of an understatement. The quest for eternity was the *raison d'être* of the Egyptian civilisation. Everything they did, every monument they built, every ceremony, every ritual, every writing was directly or indirectly inspired by the idea of eternity and how to connect with it. And if one needs reminding, then all one has to do is look at the pyramids of Giza.[2] Nothing else can really explain their brooding presence. But if the pyramids are symbols to eternity, then its very manifestation must surely be the never-ending flow of the River Nile and, perhaps even more so, its cyclical flood. The fifth century BC historian Herodotus called Egypt 'the gift of the Nile'. The Egyptians themselves went a lot further. They claimed that their sacred river had its source in heaven among the stars.[3] As the distinguished French Egyptologist Jean Kerisel so aptly put it, 'the mystery of the distant sources of the Nile and the inability to explain the mechanism behind the flooding of the river which followed a regular calendar . . . must have nourished the image of divinity and the sense of eternity'.[4]

The source of the Nile lies in the distant south, 4,000 kilometres into the heartland of Africa. But the ancient Egyptians never knew this. Indeed, the whereabouts of the source of the Nile – and thus the cause of the yearly flood – was not known to modern man until the late nineteenth century. It was towards this mysterious distant south, therefore, that the ancient Egyptians directed their attention, watching and waiting for the life-giving flood to come each year. As the British astronomer Allan Chapman explained, the Nile 'ran very largely from south to north, almost down the meridian, so that when one looked south, astronomical bodies always rose to the left from the desert, culminated to the meridian above the Nile, and set to the right beyond the western desert.'[5] Similar views are expressed by the American Egyptologist John A. Wilson who wrote that

> . . . (the Egyptian) took his orientation from the Nile River, the source of all life. He faced the south, from which the stream came. One of the

terms for 'south' is also the term for 'face'; the usual word for 'north' is probably related to a word which means 'the back of the face'. On his left was the east and on his right the west. The word for 'east' and 'left' is the same and the word for 'west' and 'right' is the same.[6]

In ancient Egypt the Nile was sacred, represented as a god with drooping breasts and a belly gorged with food and drink. The Egyptians believed with intense fervour that the Nile had its source not on earth but in some deep cavernous region of the underworld. Yet the underworld itself, as many of the ancient texts imply, was an interface with the world of the stars. It was called the Duat, and as many Egyptologists have demonstrated, there was an underworld Duat as well as a starry Duat. For example, J. Gwyn Griffiths informs us that 'Osiris is especially associated with the Duat, a watery celestial region where he consorts with Orion and Sothis (Sirius), heralds of inundation and fertility. He is also Lord of Eternity . . .'[7] And Mark Lehner writes that 'the word for "Netherworld" was Duat, often written with a star in a circle, a reference to Orion, the stellar expression of Osiris in the underworld. Osiris was the Lord of the Duat, which, like the celestial world (and the real Nile Valley) was both a water world and an earthly realm.'[8] But the celestial Duat and the underworld Duat were probably one and the same thing to the Egyptians. This can be explained by the observation that stars set (enter the underworld) in the western horizon each day and emerge twelve hours later in the east. In other words, they journey for half the day in the underworld and the other half in the sky above. But to the Egyptians the Nile not only had its source in the starry Duat, its yearly cycle of the flood mirrored the cycle of the stars. There was, however, a more visible feature in the sky that added to this earth–sky correlation: 'Was not the life-giving Nile itself,' points out the astronomer Alan Chapman, 'reflected in the very heavens themselves, in the form of the Milky Way?'[9] Speaking of the 'celestial world and underworld', Mark Lehner wrote:

Indeed, the sky had banks or levees on the west and in the east. The Milky Way was the 'beaten path of the stars', although it was also a watery way. Two fields were prominent in the sky, the Field of Reeds, a rather marshy area on the eastern edge, and the Field of Offerings further north near the Imperishable Ones. In fact, the vision is that of the Nile Valley at inundation.[10]

There can be little doubt that to the ancient Egyptians the shimmering white band of starry light we call the Milky Way was the celestial Nile on which the gods navigated. 'If Egypt is a reflection of the sky,' wrote the mythologist Lucy Lamie, 'then divine beings sail on the waters of the Great River which animate the cosmos: the Milky Way'.[11]

The Flood

Each year the great river would begin to swell in June and eventually overflow its banks and flood the adjacent land. This was a phenomenon that completely mystified the Egyptians. They had absolutely no idea why the Nile should do that and were the more bewildered because the flood came not in the rainy season, as might be expected, but in the height of summer when the weather was at its driest. As Herodotus noted when he visited Egypt in *c.* 450 BC:

> About why the Nile behaves precisely as it does I could get no information from the priests nor yet from anyone else. What I particularly wished to know is why the water begins to rise at the summer solstice, continues to do so for a hundred days, and then falls again at the end of that period, so that it remains low throughout the winter until the summer solstice comes round again in the following year.[12]

For a people living in a climate where the sun shone nearly throughout the year, and who were thus accustomed to seeing sunrise each morning and sunset each evening, it was inevitable that they would eventually notice that the yearly cycle of the flood seemed to be in synch with the yearly cycle of the sky. It would have become quickly obvious to them that when the sun reached its most northerly position on the horizon (at the summer solstice), the Nile would begin to swell. They also noticed that preceding the summer solstice sunrise certain constellations would always be seen dominating the eastern horizon. All this prompted them to carefully count and record the number of days between each cycle. It would have taken but a few years to convince them that the cycle was 365 days long. It would also have been entirely natural for them to consider the summer solstice as the first day of the new year and call it, aptly, the Birth of Ra.[13] This is because many celestial and terrestrial events that happened at this time of year evoked the idea of a beginning or a birth. For, as we have already seen in the Introduction, was not the Nile reborn at the summer solstice, and along with it the whole of Egypt? And did not Ra himself emerge from his journey through the Duat, the world of the dead, when he reached the summer solstice, as we have also seen in the Introduction?

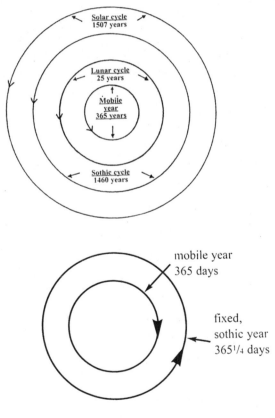

The various astronomical cycles known to the Ancient Egyptians

The East and Dawn

'The ancient Egyptians were past masters of observing nature,' wrote Anne-Sophie Bomhard.[14] They carefully observed nature, its creatures, its vegetation and its cycles. Nothing fascinated them more, however, than the observation of the celestial bodies. From earliest times they meticulously observed and recorded the rising of the sun and the stars in the east, which they called 'the place where the gods were born'.[15]

An observer looking at sunrise from the same vantage point will quickly become aware that the sun changes position along the eastern horizon throughout the year and will alternate between two extreme points: the summer solstice north of east, and the winter solstice south of east. At these two extreme points the sun appears to be stationary for a week or so, hence the term 'solstice' (from the Latin, meaning 'stationary sun'). In our modern Gregorian calendar the summer solstice falls on 21 June and the winter solstice on 21 December. Counting the days between two summer solstices will give 365 days, which we call the 'year'. Most historians of science agree that this discovery was first made in Egypt, probably in the fourth millennium BC. It was most probably around 2800 BC that a 365-day solar calendar was put into practice by the priests of the Great Sun Temple at Heliopolis.

The exact solar (tropical) year is 365.2422 days long (although the extra 0.2422 day is assumed to be 0.25, i.e. an exact quarter-day, for calendrical purposes). So to keep our modern Gregorian calendar in synch with the seasons, we add one day every four years to the month of February. This special year is called a *leap* year. The Egyptians, however, did not have a leap year. They simply let their calendar drift out of synch with the seasons. As the eminent British Egyptologist Flinders Petrie explains:

We are all familiar with the leap year, when we put an extra day in the calendar to keep the account true. The whole checking of the chronology rests on the unquestioned fact that the Egyptians ignored the leap year, and counted only 365 days . . . Now the Egyptian slipped his months backward a quarter of a day each year, by not keeping up the enumeration as we do with a 29th of February. As the months thus slipped backward, or the seasons appeared to slip forward in the calendar, in 1460 years the [calendar] months shifted round all the seasons.[16]

This 'unquestioned fact' that the ancient Egyptians ignored the leap year meant that a cycle was created of 1,460 years which can be seen as a Great Year. The value of 1,460 years is obtained by simply dividing 365 by 0.25. And although it is this value that is given by Petrie and also quoted by modern Egyptologists for the resynch of the calendar with the seasons, they are all assuming a yearly drift of the calendar of 0.25 days, which, of course, is not the case precisely. The true rate of drift is 0.2422 days, which gives us 1506 years (365 divided by 0.2422), which can be seen as a Great Solar Cycle. Actually the value of 1,460 years quoted by Petrie is not the resynch of the calendar with the seasons but rather with the heliacal rising of Sirius, an event which was called by the Egyptians *wp rnpt*, meaning 'opener of the year'[17] (see below). The heliacal rising – or first dawn – rising of Sirius had two peculiarities which the Egyptians were quick to notice: first, it took place near the summer solstice, which also happened to be the start of the flood season; and second, it drifted forward by *exactly* one day every four years with respect to the calendar.[18] And although the ancient Egyptians were fully aware of this drift of the calendar, they made no attempt to correct it by having a leap year. This non-adjustment policy had immense repercussions on the way the Egyptians perceived time and the order of the universe. For although it is nearly certain that at one time in their past they had considered the heliacal rising of Sirius as being the first day of their calendar, and indeed called this event the 'opener of the year' throughout their 3,000-year history, they nonetheless obstinately refused to have a leap year. The question begs the asking: why such obstinacy? Why didn't they simply add an extra day every four years to keep the calendar in synch with the heliacal rising of Sirius?

The answer, as we shall now see, lies in the simple fact that the ancient Egyptians did not compute their calendar in a linear manner starting from some event (such as the birth of Christ) and moving towards infinity, but in a cycle that always returned to its point of origin. In other words, to the Egyptians time was not linear but cyclical.

Year Zero: The Great Return

Our Western Christian culture has fixed 'year zero' of our calendar with the birth of Jesus, which is assumed to have happened 2,005 years ago (as I am writing this).

When was the 'year zero' of the ancient Egyptians?

Before we look into this, I first want to dispense with a misnomer regarding the Egyptian calendar. Modern Egyptologists call the ancient Egyptian calendar the 'civil calendar', which, annoyingly, gives the impression that the ancient Egyptians were essentially dull civil servants who devised a calendar fixing work and feast days and for levying taxes on livestock and suchlike tedious municipal and administrative tasks. This, of course, couldn't be further from the truth. For one, the term *civil calendar* is not from the ancient Egyptians but comes from the more pedestrian Romans. It first appeared in the third century AD in a book titled *Die Natali* by the Roman chronicler Censorinus who prosaically wrote that 'their (the Egyptians') complete civil year has 365 days without a single intercalary day'.[19] But the truth is that the Egyptian calendar was predominantly religious and was thought of as some kind of cosmic instrument with which the cosmic order could be regulated on earth. The Egyptian calendar was not civil but divine. I shall, however, reluctantly stick to the term 'civil calendar' to avoid confusion.

The civil calendar was divided in the following manner: 12 months of 30 days, with each month having three weeks or 'decades' of 10 days. The 12 months amounted to 360 days, to which were then added five days known as the Epagomenal Days or 'Five Days upon the Year', thus making up the full 365-day year. The Egyptian year had only three seasons of four months each. These were: First Season, called Akhet, meaning inundation, from months I to IV; Second Season called Peret or Proyet, meaning emergence or coming forth, from months V to VIII; Third Season, called Shemu, meaning harvest, from months IX to XII. Originally the months were not given names but only numbers from one to twelve. The first day of the first month of the First Season was known as I Akhet 1, i.e. month I, season Akhet, day 1. Later in the New Kingdom the months received official names: I Thoth, II Phaopi, III Athyr, IV Choiak, V Tybi, VI Mechir, VII Phamenoth, VIII Pharmuti, IX Pachons, X Payni, XI Epiphi and XII Mesore.[20] Egyptologists and historians can never agree how old the Egyptian calendar is. There is, however, much evidence to support the conclusion that it was already in place during the Old Kingdom, for in the Pyramid Texts there are several passages that allude to it indirectly:

Osiris appears, the sceptre is pure, the Lord of Right is exalted at the First of the Year . . . The Lord of wine in flood, his season has recognised him . . . The sky has conceived him, the dawn has reborn him, and this king is conceived with him in the sky, this king is reborn with him in the sky . . . the king has gone up from the east of the sky . . .[21]

The king passes the night (in his tomb) . . . and the shrine is opened for him when Ra (the sun) shines. The king ascends . . . in the presence of Ra on that day of the Festival of the Year . . .[22]

O king, you have not died the death; live among them the Imperishable Spirits; when the season of Inundation (Akhet) comes, provide the efflux which issues from Osiris . . [23]

The king is bound for the eastern side of the sky, for the king was conceived there and the king was born there. The Prince (successor of the king) ascends in a great storm from the inner horizon; he sees the preparation of the festival, the making of the brazier, the birth of the gods before you in the *Five Epagomenal Days* . . .[24]

More direct evidence of the civil calendar in the Old Kingdom is found in the Fourth Dynasty (*c.* 2500 BC) tomb of Princess Mersyankh III, a daughter of King Khufu, the builder of the Great Pyramid. An inscription on the entrance to her tomb at Giza, which was studied by the American Egyptologists Dows Dunham and William Kelly Simpson in 1974, gives the date of her death (referred to as 'proceeding to the House of Purification') and the date of her burial (referred to as 'proceeding to her beautiful tomb'):

> King's daughter Mersyankh, Year 1, month 1 of Shemu, day 21: the resting of her Ka and her proceeding to the House of Purification.

> King's daughter Mersyankh, Year 2, month 2 of Proyet, day 18: her proceeding to her beautiful tomb.[25]

Oddly, the time between Mersyankh's death and her burial was 273 days,[26] a figure that comes very close to nine months. This has been taken by some scholars to refer probably to a 'gestation period' of the mummy (as a sort of 'foetus') awaiting rebirth in the tomb. But whatever the meaning of this time lapse between Mersyankh's death and burial, it is undeniable that the ancient scribe was using the civil calendar when he carved the inscription. But how old was this calendar? How long before Mersyankh's death was it first put into use?

This is where the drift of the calendar relative to the heliacal rising of Sirius comes in handy.

The 'Rebirth' of Sirius

In many ancient cultures the star Sirius was known as 'the sparkling one', the 'scorching one' or, less flatteringly in Roman times, the 'dog star'. These odd names are because its heliacal rising occurred in the height of summer when the sun was at its hottest, the 'dog days' of the Roman year. The Greeks, however, called this star 'Sothis'.[27] Modern astronomers know it as Alpha Canis Major or by its common name Sirius.[28] The American astronomer Robert Burnham Jr describes it as being

> ... the brightest of the fixed stars, 'the leader of the host of heaven', and a splendid object throughout the winter months for observers in the

northern hemisphere. To Americans the coming of Sirius heralds the approach of the Christmas season and conjures up visions of sparkling frosty nights . . . On New Year's Eve (it) dominates the southern sky, reaching culmination just at midnight.[29]

Sirius, however, does not stand alone. It is, in fact, part of a bright constellation we call Canis Major, commonly known as the Great Dog, which trails behind Orion the Hunter. Being the brightest of all the visible stars, Sirius is classed as a first-magnitude star with a value of -1.42. This makes it nine times more brilliant than any other of the first-magnitude stars. It is even said that it can be seen in broad daylight with the aid of a small telescope. Its colour is a brilliant bluish-white, sometimes with pulsating faint flashes of blue. Sirius, quite simply, is the Kohinoor of the starry world. In cosmic terms, being only 8.7 light-years away, it is in our back yard. It is the second nearest star to us after Alpha Centauri.

Today, seen from the latitude of Giza, Sirius rises some 20° south of east. This will hold fairly true for the span of a human life. But eventually Sirius will be seen rising a little further south because of the effect of precession (see Appendix 2). When Imhotep built the Step Pyramid complex at Saqqara in c. 2650 BC, Sirius rose 26° south of east. In 5000 BC it rose 37° south of east. In 8000 BC it rose 58° south of east and at the remote date of 11,500 BC it would have risen almost due south (90° south of east). It is an undisputed fact that the Egyptians observed Sirius avidly, especially when it was rising in the east. It was probably observed more than any other object in the sky, perhaps even more than the sun. Let us see why.

The Heliacal Rising of Sirius

The rising time of stars is delayed by nearly four minutes each day. So if you watch, say, Sirius's rising in early August it will be at dawn. Watch it rising again in late October and it will be at midnight. Yet watch Sirius rising in early January and it will be at dusk. There is a period from late January to late May during which Sirius has already risen in daylight and now seems to 'emerge' out of the sky as it darkens after sunset (i.e., the sky becomes dark enough for the spot of light that is the star to be seen). If you were at the Giza pyramids in early March and were looking due south at dusk, Sirius would emerge out of the sky right over the Great Pyramid.[30] There comes a time in the year when Sirius will be seen hovering just over the western horizon after sunset. This happens in late May. In days that follow it will not be seen any more because it is now too close to the glare of the sun's light for its own light to be seen. It will remain 'invisible' for about 70 days, until 5 August. On this day it will rise anew before sunrise in the eastern horizon. This first dawn rising is technically known as the heliacal rising of Sirius, seen by the Egyptians as the rebirth of the star.

Because of the effect of precession, the heliacal rising of Sirius will slowly change in relation to the seasons. Today it happens in August, which is late summer. In 2781 BC it happened on 21 June, the day of the summer solstice.[31] This was a concurrence that certainly must have impressed the ancient star-gazers of the Nile. And what made this concurrence even more spectacular was the fact that the Nile's water also began to rise at this time of year. It was inevitable that this tripartite concurrence – summer solstice, heliacal rising of Sirius, and start of the flood season – would have been regarded as proof that the rebirth of the sun and of Sirius on that same day was the cosmic trigger that unleashed the Nile flood. Not surprisingly, the Egyptians saw those mysterious 70 days that preceded the rebirth of the Nile as a magical transformation in the underworld Duat which took them from death to rebirth. In the Carlsberg Papyrus I (an ancient Egyptian manuscript copied from the cenotaph of Seti I dating from *c.* 1150 BC), it is proclaimed that 'Sirius . . . customarily spends 70 days in the Duat . . . (its) burial takes place like those of men . . . that is to say (in) the likeness of the burial-days which are for men today . . . 70 days which they pass in the embalming-house . . . this is what is done by dying . . .'[32] It is not too difficult to see why the ancient astronomer-priests began to speculate that if the same cosmic 'magic' that caused the stars to be reborn after 70 days in the underworld Duat could also be applied their dead Horus-king, then he, too, could experience rebirth after 70 days in the 'embalming house'.

Horus the Son of Osiris

In the creation myth of Heliopolis we are given the genealogy of the pantheon – also known as the Great Ennead or Great Council of Nine – which was made up of four generations of gods. At the head is Ra-Atum, who became manifest in the sun. Then by masturbation or spitting, Ra-Atum created Shu and Tefnet, the air-god and the moisture-goddess. From them came Geb, the earth-god, and Nut, the sky-goddess. Geb and Nut were united and from them were born four children: Osiris, Isis, Seth and Nephtys. Then Geb and Nut were pulled apart by the air-god, Shu (this is probably where the idea came from that the image of the sky had been imprinted on the land and made Egypt 'the image of Heaven').[33] The myth now enters its second phase, sometimes known as the Osirian myth. It reveals how Osiris and Isis became lovers and ruled Egypt as the first pharaoh and queen. It then goes on to tell how Seth, their jealous brother, plotted the murder of Osiris. One version has Seth drowning Osiris in the Nile, while another has him cutting Osiris's body into 14 parts, which he then scatters all over Egypt. Seth takes the throne while Isis, almost mad with grief, searches frantically for Osiris, finds him and, with her magical powers, brings him back to life long enough to take his seed and become pregnant. She then hides in the bulrushes of the Delta and gives birth to a son, Horus. When Horus grows up, he challenges Seth to a duel. A great battle ensues. The Great Council of Nine, represented by Geb, interferes and divides Egypt between the two contenders. But the decision is reversed by Geb, who decides that Horus, 'the son of Osiris', will rule the whole of Egypt and that Seth will be banished into the desert. As for Osiris himself, we are told that he ascended to the stellar world and established a kingdom for the dead called the Duat.

Egyptologists have long known that in ancient Egyptian cosmology Osiris was identified with the constellation of Orion.[34] They have all agreed, too, that his wife-sister Isis was identified with the star Sirius called *spdt* or *sopdet* by the ancient Egyptians. Thus in *The British Museum Dictionary of Ancient Egypt*, for example, we are given this characteristic definition: 'Along with her husband

SAH (Orion) and her son SOPED, *Sopdet* was part of a triad that paralleled the family of Osiris, Isis, and Horus. She was therefore described in the Pyramid Texts as having united with Osiris to give birth to the Morning Star.'[35] According to the archaeoastronomer Edwin C. Krupp:

In ancient Egypt this annual reappearance of Sirius fell close to the summer solstice and coincided with the time of the Nile's inundation. Isis, as Sirius, was the 'mistress of the year's beginning', for the Egyptian New Year was set by this event. New Year's ceremony texts at Dendera say Isis coaxed out the Nile and caused it to swell. The metaphor is astronomical, hydraulic and sexual, and it parallels the function of Isis in the myth. Sirius revives the Nile just as Isis revives Osiris. Her time of hiding from Set is when Sirius is gone from the night sky. She gives birth to her son Horus, as Sirius gives birth to the New Year, and in texts Horus and the new year are equated. She is the vehicle for renewal of life and order. Shining for a moment, one morning in summer, she stimulates the Nile and starts the year.[36]

A word of caution: many Egyptologists tend to use the Greek name Sothis to denote the star Sirius. For example, a typical passage from the Pyramid Texts translated by British philologist R.O. Faulkner reads: 'O Osiris the king, arise, lift yourself up . . . Your sister Isis comes to you rejoicing for love of you. You have placed her on your phallus and your seed issues into her, she being ready as Sothis, and *Horus-Spd* has come forth from you as "Horus who is in Sothis"'[37]. Although Faulkner did admit that 'Horus-Spd' was also a star, he failed to give an adequate explanation of why this unidentified star was said to 'come forth' from the star Sothis, i.e. Sirius. Such a statement simply makes no sense.

In 1994 a young French Egyptologist called Natalie Beaux decided to challenge Faulkner's translation. Working closely with the American Egyptologist Virginia L. Davis of Yale University, an accredited authority on ancient Egyptian astronomy, she noted that in the Pyramid Texts there were not one but *two* names that seemed to refer to the star Sirius: one was *spd*, and the other had the addition of the suffix 't' to give the feminine variant *spd-t*. But how could this be? The explanation to this mystery is given by Natalie Beaux:

> It is evident that there originally existed a masculine form, *Spd*, and also a feminine form, *Spd-t*, and it would be logical that they refer to two different stellar entities. Dr V.L. Davis has proposed that the second form (i.e. Spd-t) is the name of the constellation to which belongs Sirius, in view that most constellations carry feminine names. This proposal has the advantage to make comprehensible texts which, without this distinction, do not make sense as in line 458a (Unas) '*Spd is alive, because Unas is alive, the son of Spd-t*', where it is clearly demonstrated that the filial relationship Spd/Spd-t represents the belonging of the star to the constellation.[38]

Beaux then requotes the same passage from the Pyramid Texts used by Faulkner, with her new interpretation for *spd-t* and *spd*: 'O Osiris (as Orion) the king, arise, lift yourself up . . . Your sister (wife) Isis comes to you rejoicing for love of you. You have placed her on your phallus and your seed issues into her, she being ready as Spd-t (Canis Major), and Horus-*Spd* (Sirius) has come forth from you as "Horus who is in Spd-t" (Sirius which is in Canis Major).'[39] The passage now clearly makes sense. It also provides us with the correct metaphor to describe an actual astronomical observation. For when the ancient priests described Horus-*spd* as being 'in *Spd-t*', what they really meant was that the star Sirius was in Canis Major, or, in their mythic parlance, Horus was in the womb of Isis. This clever interpretation by Beaux and Davis also provides us with the correct correlation between the astral triad Orion, Canis Major and Sirius and the mythic triad Osiris, Isis and Horus.

By testing Beaux's interpretation of *spd* in *spd-t* on other passages from the Pyramid Texts, it is clear that it is correct. For example:

> Orion is enveloped by the dawn-light, while the 'Living One' washes himself in the Horizon. Canis Major (Spd-t) is enveloped by the dawn-light, while the 'Living One' washes himself in the Horizon. This king

Unas is enveloped by the dawn-light, while the 'Living One' washes himself in the Horizon.

Let the sky brighten, let Sirius (Spd) live, for this king Unas is the 'Living One', the son of Canis Major (Spd-t).

The 'Living One' is obviously the Horus-king (Unas in this case) who is reborn as the star Sirius, i.e. *spd*, which is within Canis Major, i.e. *spd-t*.[40] The original hieroglyphs read: *nh spd n wnjs js nh s3 spd.t* (*spd* is alive because Unas is the Living One, the son of *spd-t*).[41] Now had Natalie Beaux also been investigating the orientation of Djoser's *serdab*, as I had been doing, she would surely have noticed that at the precise moment of the rebirth of *spd*, i.e. the rising of Sirius in the east, if one turned north one would see the star Al Kaid in the bull's thigh (the Plough) positioned at about 4° 35′ to the east of north and some 16° above the horizon – the very same spot in the northern sky which was in alignment with the *ka* statue in the *serdab*, the latter being part of the Step Pyramid bearing the name 'Horus is the Star at the Head of the Sky'. And although looking at this spot in the sky in isolation does not appear at first to have any particular significance, it becomes a sort of 'trigger' when occupied by the star Al Kaid, the 'hoof' of the celestial bull, to induce, as it were, the rebirth of Sirius, the star of Horus.

Clearly the term 'Horus is the Star' is the same as Horus-*spd*, i.e. Horus-Sirius. Could the Step Pyramid complex, then, be a sort of architectural symbol of Sirius and its special cycles?

How?

Why?

The Egyptian Phoenix: the Harbinger of Good Tidings

'Ultimately,' wrote the astronomer R.W. Stoley, 'our clocks are really timed by the stars. The master-clock is our earth, turning on its axis relative to the fixed stars.'[42] Stoley, of course, is telling us that we often tend to forget that time is not the moving hands on a wristwatch or the flipping of a sheet of a calendar hung on a kitchen wall, but the actual observation of the majestic movement of the celestial canopy around the earth. And the astronomer Edwin Krupp also reminds us that 'celestial aligned architecture and celestially timed ceremonies tell us our ancestors watched the sky accurately and systematically.'[43] It should now be obvious that the Step Pyramid complex was ingeniously designed with a celestially aligned architecture in mind to service 'celestially timed ceremonies' most probably to do with the star Sirius. The scale of the complex, however, should also compel us to consider not merely the yearly cycle of this star, but also its longer cycle of 1,460 years. This long cycle is known as the Sothic cycle and as we have seen earlier is caused by the quarter-day 'slippage' per year of the civil calendar in relation to the heliacal rising of Sirius.[44] In AD 239 the Roman chronologist Censorinus wrote that

> The beginnings of these years are always reckoned from the first day of that month which is called by the Egyptians Thoth, which happened this year upon the 7th of the kalends of July [25 June]. For a hundred years ago from the present year the same fell upon the 12th of the kalends of August [21 July], on which day Canicula [Sirius] regularly rises in Egypt.[45]

What Censorinus was saying in so many words was that a Sothic cycle began on 21 July AD 139, when 1 Thoth of the civil calendar (I Akhet 1), which was the first day of the new year, coincided with the heliacal rising of Sirius. A quick check with StarryNight Pro. V.4 confirms that this statement is correct. Sirius did rise heliacally on 21 July according to the Julian calendar in the year AD 139 as witnessed from the city of Alexandria, from where the observation was most probably made, since it was the capital city of Egypt at that time and the seat of learning and calendrical time-keeping.[46] Censorinus has thus provided future chronologists with an anchorage point from which other Sothic cycles could be determined by subtracting increments of 1,460 years starting from the year AD 139. This gives us the dates of 1321 BC, 2781 BC, 4241 BC and so forth for the start of Sothic cycles. It follows, therefore, that the Egyptian civil calendar *must* have started at one of these dates. We can immediately discount the date 1321 BC because the calendar was operational much earlier, as confirmed by the Pyramid Texts. Most Egyptologists accept 2781 BC as the starting point of the Egyptian calendar. Few, if any, are willing to consider the previous date of 4241 BC because, in the words of one chronologist, Marshall Clagett, the Egyptians were 'at an underdeveloped level of sophistication'.[47]

But not everyone agrees with this. For example, the historian David E. Duncan, in his popular book *The Calendar*, ventures that the Egyptian calendar could be 'as early as 4241 BC'.[48] And the Oxford astronomer Allan Chapman seems confident when he asserts that 'from perhaps as early as 4500 BC, the Egyptians had noticed that just as the Nile was about to flood in early June, the star . . . (Sirius) rose just before the sun'.[49] Similar views were also held by the late German chronologist Eduard Meyer and the Welsh historian J.E. Machip-White, both of whom boldly fixed the invention of the Egyptian civil calendar to 4241 BC.[50] The issue of the origin of the Egyptian civil calendar, therefore, remain an open one. But I feel that it is safe to assume that although the Egyptians probably did observe and record the movement of the celestial bodies as early as – and perhaps even earlier than – 4241 BC, it was not till 2781 BC that they decided to formally adopt the calendar as an *official* time-keeping instrument for fixing religious festivals and events. There is much to suggest that it was the conjunction of the summer solstice sunrise and the heliacal rising of Sirius in 2781 BC that prompted this decision. Bearing this in mind, the astronomer E.C. Krupp makes a very interesting comment that provides a clue as to how the ancient sun-priests of Heliopolis may have interpreted the heliacal rising of Sirius: 'The world began in earnest there (at Heliopolis) when Sirius, the stellar signal for the Nile Flood, in its first return to the predawn sky, alighted as the bennu, the bird of creation, upon the benben and then took wings as the sun followed it into the heaven to bring light, life, and order to the cosmos.'[51]

The *bennu* or 'bird of creation' which Krupp is alluding to was the Egyptian phoenix. There was a 'temple of the phoenix' at Heliopolis which is mentioned in the Pyramid Texts.[52] According to legend the phoenix returned to Heliopolis in long cycles of time to usher in a new calendrical age. Could there be a link, therefore, between the return of the phoenix to Heliopolis and the return of the heliacal rising of Sirius when 1 Thoth (New Year's Day) resynchronised in cycles of 1,460 years? Krupp certainly seems to imply this. The temple of Heliopolis was, after all, the centre of time-keeping and calendrics, and it is known with certainty that it was especially at Heliopolis that the heliacal rising of Sirius, which the astronomer Anthony J. Spalinger calls 'the ideal New Year's Day',[53] was celebrated. There is, in fact, a statement made by the first-century Roman historian Cornelius Tacitus which suggests that the return of the Egyptian phoenix to Heliopolis was none other than the 'ideal New Year's Day' of the star Sirius which took place every 1,460 years:[54]

> the bird called the phoenix, after a long succession of ages, appeared in Egypt and furnished the most learned men of that country and of Greece with abundant matter for the discussion of the marvellous phenomenon . . . it is a creature sacred to the sun, differing from all other birds in its beak and in the tints of its plumage, is held unanimously by those who have described its nature . . . Some maintain that it is seen at intervals of 1,461 years, and that the former birds flew into the city called Heliopolis . . .[55]

Commenting on Tacitus's statement, the Egyptologist Stephen Quirke, curator at the Petrie Museum of Egyptian Archaeology in London, wrote thus:

> Intriguingly, the Roman author Tacitus refers to a cycle of 1,461 years, which is four times 365 and a quarter. This number carried hidden significance for Egypt, where the ancient calendar rounded off the actual solar year. The earth in fact takes 365 and a quarter days to go around the sun, but the round number has advantages for accountancy, and the Egyptians did not feel the need to add a day in the manner of our leap year. Every 1,461 years the New Year of the Egyptian calendar would coincide again with the 'real' New Year of the solar, and so of the agricultural calendar. This suggests a Nilotic origin for the phoenix at least in the version recorded by Tacitus.[56]

We should also note that the 1,460–1 years, or Sothic cycle, was sometimes called the Great Year. Bearing this in mind, there is a commentary by Pliny the Elder (AD 23–79) on Manilus that affirms that 'the eminent senator famed for his extreme and varied learning acquired without a teacher . . . states that the period of the Great Year coincides with the life of this bird (i.e. the phoenix), and that the same indications of the seasons and stars return again . . .'[57] Clearly, then, the cycle of the phoenix and that of Sirius were one and the same to Tacitus and Pliny. Giving support to this view is the Egyptologist R.T. Rundle Clark, who wrote that

Underlying all Egyptian speculation is the belief that time is composed of recurrent cycles which are divinely appointed: the day, the week of ten days, the month, the year (and) even longer periods . . . 1,460 years, determined according to the conjunction of sun, moon, stars and inundation. In a sense, when the Phoenix gave out its primeval call it initiated all these cycles, so it is the patron of all divisions of time, and its temple at Heliopolis became the centre of calendrical regulation. As the herald of each new dispensation, it becomes, optimistically, the harbinger of good tidings.[58]

Was the Step Pyramid complex, the 'Star of Horus', built as a sort of a calendrical centre locked into the 'ideal New Year's Day' and the Sothic cycle?

The Oath of the Horus-King and the Calendar

Not long ago I hosted a group of British visitors to Egypt. Among them was Dr John Brown, the Astronomer Royal for Scotland.[59] It was his first visit to Egypt and he was keen to see the ancient sites that were reputed to have astronomical features. During a visit to the Temple of Isis at Philae at dawn, we watched the sunrise and were inspired to talk about the Egyptian civil/solar calendar. But when I told Dr Brown that the ancient Egyptians did not make any adjustments to their calendar for the quarter-day difference in the year *even though they were aware of it*, he found this very hard to understand. Perhaps, he ventured, they were not, after all, aware of the quarter-day difference. I told him that this was not so, and that Egyptologists had hard evidence that the Egyptians were aware of the drift of their calendar relative to the seasons. I quoted the words of Professor Rolf Krause, an expert in this field, who asserts that 'one can no longer maintain that the Egyptians did not realise the lack of ¼ day in their mobile year . . . the 365-day calendar was intentionally planned and inaugurated as a calendar which moved forward through the seasons'.[60]

'Why did they not make the correction then?' asked Dr Brown. Being a scientist, he found their obstinacy most trying. The answer, I informed him, was not a scientific one but a religious one: the Egyptians regarded their calendar 'as a gift from the gods', and thus sacred and not to be tampered with. To them it was not the calendar that drifted relative to the seasons, but the other way round: the seasons – and thus the declination and right ascension of the sun – drifted relative to the calendar. If the cosmic order required that the sun change position by one day every four years, then so be it. This was Maat, the cosmic order, and no one, not even the pharaoh, could or should make additions or deductions to it, no matter how illogical this might seem to us today.

The American Egyptologist Donald Redford, after giving a definition of Maat as 'the ethical conceptions of truth and order, and cosmic balance', went on to say that,

> One of the primary duties of the king was to maintain the order of the cosmos, effected by upholding the principle of Maat through correct and just rule and through service to the gods. The people of Egypt had an obligation to uphold Maat, through obedience to the king, who served as an intermediary between the divine and profane spheres.[61]

The British Egyptologist Cyril Aldred was to remark that '. . . the king was the personification of Maat, a word which we translate as "truth" or "justice", but has an extended meaning of the proper cosmic order at the time of its establishment by the Creator'.[62] Thus the king was not merely expected to uphold Maat, he actually embodied Maat, and his primary role was to ensure through his divine power that no changes were made to it. But how could the king, or indeed anyone, 'change' the cosmic order? A clue is provided by the Macedonian poet Aratus, who visited Egypt in the third century BC as a guest of King Ptolemy Philadesphus, and wrote that: 'each Egyptian king on his accession to the throne, bound himself by oath before the priests . . . not to intercalate either days or months, but to retain the year of 365 days as decreed by the ancients.'[63] And Sir Norman Lockyer was among the first modern scientists to fully appreciate that 'to retain this year of 365 days, then, became the first law for the king, and, indeed, the pharaohs; thenceforth the whole course of Egyptian history adhered to it, in spite of their being subsequently convinced . . . of its inadequacy'.[64]

In 238 BC, one 'Greek' pharaoh, Ptolemy III, did, in fact, attempt to enforce a leap year to the calendar, but he was met with such fierce opposition by the Egyptian priests that the idea was quickly abandoned.[65] Julius Caesar made another attempt in 48 BC, but even this new 'Julian Calendar' was rejected by the native priests. It was not until the arrival of Augustus Caesar in Egypt in 30 BC that the leap year was finally enforced.[66] Such intractable behaviour on the part of the Egyptian priests can only be explained by their unflinching commitment not to alter Maat. Recently scholars have also come to appreciate that a 'drifting' year of 365 days will, in fact, readjust itself ad infinitum much better than any man-made calendar which may include a leap year or other fine-tuning. Let us see how.

Anne-Sophie Bomhard, in her book *The Egyptian Calendar: A Work for Eternity*, called the Egyptian calendar 'the gliding calendar' because this is precisely what it did: 'glide' around the seasons. Simple calculation shows that if left free to glide in this way, the calendar returns to its starting point every 1,506 years and resynchronises itself perfectly with the seasons.[67] This, Bomhard argued, made it needless to add a leap year or any other mathematical adjustments for fine-tuning, because, in her words, this is 'the most difficult stumbling block for any calendaric construction'. For example, even though we add a leap year to our Gregorian calendar, this will still not perfectly retune with the seasons, because we assume the seasonal year to be

365.25 days whereas it is, in fact, 365.2422 days. So there is still a need to make some extra minuscule adjustments every so often. Yet even with the best of fine-tuning, absolute perfection is still not possible, and it is calculated that our calendar will lose a whole day every 3,000 years or so and, consequently, need another adjustment. On the other hand, as Bomhard correctly argues, by leaving their own 365-day civil calendar to drift through the seasons, the ancient Egyptians achieved a perfect system of long-term time-keeping because their civil calendar naturally resynchronised every 1,506 years, making it a much better calendrical instrument than our Gregorian calendar which requires constant mathematical adjustments to keep it running as close as possible (but never perfectly) to the true solar year.[68]

The stark reality is that our planet revolves around the sun in an inexact number of days.[69] Counting the days from sunrise on 1 January to the next 1 January, one will have to wait a further six hours (till around noon) for the true solar year to end. But this kind of reckoning goes against the way in which we perceive a 'day'. In our mind a day is a day, that is from sunrise to sunrise (or sunset to sunset, as the Jews prefer), and our mental perception is hard pressed to envision it being a fraction of this length. The ancient Egyptians were no different from us. Where we do differ, however, is in the way we think of the sun: to the ancients it was the manifestation of the supreme god, who, for reasons known only to him, chose to glide around the seasons in a majestic slow cycle of 1,506 years (which we have termed the Great Solar Cycle). And since the pharaoh was the manifestation of the sun on earth, and that his primary duty was to maintain the cosmic order, he had to resist any attempt to alter this incontrovertible fact. Indeed, as we have already seen, at his coronation the pharaoh had to take a solemn oath not to change the 'year'. This resulted in an observable phenomenon: starting from New Year's Day (1 Thoth), the sun would very slowly glide in time along the eastern horizon. From its original place at the summer solstice 28° north of east, the sunrise would glide to the winter solstice at 28° *south* of east, and then slowly back again, the whole process taking 1,506 years. In other words, the place of 'birth of Ra-Horakhti' changed from a point in the north to a point in the south and back again in a cycle of 1,506 years, i.e. the Great Solar Cycle. This cycle, as we shall see later, may have been the cause of the curious cyclical migration of the sun-priests from north to south and back again that took place in Egypt's 3,000-year-long history.

But more on this later. Meanwhile let us look again at Djoser's Step Pyramid complex, but this time with these long-term cycles in mind. We have seen how the Step Pyramid is orientated in such a way that it could have served as a time-marker for the rising of Sirius. This feature, as well as its name, 'Horus is the Star at the Head of the Sky', certainly suggests, if not confirms, that it was symbolic of Sirius. This conclusion may not be as far-fetched as it first appears, for the principal occupation of its designer, Imhotep (who was the high priest of Heliopolis), was the observation and recording of the cycles of Sirius in connection to the rebirth of the pharaoh and the flooding of the Nile. Heliopolis, after all, was the centre of calendrical studies, and also the place where the phoenix returned every 1,460 years – an event that was probably equated to the return of the Sothic cycle, i.e. the return of the heliacal rising of Sirius to 1 Thoth every 1,460 years.

Could the Step Pyramid complex be an architectural expression of the phoenix?

The Sothic Cycle and the Wall

Since the mid-1980s I have been using the facilities of the library of the Griffith Institute at Oxford (now part of the new Sackler's Library). The Griffith is conveniently located less than an hour's drive from my home, and it has the advantage of being part of the Ashmolean Museum which has an excellent collection of Egyptian antiquities. I have known its director, Dr Jaromir Malek, since 1987.[70] The Griffith Institute has a wide range of books, monographs and articles on Egyptology, and there is a large section on pyramid research and exploration that I particularly enjoy. It was during one of my browsing sessions there that I pulled out by chance a book written by a French researcher. As I was about to put it back in its place, fate would have it that it fell from my hands and lay open at a page with the title: 'Le complexe calendaire de Djeser à Saqqara' (The calendrical

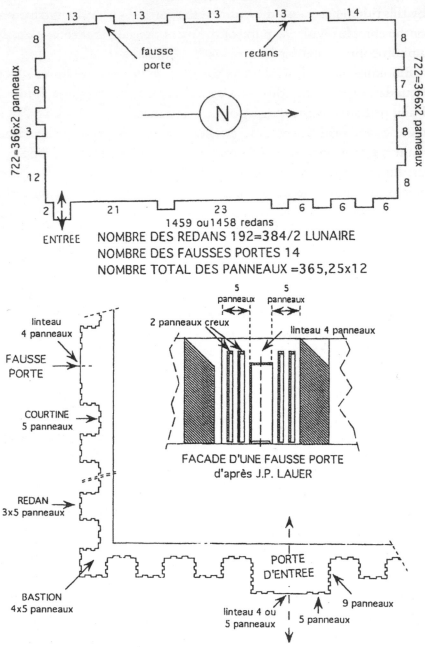

Details of the boundary wall of the Djoser complex

complex of Djoser at Saqqara). I was, of course, immediately intrigued by this title. There was, to my surprise, a diagram of the boundary wall of the complex with the number 1,461 next to it. I immediately made a photocopy of this diagram and took it home with me.

Looking more closely at the curious architectural features of the boundary wall of the complex based on a reconstructed plan by Jean-Philippe Lauer, it could be easily deduced that there was a total of 192 recesses and protrusions, 14 false doors, four corner bastions and one main entrance. Few researchers, however, had paid much attention to the hundreds of slender horizontal panels that were also an integral part of the design. What was most intriguing about these panels was that the west side of the boundary wall contained 1,461 of them, and the east side 1,459. The uncanny similarity of these values to the Sothic cycle of 1,460–1 years was obvious. In my mind this could not be a coincidence, not with the conclusions I had arrived at regarding the connection between the Step Pyramid and Sirius. But what could be the meaning and purpose of it?

A Jubilee Centre for Eternity?

On the eastern side of the Step Pyramid complex there are four stone pavilions set in a row which are referred to by Egyptologists as 'dummy structures'. They are, in fact, models of movable wooden pavilions that were used for the so-called *heb-sed* festivals, or jubilees of the king. According to the consensus these dummy pavilions were intended for the *heb-sed* festivals that the king wished to celebrate in his eternal afterlife. As Egyptologists Ian Shaw and Paul Nicholson asserted, '. . . the first mortuary complexes were concerned with the king's enactment of the sed-festival. The eastern side of the step pyramid complex of Djoser at Saqqara incorporates the earliest architectural setting for the festival.'[71] In his description of the Step Pyramid complex, Mark Lehner remarks that the 'tomb building appears to have been part of a larger ceremonial cycle . . . the fictive architecture served the king's Ka in the afterlife.'[72] In other words, the Step Pyramid complex, or at least a large part of it, was a jubilee centre for eternity.

The *heb-sed* festival (sometimes called simply *heb-sed* or *sed-festival*) is generally described by Egyptologists as a royal jubilee. In reality, however, it was much more than that. In early times the king's future reign, and perhaps even his own life, depended on its success. For this festival was a sort of fitness test that the king had to endure from time to time to reassure the people that he still possessed the full faculties and sexual potency required to rule Egypt as a god and, more importantly, to be fit and able to maintain the cosmic order. As Egyptologist G.A. Wainwright explains:

> . . . nothing is more certain than that the pharaoh was divine . . . Kings of this type contained within themselves the power that produced prosperity . . . To do all this, a divine fertility-king must keep himself in good health and live a well-ordered life. For as he functions regularly and in good order, so will the universe remain stable and continue in its allotted course, for he is himself the universe. The service rendered by such kings has always been to ensure the fruitfulness of the earth, and consequent health of the people . . .[73]

The first *heb-sed* festival for a king was normally celebrated after the thirtieth year of his reign, but there are many indications that it could take place at shorter intervals. According to Wainwright, originally it took place after seven years.[74] Wainwright was of the opinion that the *heb-sed* festival stemmed from the old sky and fertility religion, in which the fertility of the crops and livestock depended on the ability of the king to control the weather and the Nile – a concept that is known to hark back to very ancient times.[75] At any rate, Egyptologists are in agreement that the *heb-sed* was practised as early as the First Dynasty.

There are few inscriptions that give details of what actually took place during this important festival, and interpretations by modern scholars are usually based on pictorials. The earliest of these so-called *heb-sed* scenes is found on an ebony tablet from Abydos attributed to King Den of the First Dynasty (*c.* 2900 BC). On the left part of the scene, Den is shown wearing the double crown of Upper and Lower Egypt and seated on a throne under a *sed*-pavilion resembling the dummy ones at Saqqara. The right part of the scene shows the king running between two sets of cairns that represent the boundaries of his kingdom. This most important ritual of the *heb-sed* required the king to race around a courtyard or perhaps even the boundary wall of the ceremonial complex. As Wainwright further explains:

> (the heb-sed) consisted essentially in a running ceremony, performed in archaic times before the king and from the First Dynasty onwards by the king himself . . . several of the old sky-gods figure in the ceremony . . . The ceremony clearly went back at least into Prehistoric times . . . Physical activity is essential in fertility-rites such as these clearly show. No doubt the king's agility here brought fertility to the fields, and induced the necessary activities in the skies in providing the water required . . . Thus we find that the Pharaohs were divine; controlled the activities of the sky; kept their people in health; hoed the ground; reaped the harvest; carried out a ceremony for the fertility of the fields, and concerned themselves with the opening of the dykes for the inundation . . . The Pharaohs were in fact fertility-kings, upon whose health and proper observance of the rites the health and wealth of the country depended . . .[76]

Further evidence that the Step Pyramid complex was meant to serve as an eternal *heb-sed* centre is provided by the king's apartments under the pyramid and also by the so-called South Tomb next to the Step Pyramid. Here there are reliefs that show King Djoser performing the ritual race. According to Egyptologist Donald Redford the *heb-sed* 'complex took on the character of a microcosm of Egypt itself . . . the symbolism is clear: the racecourse is Egypt'.[77] Apparently during the race – which was run four times around the open courtyard – the king made various proclamations evoking his connection with the gods of Egypt, one of which was 'I have passed through the land and touched its four sides'. The 'four sides' are, most probably, the four cardinal points of the compass. An inscription also states that the king 'runs crossing the ocean (the sky) and the four sides of heaven, going as far as the rays of the sun disc, passing over the earth'.[78] The same 'four sides of heaven' are also evoked when the king is made to shoot four arrows towards the four cardinal points of the compass.[79] According to Greg Reeder, the editor of *KMT* magazine,[80]

> Two paired glyphs that look like swinging doors, but are actually the two halves of the sky, are often shown in direct association with the three cairn-shaped glyphs which identify the territorial markers which the king rounded during his run-of-the-field event of the Heb-sed. Thus the celebrant not only traversed the field (i.e. Egypt) in a public ceremony but also traversed the heavens in, understandably, a less public form.

In support of this sky–ground correlation of the *heb-sed* rituals, Reeder quotes from the Pyramid Texts: 'the king has gone round the entire two skies, he has circumambulated the Two Banks.' Reeder also sees the king's assimilation to the god Horus as part of the ritual, as indicated in another passage of the Pyramid Texts: 'O King, free course is given to you by Horus, you flash as the lone star in the midst of the sky, you have grown wings as a great-breasted falcon, as a hawk seen in the evening traversing the sky. May you cross the firmament by the waterway of Ra-Horakhti.' All the above implies, if not confirms, that the *heb-sed* was principally an event that took place in a symbolic landscape, a sort of cosmic environment in which the king tracked the circuit of the sun-god Ra-Horakhti, Ra-Horus-of-the-Horizon. The sun's circuit is, of course, its annual cycle around the ecliptic in 365¼ days. This suggests that the circuit of the racecourse during the *heb-sed* was in some way calendrical. Now it stands to reason that the Step Pyramid complex was not built for a one-off *heb-sed* event. A project on such a massive scale suggests a very long-term function. Did Imhotep design the complex in such a way that it would service 'super' jubilees every 1,460 years marking the 'return of the phoenix'? Is this why the phoenix was sometimes called 'Lord of Jubilees'?[81]

The idea that the *sed* festival could have been computed using the Great Year of Sirius is not as fanciful as it might at first seem. In fact it comes from Sir Flinders Petrie, Britain's most revered Egyptologist, who undertook precisely such a study in 1906 on the connection between the *sed* festival and the Sothic cycle of Sirius. Petrie's conclusions appeared in a book titled, oddly, *Research in Sinai*, in which he wrote: 'In connection with the question of the rising of Sirius in their chronological relation, we must also take notice of the great festival of the sed, or ending, which was a royal observance of the first importance.' He then went on to discuss how, as a rule, all Egyptologists agree that the *sed* festival came after a period of 30 years of a king's reign, but added that he was not convinced that this period referred to the years of reign because there was much evidence that kings whose reigns had lasted much less than 30 years had also celebrated *sed*-festivals. Petrie was of the opinion that there was much 'reason for associating these festivals with a fixed period'. In this respect he pointed out how 'important was the observation of Sirius for regulating the year, and how the whole cycle of months shifted around the seasons, and was connected to the rising of Sirius. If, then, the months were thus linked to a cycle of 1,460 years, what is more likely than the shifting of the months would be noticed?'[82]

The Egyptian calendar, we recall, had months of 30 days each. In the Sothic cycle or Great Year of Sirius this would correspond to 120 years ($30 \div 0.25 = 120$). This means that each month took the place of the previous one every 120 years in relation to the seasons. It follows that the heliacal rising of Sirius would fall at the beginning of each month every 120 years, a fact that Petrie felt would certainly not have gone unnoticed by the astronomer-priests of Egypt. Petrie then found evidence that

> (a *sed* festival of) 120 years is recognised as having taken place; it was named the henti, and was determined by the hieroglyphic of a road and two suns, suggesting that it belonged to the passage of time . . . Can we, then, dissociate a feast of 30 years from that of 120 years? The 120 years is the interval of one month's shift; the 30 years is the interval of one week's shift. Having a shifting calendar it would be strange if no notice was taken of the periods of reoccurrence in it, and feasts of 120 years and another of 30 years are the natural accompaniments of such a system.

In the Sothic cycle of 1,460 years, a day corresponds to four years, a 'decade' or 10-day week corresponds to 40.53 years, and a month corresponds to 121.66 years. So a period of 30 years would correspond to 7.5 Sothic days, which could be rounded down to seven days. We have seen how in the archaic era the 'life period' that the goddess Seshat allocated to the king during the *sed* festival was seven years, whereas in later times the period of reign linked to the *sed* festival is said to be 30 years. Could the idea of a 30-year festival come from calendrical computations? According to Wallis Budge:

> . . . she (Seshat) appears in the character of the chronographer and chronologist; the use of the notched palm-branch as a symbol of the counting of years taking us back to a custom probably prevalent in predynastic times. In yet another scene we find the goddess standing before a column of hieroglyphics meaning 'life' and 'power' and 'thirty-year festivals' (the Heb Sed) which rest upon a seated figure who holds in each hand 'life' and who typifies 'millions of years'. In connection with this must be noted a passage in a text in which she declares to a king that she has inscribed on her register on his behalf a period of life which shall be 'hundreds of thousands of Thirty-Years periods' and has ordained that his years shall be upon the earth like the years of *Ra* i.e. that he shall live forever.[83]

Yet G. A. Wainwright was adamant that the life period allocated to the king was seven years, which could be renewed at his *sed* festivals. Also according to Wainwright, Seshat 'clearly brought the ancient gift of a reign of seven years, relics of which may be found throughout pharaonic days. In granting a period of life that is not eternity, Seshat fixes the king's fate and decides the time of his death.'[84] But why seven years? According to Wainwright, 'all through the Old Kingdom and indeed until the Nineteenth Dynasty, Seshat's symbol invariably had seven petals, leaves, rays, or whatever the object may have been . . . Seshat is therefore very definitely related to the number seven.' We should also recall that Seshat performed the 'stretching of the cord' ceremony which involved the astronomical sighting of the Plough. In this respect the astronomer E.C. Krupp was quick to note that the number seven may also have something to do with the seven stars of this constellation:

> Usually Seshat was portrayed with a seven-pointed star (although some have likened it to a seven-petaled flower) supported by a rod balanced upright upon her head. Like a canopy over her star hangs what may be a pair of upturned horns of a cow or bull. This emblem was also the hieroglyph for her name. Both the horns and the seven points of the star seem to have something to do with the Big Dipper. We already know that the Bull's Thigh, or Meskhetiu, was the Big Dipper, and the Dipper contains seven stars. It is certain that the Egyptians associated the number seven with the Big Dipper because several portrayals of Meskhetiu – at Dendera, Edfu, Esna and Philae – surround the picture of the bull's leg with seven stars.[85]

The Step Pyramid, which is aligned to the Plough, also has seven tiers (six steps plus the capstone) and the perimeter wall of the complex has 14 (2 × 7) 'false gates'. Egyptologist Ali Radwan explains this by saying that 'seven was always considered a sacred number (for example Re had seven Bas), and its multiples must have had the same connotations'.[86] The possible link between Seshat, the *heb-sed* and the calendar is further confirmed by the Egyptologist Jean Yoyotte, who wrote that

> The year is called *rnpet*, which derives from the word *rnep* 'to be young, to rejuvenate' in the sense as does the world of plants and animals, of men and the gods and stars, and which is often interpreted as 'new' in the context of the return of the flood of the Nile. The hieroglyphic sign describing this word, and serving as an ideogram for our 'year', is a branch of the palm tree without leaves, on which a little excrescence represents a kind of notch. This is the simplified form which the gods present to the king to offer him hundreds of thousands of thirty-year jubilees: a promise of eternity. The hieroglyph describing the jubilee (*heb-sed*) is often shown suspended from its upper tip. At the lower tip can be seen the tadpole (the symbol for 100,000) resting on a circular sign (*shen*) which represents the universe as Ra wanders across it and

pharaoh rules it. On this stem, Thoth – the lunar god who reckons time, protector of the learned and the scribes, who possess knowledge and administer the creation, and Seshat, the goddess who watches over the royal inscriptions and books, and architectural plans and drawings – count the years back into the past, and forward into the future.[87]

Could these 'hundred of thousands' of *sed* festivals have something to do with the Sothic period of ad infinitum cycles of 1,460 years? Was the Step Pyramid complex meant for these 'eternal' cycles?

The Genesis of the Sothic Cycles

Although it is true to say that the ancient Egyptians believed in eternity and sought to connect with it in every way they could, it is also true that they believed in a *beginning* of time which they called *zep tepi*, literally 'the first time', and which was intrinsically tied to their beliefs in creation and the return of the phoenix.

The Egyptologist Richard Wilkinson was of the opinion that from very early times 'three great themes – original cosmic structure, ongoing cosmic function and cosmic regeneration – may be seen to be recurrent in Egyptian temple symbolism',[88] and his colleague R.T. Rundle Clark also concluded that all rituals and feasts were 'a repetition of an event that took place at the beginning of the world.'[89] Also according to Clark:

> The basic principles of life, nature and society were determined by the gods long ago, before the establishment of kingship. This epoch – *zep tepi* – 'the First Time' – stretched from the first stirring of the High God in the Primeval Waters to the settling of Horus upon the throne and the redemption of Osiris. All proper myths relate events or manifestations of this epoch. Anything whose existence or authority had to be justified or explained must be referred to the 'First Time'. This was true for natural phenomena, rituals, royal insignia, the plans of temples, magical or medical formulae, the hieroglyphic system of writing, the calendar – the whole paraphernalia of the civilization . . . all that was good or efficacious was established on the principles laid down in the 'First

Time' – which was, therefore, a golden age of absolute perfection – 'before rage or clamour or strife or uproar had come about'. No death, disease or disaster occurred in this blissful epoch, known variously as 'the time of Re', 'the time of Osiris', or 'the time of Horus'.[90]

Would it thus not be in keeping with such potent beliefs to consider that the *heb-sed* festival was also anchored to the 'First Time'? Support for this hypothesis comes in the names given to some of the *heb-sed* festivals, such as *zep tepi heb-sed*, which translates as 'the *heb-sed* of the First Time' and also *zep tepi uahem heb-sed*, 'the repetition of the *heb-sed* of the First Time'.[91] Now the Sothic cycle, as we have seen, had anchorage points every 1,460 years. Counting back in increments of 1,460 years from AD 139, we get the anchor dates of 1321 BC; 2781 BC; 4241 BC; 5701 BC; 7160 BC; 8621 BC; 10,081 BC; 11,451 BC and so on. Which of these could be regarded as *zep tepi*, the 'First Time'?

If one watches the star Sirius cross the southern meridian over the Great Pyramid, today it will be at 43° above the horizon. Had the observation been made in 2500 BC when the Great Pyramid had just been built, Sirius would have culminated at 36° above the horizon. Going back much further to about 11,500 BC it would culminate 1° above the horizon. Before this epoch it would not have been seen at all. This is because it would have been rising below the horizon. What, then, would have been the reaction of the ancient sky-watchers of Egypt who might have been there to witness the very first appearance of Sirius in the Egyptian sky in about 11,500 BC? Was this event seen as the 'First Time'?

At precisely the time that Sirius showed itself in the distant south, if the observer turned to look due east he would have witnessed another magnificent constellation also rising. As the astronomer Nancy Hathaway once remarked, 'Leo resembles the animal after which it is named. A right triangle of stars outline the back legs . . . the front of the constellation, like a giant backward question mark, defines the head, mane, and front legs. At the base of the question mark is Regulus, the heart of the lion . . .'[92] In other words, Leo resembles a recumbent lion with a bright star, Regulus, on its chest. On the Giza plateau there is a recumbent lion we call the Great Sphinx of Giza. It too is looking due east. Between its paws there is a large stone covered with inscriptions. One line reads: 'This is the Splendid Place of the First Time'.

I took out a map of the Memphite region showing all the pyramid fields on the west side of the Nile, and on the east side the solar city of Heliopolis from where had emanated, in all probability, the impulse to build all those giant pyramids that were scattered seemingly randomly in the desert. I gazed intently at the location of Heliopolis, then at the Giza pyramids, then at the other pyramid fields further south. There was a ghost hidden in this map. I could feel it, almost see it. Slowly a mist began to lift in my mind and also from the whole Memphite region. Beneath it shimmered a weird starry landscape. Suddenly I knew that I was looking at the 'Splendid Place of the First Time' . . .

CHAPTER THREE

The Duat of Memphis

Did the Egyptians of the Pyramid Age have much more astronomical and geographical knowledge than hitherto assumed by us?
George Goyon, *Kheops: Le Secret des Batiseurs des Grandes Pyramides*

The idea that the distribution of the pyramids is governed by definable ideological (religious, astronomical, or similar) considerations is attractive. After all, if there were such reasons for the design of the pyramid and for the relationship of monuments at one site, why should we shut our eyes to the possibility that similar thinking was behind the apparently almost perverse scatter of the pyramids over the Memphite area? The argument that the Egyptians would not have been able to achieve this had they set their mind to it cannot be seriously entertained.
J. Malek, 'Orion and the Giza Pyramids'

Musical Chairs with Pyramids

The founder of the great Fourth Dynasty was the pharaoh Snefru, the son of Djoser. But instead of building a step pyramid like his father at Saqqara, Snefru invented the new design of the 'true' or smooth-faced pyramid and built not one but two pyramids seven kilometres south of Saqqara, at a site called Dashur. Oddly enough, the site of Dashur is not on a promontory like Saqqara, nor does it have any special geological features that may have warranted a move so far away from the Step Pyramid. Immediately after Snefru died, his son, the pharaoh

Khufu, did the opposite of his father: he moved 12 kilometres *north* of Saqqara, and built his giant pyramid on the high promontory we call the Giza plateau. This curious moving around continued with his son, Djedefra, who decamped another eight kilometres north and built his own pyramid at a place called Abu Ruwash. His two successors, Khafra and Menkaura, returned to Giza and build their pyramids next to Khufu's. Then the Fifth Dynasty came along. Its first pharaoh, Userkaf, returned to Saqqara and built his pyramid next to Djoser's Step Pyramid. His six successors, however, all moved north of Saqqara and raised their pyramids at a place called Abusir. Yet the last king of the Fifth Dynasty returned to Saqqara to build his pyramid south of the Step Pyramid of Djoser.

What drove these kings to play musical chairs with their pyramids all over the Memphite region? Take the case of Khufu. The standard explanation is that he chose the Giza plateau because it had a commanding view over the whole Memphite region. But if that was the true motive behind his choice of location, then we may well ask why his father Snefru or, for that matter, his grandfather Djoser, did not grab this prime afterlife site for themselves. Miroslav Verner, the eminent Czech Egyptologist, puzzled over this enigma in another way:

> The reasons why the ancient Egyptians buried their dead on the edge of the desert on the western bank of the Nile are evident enough. The same, however, cannot be said of the reasons for their particular choice of sites for pyramid-building. Why, for example, did the founder of the Fourth Dynasty, Snefru, build his first pyramid at Meydum then abandoned the place, building another two of his pyramids approximately 50 kilometres further north of Dashur? Why did his son Khufu build his tomb, the celebrated Great Pyramid, still further to the north in Giza? . . . the questions are numerous, and, as a rule, answers to them remain on the level of conjecture.[1]

In 1983 I came up with some conjecture of my own. I wrote to a selection of eminent Egyptologists and suggested to them that the reason for this apparent unruly scattering of pyramids along the

40-kilometre strip of desert they call the Memphite Necropolis had little if anything to do with engineering or geological practicalities, as is often suggested, but rather with religion. To be more specific, I proposed a controversial new idea: that the religious motive was to replicate on the land the scattering of stars that were said to be in the Duat. Not too unexpectedly, I was patronisingly told to mind my own business.[2] In any case, according to Egyptologists the pyramids had nothing or very little to do with the stars, but were symbols of the sun. This 'solar' tag was so entrenched in Egyptology that anyone suggesting otherwise, and especially an outsider speaking of a connection with the stars, was bound to be ignored at best or severely pilloried and ridiculed at worst. As for the bizarre random scattering of pyramids in clusters in the open desert, this, virtually all Egyptologists insisted, had nothing to do with imaginary stellar plans (or any plan for that matter), but rather with a pharaoh's whim to have his pyramid near his palace or because of the discovery of a better supply of limestone. There was, however, no convincing evidence that the pharaohs had palaces at different locations, and as Miroslav Verner argued, 'limestone occurs almost everywhere in the area of the Memphite necropolis and the technical difficulties in obtaining it and transporting it to the building site did not vary substantially between the different places'.[3]

By 1994, however, some second thoughts on the 'religious' idea were beginning to be aired. We have seen how the director of the Griffith Institute at Oxford, Dr. Jasomir Malek, after reviewing my book *The Orion Mystery*, felt that 'the idea that the distribution of the pyramids is governed by definable ideological (religious, astronomical, or similar) considerations is attractive.'[4]

Mark Lehner also relented a little by offering that 'some religious or cosmic impulse beyond the purely practical may also have influenced the ancient surveyors', although he remained sceptical about a stellar-based plan.[5] As far as Lehner is concerned, the possible 'cosmic impulse' that may have influenced the choice of location for a pyramid site came from the emerging powerful sun-religion of Ra at Heliopolis that had apparently reached its peak in the Fourth Dynasty. His

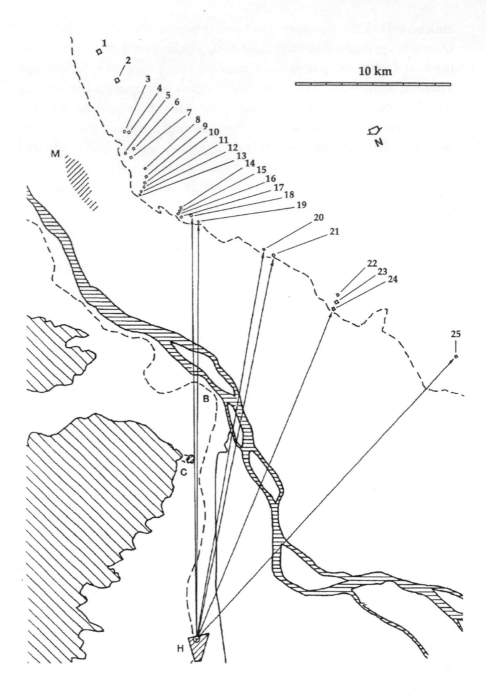

Map of the Memphite Necropolis. 14, 15, 16 and 17 are the Abusir Pyramids. 18 and 19 are the Sun Temples of Abu Ghorab. 22, 23 and 24 are the Giza Pyramids.

colleague Dr Zahi Hawass even went so far as to claim that Khufu, its second king, demanded to be venerated as Ra on earth – a theory that, for a while at least, gained much support among other Egyptologists. There is, admittedly, much that invites such views. For example, it is true that after Khufu's death, many of his successors incorporated the name of Ra to their own – Djedefra, Khafra, Menkaura, Sahura and so on. They also took the title 'Son of Ra'.[6] According to Mark Lehner:

> . . . the pyramid built by Djededfre, Khufu's son and successor, [is] 8 km (5 miles) to the north on a hillock overlooking the Giza plateau. By moving to this spot (Abu Roash), Djedefre's pyramid was nearer due west of Heliopolis, centre of the sun cult, than Giza. Perhaps he was motivated by religious reasons since Djedefre is the first pharaoh to take the title 'Son of Re'.[7]

Lehner might be right in this supposition. Saying, however, that Djedefra's pyramid was 'nearer due west' of Heliopolis is somewhat off the mark. Measuring from a scaled map of the Memphite Necropolis,[8] it is obvious that Djedefra's pyramid is nearer 27° south-of-west from Heliopolis. At this latitude this is the orientation of the setting sun at the winter solstice. Alternatively, an observer at Djedefra's pyramid looking east towards Heliopolis would have seen the sun rising directly over Heliopolis on or very near the day of the summer solstice,[9] which can hardly be taken as a coincidence in these circumstances. The reader will recall from Chapter Two how important the summer solstice was to the feast of the 'Birth of Ra', when the civil calendar was inaugurated. At any rate, the transition from the Fourth to the Fifth Dynasty may also have been due to a dynastic *coup d'état* when a priestess called Rudjdjedet, wife of the high priest of Heliopolis, gave birth to triplets which she claimed had been conceived by Ra himself.[10] All three were to become kings. Two of these sun-kings, Sahura and Neferikara, incorporated the name of Ra to their own, and although the third, Userkaf, did not, he nonetheless took the unprecedented step of building a sun temple that was modelled on the great temple of Ra at Heliopolis.[11] The curious thing about Userkaf's sun temple, however, is that it was not built

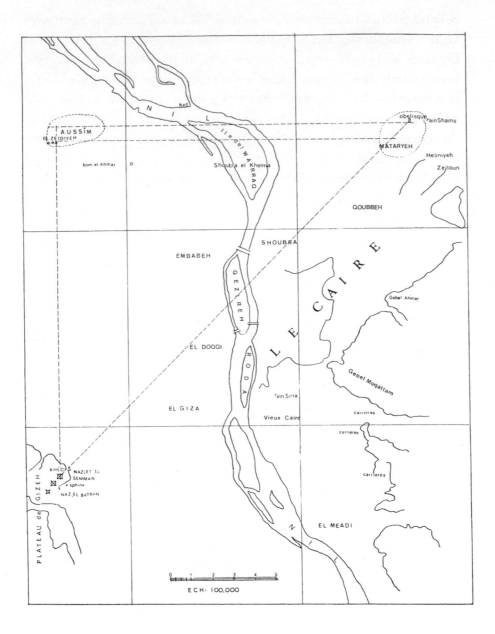

Map of the Giza-Ausim-Heliopolis region

72

near his pyramid at Saqqara but at Abu Ghorab, some three kilometres away to the north. Indeed five of the so-called sun-kings of the Fifth Dynasty who followed Userkaf also built temples at Abu Ghorab, even though their pyramids were raised a kilometre or so to the south at Abusir (nearer Saqqara).[12] Until recently no one quite understood why these sun temples were built at all and why, more intriguingly, they were placed away from their corresponding pyramids. Only two of the six have been found by archaeologists – Userkaf's and Niussera's. We know of the others only by their names found in contemporary inscriptions: 'The stronghold of Ra', 'The Offering Fields of Ra', 'The Favourite Place of Ra', 'The Offering Table of Ra', 'The Delight of Ra', and 'The Horizon of Ra'. This very obvious connection with the sun-god of Heliopolis, however, was not merely spiritual. According to a new theory by British Egyptologist David Jeffreys, it was all about their exact location relative to Heliopolis.

In the late 1990s, Jeffreys was conducting a survey in the area of Memphis on behalf of the Egypt Exploration Society. Armed with the latest topographical maps and good surveying equipment, he was puzzled by the fact that whereas from the sun temples of Userkaf and Niussera he had an unobstructed line of sight to Heliopolis, if he moved just a little further south towards the Abusir pyramids, his view was cut off by the Muqattam hills.[13] In a flash of inspiration Jeffreys realised that perhaps this was the reason why the sun temples were built some distance north of their corresponding pyramids. This also meant, of course, that all the pyramids *north* of Abu Ghorab (which included Zawyat Al Aryan, Giza and Abu Ruwash) also had clear unobstructed views to Heliopolis, whereas those *south* of Abu Ghorab (including Abusir, Saqqara, Dashur and all others up to Meydum) simply did not. It struck him that only the Fourth Dynasty pyramids and Fifth Dynasty sun temples had unobstructed lines of sight to Heliopolis, and that it was these two dynasties that allegedly had special reverence for the sun-god Ra of Heliopolis. In Jeffreys' own words:

A re-examination of the location of Pyramids whose owners claim or display a special association with the solar cult betrays a cluster pattern for which a political and religious explanation suggests itself . . . The Giza pyramids could also be seen from Heliopolis . . . It is therefore appropriate to ask, in a landscape as prospect-dominated as the Nile Valley, which sites and monuments were mutually visible and whether their respective locations, horizons and vistas are owed to something more than mere coincidence.[14]

At long last here was a prominent and well-respected Egyptologist who was proposing nothing less than 'a re-examination of the location' of the pyramids which could account for 'the oscillation in the location of pyramid sites' or, in other words, the scattering of pyramid clusters along the 40-kilometre strip of desert which is the Memphite Necropolis. It was nothing short of a major breakthrough. This is because it brought on to the academic table the strong possibility that pyramids – at the very least those with lines of sight to Heliopolis – were interrelated by the same surveying motive, implying a master plan that took into account the vast area encompassed by the Memphite Necropolis and Heliopolis.

The Master Plan

Having worked in the construction industry for many years in the Middle East, often surveying vast areas of open desert for new roads and remote military bases, I knew that a project as vast as that suggested above would require a fixed point or datum from which a topographic survey grid could emanate. The location of this datum point would, ideally, be at the intersection of a prime latitude and a prime meridian that would become the X–Y axes of a huge grid. Since the principal objective of the project would be the positioning of pyramids along a strip of desert running from Abu Ruwash to Abusir, with the added requirement of them having clear lines of sight to Heliopolis, the ideal location for this datum point would be somewhere due west of Heliopolis and due north of Giza. Working with a good map of the region, I easily established that this point would fall within the modern town of Ausim, once called by the Greeks Letopolis and Khem by the ancient Egyptians.

Little is known about Letopolis other than that it had been an important religious centre dedicated to the god Horus the Elder as early as the First or Second Dynasties, perhaps even harking back to the late prehistoric period. Today nothing remains of Letopolis except for a few dilapidated ruins dating from the late period attributed to the last indigenous pharaohs, including Nectanebo I (380–362 BC). Ausim is now a typical slum of Greater Cairo (sadly the same fate has befallen ancient Heliopolis, the modern Matareya).[15] At any rate, it is very tempting to postulate that there might once have existed here at Letopolis an observation tower from which the ancient surveyors could have projected their grid lines towards Heliopolis in the east and the various pyramid fields in the south. George Goyon, the director of the Centre National de Recherches Scientifiques in Paris and professor at the Collège de France, certainly thinks so . . .

The Observatory of Eudoxus at Letopolis

In the early 1970s George Goyon took a keen interest in the writings of the Roman geographer Strabo, who had visited Egypt in c. AD 30. According to Strabo:

> . . . the city of Kerkasore, which is located near the observatory of Eudoxus, is in the Libyan side (i.e. western bank) of the Nile, where there is a sort of watch-tower which can be seen from Heliopolis [and] from which Eudoxus made his observations of the movement of the celestial bodies. There is the Letopolite Nome.[16]

Goyon had not heard before of this mysterious city of Kerkasore, but because of the description and location details that Strabo gave, Goyon suspected that he was in fact talking about the ancient site of Letopolis, and that the watch tower he was referring to was some kind of observation tower used by the ancient astronomer-priests of Heliopolis. Since Strabo had called this tower the 'observatory of Eudoxus', Goyon decided to investigate whether it was indeed at Letopolis that Eudoxus might have made his famous observations of 'the movement of the celestial bodies'.

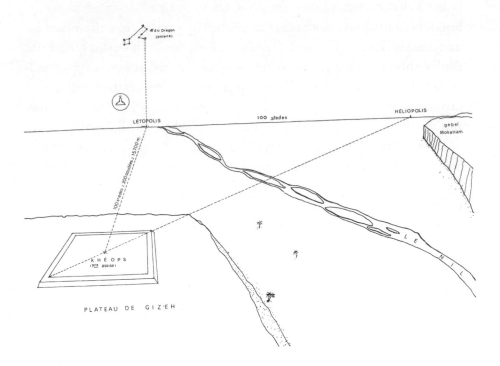

Labels in figure:
α du Dragon (polaire)
LÉTOPOLIS
100 stades
HÉLIOPOLIS
gebel Mokattam
100 stades = 300 coudées = 15,700 m
KHÉOPS (1ère assise)
PLATEAU DE GIZEH
LE NIL

Isometric view of the Giza Plateau, Letopolis and Heliopolis

Eudoxus of Cnidus (408–355 BC) was one of Greece's most eminent mathematicians, and it is recorded that he visited Egypt in *c.* 370 BC for two years as a student at the sun temple of Heliopolis, there to learn the science of astronomy from the Egyptian priests. From an analysis of Strabo's commentary and also those of other ancient writers who mentioned the mysterious location of Kerkasore in passing (Herodotus, Pomponius Mela, and Quintus Curtius), Goyon was able to establish that it had been located about 100 stadium (15.7 kilometres) due north of Giza and 100 stadium due west of Heliopolis. These coordinates mark a spot very near the present modern town of Ausim. Seeing that Ausim was due north of the Great Pyramid, Goyon became convinced that the tower from which Eudoxus had studied the stars might have been the remnants of a very ancient bollard that had served as a sighting point for the ancient pyramid-builders to maintain the monument in a true north orientation during its construction.[17] He suggested that the Eudoxus tower had been, in probability, very similar to the squat obelisk-shaped towers that stood at the sun temples at Abu Ghorab, and that, like them, its top was probably fitted with a polished metal disc from which reflected the sun's rays like that of a lighthouse.[18]

What made Goyon's hypothesis so convincing was that it was well-known that Letopolis, since earliest times, had been the capital of the second Nome of Lower Egypt, whose emblem was a bull's thigh, which, according to Goyon, 'means the constellation of Ursa Major' (or rather the Plough, as we have seen earlier).[19] British Egyptologist G.A. Wainwright had also shown that the deity known as 'Horus of Letopolis' was the traditional keeper of the ritualistic adze used in the 'opening of the mouth' that was shaped like the Plough and bore the same name, i.e. *meskhetiu*, or bull's thigh.[20] We should recall that this constellation was, of course, the celestial target for the 'stretching of the cord' ceremony to align pyramids and temples towards the north. But there was, too, another important constellation involved in this alignment ceremony and which, according to Richard Wilkinson, relied on sightings not only of the Great Bear but also of 'the Orion constellations'.[21] Evidence of such astronomical symbolism to denote the north and south of a place is found at the temple of Horus at Edfu, where an inscription referring to the 'stretching of the cord' ceremony also states that the north side of the temple was the 'bull's thigh' and the south side was 'Orion'.[22] The same north–south symbolism is also found in many of the so-called astronomical ceilings of the New Kingdom where north is symbolised by the bull's thigh and south by Orion (and also Sirius).

Bearing this in mind, it follows that an ancient observer placed at the Giza plateau at night looking due north would have seen the Plough transiting directly over Letopolis, while another observer placed at Letopolis looking due south would have seen Orion's belt transiting over the Great Pyramid. Giza and Letopolis are thus interrelated, and the latter, which is also due west of Heliopolis, must by necessity be added to the master plan that I am proposing. These three locations – Giza, Letopolis and Heliopolis – form a huge Pythagorean triangle, with two of its corners – the north at Letopolis and the south at Giza – appearing to represent two prominent constellations, the Plough and Orion's belt, on the ground. These two constellations are on the west bank of the Milky Way. Could the third corner of the triangle, at Heliopolis, which lies across the Nile some 18 kilometres due east of Letopolis, also be denoting a prominent constellation that is on the eastern bank of the Milky Way and is seen due east from Letopolis? Which constellation could that be? A fortuitous inscription that refers to the 'stretching of the cord' ceremony gives us a clue: 'The king has built the Great Temple of Ra-Horakhti in conformity with the horizon which bears his disc; the cord was stretched by his Majesty himself, having held the rod in his hand with Seshat . . .'[23]

Could the Great Temple of Ra-Horakhti – a name applied specifically to the Great Temple of Heliopolis – have represented a prominent constellation that coalesced with the sun disc in the eastern horizon at dawn?

The Coalescing of Ra and Horakhti in the East

'An important mythological aspect of the solar god in the heavens,' wrote Egyptologist Richard Wilkinson, 'is found in his identity as a cosmic lion.' Furthermore, Wilkinson was of the opinion that 'the stellar constellation now known as Leo was also recognised by the Egyptians as being in the form of a recumbent lion . . . (and that) the constellation was directly associated with the sun god'.[24] Wilkinson proposed that when the sun god Ra rose to prominence during the Fourth Dynasty, he was 'coalesced' with the primitive god Horakhti thus 'becoming Ra-Horakhti as the morning sun'.[25]

Most Egyptologists will agree with Wilkinson on his last statement, namely that Horakhti (Horus-of-the-Horizon) was coalesced with the sun-god Ra to become Ra-Horakhti, together a symbol of the rising sun in the east. This is, in any case, confirmed by the Pyramid Texts, which refer to the rising of Ra-Horakhti in the 'eastern side of the sky . . . the place where the gods are born (i.e rise)'.[26] Egyptologists

The Step Pyramid Complex at Saqqara.

The Step Pyramid of Djoser at Saqqara.

Details of panelled
boundary wall of
the Step Pyramid
Complex at Saqqara.

Robert Bauval measuring
the inclination of the Serdab.

Night photograph of the Serdab with the statue of King Djoser gazing towards the circumpolar stars.

Looking through the peephole at the Statue of King Djoser in the Serdab at Saqqara.

The Giza Pyramids during
the flood season.

The Nile at Aswan
during the flood season.

The solstices and equinoxes as
seen in a flat desert landscape.

21 March

22 September

DUE EAST

21 June

21 Decembe

The sky-region of the Duat, showing Sirius (lower left of frame), the Pleiades (on middle right of frame), Orion (middle of frame) and the Milky Way.

(*Facing page*)
The Big Dipper
seen upright.

The *Bull's Thigh* constellation of the
ancient Egyptians (Big Dipper) on the
lid of the Asyut coffin, 10th dynasty
(c. 2050 BC).

The goddess Isis with
the Star Sothis (Sirius),
Temple of Dendera
(courtesy Sarite).

The goddess Isis suckling the
infant Horus in the bullrushes,
Temple of Horus at Edfu.

Sirius rising (lower left). Note Orion above the two persons.

The sun's journey through the Duat: entry at the Pleiades (Spring Equinox) and exit at Leo (Summer Solstice).

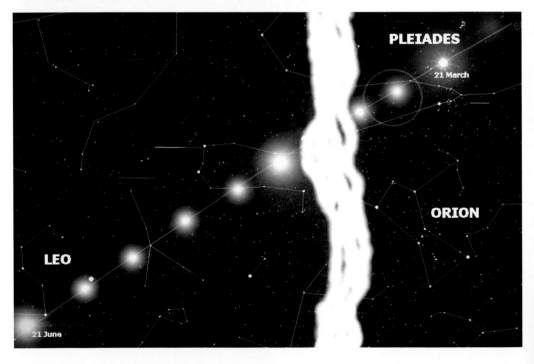

will also readily agree that an important mythological aspect of the sun-god, especially at sunrise and sunset, was that of the cosmic lion. Indeed, as Ian Shaw and Paul Nicholson pointed out:

> Since lions (in Egypt) characteristically lived on the desert margins, they came to be considered as the guardians of the eastern and western horizons, the places of sunrise and sunset. In this connection, they sometimes replaced the eastern and western mountains, symbolic of past and future, on either sign of the 'horizon' hieroglyph (*Akhet*) . . . Since the sun itself could be represented as a lion, Chapter 62 of the Book of the Dead states: 'May I be granted power over the waters . . . for I am he who crosses the sky, I am the lion of Ra' . . .[27]

Few, however, have found any significance in the fact that the word *akhet* means both 'the horizon' and 'the flood season'. It was at this special time of year that the constellation of Leo was seen rising at dawn in the eastern horizon, or, as astrologers would say, the sun was coalesced in Leo. In spite of such tantalising clues, however, hardly any Egyptologists agree with Wilkinson that the solar lion of the ancient Egyptians can be equated to our constellation of Leo. But I do. I side with Wilkinson on this issue because I am convinced that the solar lion mentioned in many ancient Egyptian texts and depicted on their astronomical drawings was, in fact, the constellation Leo. I am also convinced that this can be proved.

The Lifeblood of Egypt

The very existence of Egypt, its agriculture, its ecology and the survival of its people, depended on the flood. If ever the flood waters failed to come, total disaster would ensue. Indeed, it would not be any exaggeration to say that the flood was the very lifeblood of Egypt, and that nothing terrorised the ancient Egyptians more than the thought that it would one day fail to arrive, or that its waters would fail to rise to the optimum level measured at Elephantine near Aswan. As Ian Shaw and Paul Nicholson explain:

Egypt's agricultural prosperity depended on the annual inundation of the Nile. For crops to flourish it was desirable that the Nile should rise about eight metres above a zero point at the first cataract near Aswan. A rise of only seven metres would produce a lean year, while six metres would lead to famine. That such famines actually occurred in ancient Egypt is well documented from a number of sources, both literary and artistic.[28]

On the small rocky island of Sehel south of Elephantine is the so-called 'famine stela', on which is inscribed the story of a terrible seven-year famine that decimated the population and livestock of Egypt during the reign of Djoser. Another protracted famine must have occurred some time during the Fifth Dynasty, for depictions of starving people were found on the walls of the causeway of the pyramid of Unas at Saqqara.[29] These terrible famines were surely caused by too weak a flood. But it was no great boon to have too strong a flood either, for this also spelt a tragedy on a different scale with the torrential waters drowning crops and destroying villages along their ruthless path. The flood, quite simply, had to be just right. Not too weak and not too strong. Yet it was not only that the water level had to rise eight metres at Elephantine, but also, and perhaps more so, that the celestial signs had to be manifest at the right time of year. This right time of year was, of course, the summer solstice, when the sun reached its apogee. Only when these two essential requirements were fulfilled would there be a perfect flood.

Fortunately for the Egyptians, more often than not the flood was good and all went well. Nonetheless, the fear of a bad flood and the havoc and death it would bring was never too far away from the thoughts of the ancient Egyptians, and it hung precariously like some giant sword of Damocles over the very heart of Elephantine, where they believed the flood waters emerged. It was natural, therefore, that their astronomer-priests would pay special attention to the climatic conditions as well as the celestial events that took place around this crucial time of the year. And this entailed avid observation of the stars, especially at dawn, in order to see which constellation preceded the sun. It is beyond any doubt that the astronomer-priests of Heliopolis observed in particular the dawn rising of Orion and Canis Major, which took place at the start of the flood season, and equated these astral deities to Osiris and Isis, the harbingers of rebirth and regeneration. The question must arise, therefore, as to whether or not they also observed with which constellation the sun coalesced at this crucial time of year. To be more precise, did the ancient star-gazers of Egypt take heed that the summer solstice occurred in the constellation of Leo? It would seem very odd if they didn't. Wilkinson's assertion that the Egyptians *knew* the constellation of Leo as a recumbent lion must be reconciled with the fact that in the minds of the sun-priests of Heliopolis, the more primitive god Horakhti had coalesced with the sun-god Ra to become Ra-Horakhti. Egyptologists translate the name Horakhti as Horus-of-the-Horizon, but there may be a word play here with Akhet, the flood season, which would evoke a celestial figure that coalesced with the sun in the horizon *at the time of the flood*. Could it be, then, that Horakhti was originally a stellar god, a constellation if you will, that was actually seen coalescing with the sun at the time of the flood when the Ra cult rose to prominence at Heliopolis? In other words, were the ancient priests celebrating the entry of the summer solstice in the constellation of Leo?

The House of the Rising Sun

That the religion of Heliopolis was stellar before it was absorbed into the solar cult by the priests of Ra is a very moot issue in Egyptology. The distinguished German Egyptologist, Hermann Kees, for example, after studying the Pyramid Texts for many years, came to the conclusion that 'the particular worship peculiar to Heliopolis was, however, that of the stars. From the worship of the stars evolved the worship of Ra in the form of "Horus of the Horizon" (Horakhti), the god of the morning sun.'[30] Kees was not alone in this way of seeing things. Already back in 1912 the influential American Egyptologist James Henry Breasted had demonstrated that the Pyramid Texts contained a stellar cult that pre-dated the solar cult at Heliopolis, and that eventually 'the stellar notion has been absorbed in the Solar'.[31] These were also later the views of Raymond O. Faulkner, the celebrated translator of the Pyramid Texts, who wrote that 'it is of course very well known that the Ancient Egyptians took a great interest in the stars . . . it is also realized that behind this lay a very ancient stratum of stellar religion . . .'[32] The point was driven home more forcefully by I.E.S. Edwards, perhaps the most prominent authority on the Pyramid Age, who declared that 'on the grounds of internal evidence alone it has been deduced that the spells in the Pyramid Texts which refer to the stars have an independent origin from the solar spells and that eventually they were merged into the Heliopolitan (solar) doctrines'.[33] Now it would be logical to suppose that the coalescing of Horakhti and Ra represents the point when the stellar religion was merged or absorbed into the new solar religion of Heliopolis. This seems to be confirmed in the Pyramid Texts, where not one but two separate divinities seen rising at the same time in the eastern horizon at dawn are joined by the dead king, one being Ra (the sun) and the other being Horakhti.

Who, then, was Horakhti?

The Pyramid Texts are implicit that these two divinities rose in the eastern horizon when the Nile began to flood, which, of course, was during the summer solstice:

[The king says]: The reed-floats of the sky are set in place for Ra that he may cross on them to the horizon; the reed-floats are set in place for Horakhti that he may cross on them to Ra; the reed-floats of the sky are set in place for me that I may cross on them to Ra; the reed-floats are set in place for me that I may cross on them to Horakhti and to Ra. The Fields of Rushes are filled (with water) and I ferry across on the Winding Waterway; I am ferried over to the eastern side of the horizon, I am ferried over to the eastern side of the sky, my sister is *Spdt* (Canis Major) . . .'[34]

The Winding Waterway is flooded that I may be ferried over thereon to the horizon, to *Horakhti* . . .[35]

The king will be the companion of Horakhti and the king's hand will be held in the sky among the followers of Ra. The fields are content, the irrigation ditches are flooded for this king today . . . Raise yourself, O King, receive your waters . . . receive this pure water of yours which issues from Elephantine (the mythical source of the Nile) . . . O King, your cool water is the Great Flood which issues from you . . .'[36]

The reed-floats of the sky are set in place for me that I may cross to the horizon, to Ra and to Horakhti. The nurse-canal is opened, the Winding Waterway is flooded, that I may be ferried over to the eastern side of the sky, to the place where the gods were born . . .'[37]

When reading these texts with the geography and ecology of the region in mind, then it is obvious that they are describing what was actually seen in the eastern horizon at dawn when the Nile waters began to rise in late June.[38] It is also obvious that the texts were written from the perspective of the Memphite Necropolis (probably Letopolis or Giza), since they present us with a vision of the Nile plains when looking towards the east; that is, towards the sacred city of Heliopolis. The time of year is confirmed by the presence in the eastern horizon at dawn of *spd-t*, i.e. Canis Major, who was the stellar counterpart of Isis, the mythical sister-wife of the departed king identified with Osiris, who, in the sky, was Orion:

Behold, he has come as Orion; behold, Osiris has come as Orion . . . O king, the sky conceives you as Orion, the dawn-light bears you like Orion . . . You will regularly ascend with Orion from the eastern region of the sky . . .'[39]

I go up (rise) on this eastern side of the sky where the gods were born, and I am born as Horus, as Him of the Horizon (Horakhti) . . . for Spdt is my sister, the Morning Star is my offspring.[40]

From the above passages of the Pyramid Texts it is clear that the time of year is around the summer solstice, and this was when the coalescing of the departed king with both Ra and Horakhti took place in the east at dawn. With StarryNight Pro it is easily verified that these celestial events took place in conjunction during the epoch 2800–2500

BC, which perfectly coincides with the time that Egyptologists say the cult of the sun-god Ra started to predominate at Heliopolis. At that epoch and at that time of year the sun was housed by the constellation that resembled a recumbent lion. It would be truly perverse on our part to suggest that such avid star-watchers as the priests of Heliopolis would not have seen in this the combined figure of Ra-Horakhti. Let us, however, familiarise ourselves with the way the sun travels against the fixed background of constellations so that we can understand this argument better.

The Zodiac

Seen from earth, the sun appears to travel along a circular path we call the ecliptic, also known as the zodiac. It so happens that along this circular path are 12 distinct constellations. These are the zodiacal constellations, so called because their shapes are suggestive of living creatures ('zodiac' comes from the Greek word *zodiakos*, meaning 'circle of animals'). The 12 zodiacal figures or signs are: Aries the ram, Taurus the bull, Gemini the twins, Cancer the crab, Leo the lion, Virgo the virgin, Libra the scales, Scorpio the scorpion, Sagittarius the man with the body of a horse, Capricorn the deer with the body of a fish, Aquarius the water-bearer and, finally, Pisces the fish.[41] In actual fact there are only two zodiacal constellations that can truly be said to bear a resemblance to the creatures they are supposed to represent: Leo as a recumbent lion, and Scorpio as a scorpion with outstretched claws.

The two solstices of summer and winter and the two equinoxes of spring and autumn will denote four points on the zodiacal circle (also called the 'zodiacal belt') which the sun eclipses. In the Pyramid Age the summer solstice point was in Leo; the autumn equinox point was in Scorpio; the winter solstice point was in Aquarius, and the spring equinox point was in Taurus (near the Pleiades). In its yearly circuit around the zodiac, the sun disc also crosses the Milky Way at two places. In the Pyramid Age, the first crossing took place around early April and the second around early October. Also at that epoch the heliacal rising of Orion's belt fell on 1 June (Gregorian), 70 days after

21 March (Gregorian), the spring equinox. On 21 March the sun would rise due east and would occupy a spot just below the small cluster of stars known as the Pleiades.[42] The twenty-first of March was thus the last day that Orion's belt would be seen in the sky before its 'rebirth' (or heliacal rising) in the east at dawn. For 70 days Orion resided in the underworld Duat where, like Osiris, it was subjected to a magic that caused it to rise anew in the east. But during that period when Orion was invisible the sun disc could be seen travelling through the mysterious region of the underworld Duat which transited across the daytime sky. For 70 days the sun travelled eastwards from a point near the Pleiades, crossing the Milky Way to finally reach a point in front of Leo's head. This was when the heliacal rising of Orion, i.e. the rebirth of Osiris, took place in the east at dawn. Three weeks later, on 21 June, the heliacal rising of Sirius took place, signalling the rebirth of Horus, the son of Osiris. We can easily see in these events the cosmic metaphors for the rebirth of the dead pharaoh as Osiris and the ascent of his son as the new Horus-king.

The heliacal rising of Sirius was the ideal New Year's Day, which marked the official start of the flood season. Here we have another powerful metaphor, with the flood water symbolising the birth-water coming out from the womb of Isis as she brings forth Horus in the bulrushes of the Nile. Being such attentive observers of the constellations to the point of obsession, and especially so on the day of the heliacal rising of Sirius, it would be very odd indeed if the priests of Heliopolis did *not* take any particular notice of the lion-shaped constellation that housed the sun at this time of year, and which was the perfect metaphor for Ra-Horakhti, the merger of Ra with the cosmic lion. Yet this is precisely what Egyptologists want us to accept. To be fair on them, it is not that they deny that the ancient astronomers of Egypt could observe and identify the constellation that housed the sun. What they deny is that these astronomers saw in the pattern of this constellation a recumbent lion. Such a curious bias stems from their entrenched conviction that the zodiac was not known to the uncouth Egyptian astronomer-priests until the arrival of the more 'sophisticated' Greeks in the fourth century BC. But the Greeks themselves insist that it was the Egyptian priests who had taught the Greek scholars who visited Egypt all about the movement of the stars and the sun. For example there is the well-known testimony by Herodotus, who visited Egypt nearly a century *before* the Greeks occupied Egypt, where we see him praise the priests of Heliopolis for their astronomical knowledge, which was much more advanced than that of the Greeks:

> ... they were the first to discover the solar year, and to portion out its course into twelve parts. They obtained this knowledge from the stars. To my mind they contrive their year much more cleverly than the Greeks, for these last every other year intercalate a whole month, but the Egyptians, dividing the year into twelve months of thirty days each, add every year a space of five days besides, whereby the circuit of the seasons is made to return with uniformity.

For a man like Herodotus, a Greek, to say that it was not the Greeks but the Egyptians who first portioned the course of the sun in the year into twelve parts by using their knowledge of the stars is practically the same as saying that they created the zodiac. For this is precisely what the zodiac is: *the portioning of the sun's annual path into twelve parts*. Further, confirmation is also given by Herodotus when he writes that it was the Egyptian priests who 'first brought into use the names of the twelve gods, which the Greeks adopted from them'. Yet in spite of such affirmation by the 'father of history', there are Egyptologists such as Wallis Budge who admonish that 'it is wrong, however, to conclude from this, as some have done, that the Egyptians were the inventors of the Zodiac, for they borrowed their knowledge of the Signs of the Zodiac, together with much else, from the Greeks'.[43] Why it is 'wrong' to do so, Wallis Budge does not explain; he seems simply to rest his case on the academic bias that favours Greek superiority in such matters. And so, most unfairly in my view, the honour for the invention of the zodiac, 'together with much else', he hands to the Greeks in one sweeping phrase. To be more specific, academics such as Wallis Budge claim that the Greek scholar Eudoxus of Cnidus, called 'the founder of scientific astronomy', was the first to identify the twelve gods with the twelve signs of the zodiac. Eudoxus probably borrowed his idea from earlier sources, although Babylonian sources rather than Egyptian are often cited by modern academics. Eudoxus, however, though he never visited Babylon, did, on the other hand, visit Egypt. Indeed he spent two years at Heliopolis during the reign of the pharaoh Nectanebo I, and was taught about the movement of the stars by the priests there. As Goyon pointed out:

In Greece, astronomy before Eudoxus was a science that was presented in metaphysical terms. The sky was not observed seriously. Eudoxus is said to be the first to have employed direct observations. But as we have seen, he had used the Egyptian observatory at Kerkasore. He made discoveries in geometry and astronomy which indicated a very advanced level of science. So advanced even, that it is impossible to think that he drew it all from within himself. Only observations and continuous recording (of the sky) during many centuries could have given them to him.[44]

To be fair, Egyptologists do not deny that the ancient Egyptians carefully observed and recorded the movement of the stars and probably portioned the solar year into twelve parts or 'months' even as early as the third millennium BC.[45] But in the same breath they do deny that the Egyptians were capable of recognising in these portions or constellations the figures of the creatures in the way the Greeks or Babylonians did. This stands in total contradiction, however, not only of the accounts of Herodotus and others, but also of contemporary archaeological evidence. For there exist drawings of ancient Egyptian cosmology showing human as well as animal figures that quite clearly represent constellations, such as Orion as Osiris, Canis Major as Isis, the Plough as a bull's thigh, Draco as a pregnant hippopotamus, and so on. Egyptologists will be quick to point out that these constellations are not zodiacal ones, i.e. they are not the twelve through which the sun passes in the course of the year. True. But also shown in the astronomical drawings from the ceilings of royal tombs dating from the Ramesside period are animal figures that are clearly zodiacal, such as a scorpion, a lion and a ram. And there is, of course, the cosmic scales which Maat personifies. Such clear evidence has on occasion brought protestation by more open-minded historians of science, such as the eminent Russian astronomer Alexander Gurshtein, for whom it was obvious that the 'ancient Egyptians were devoted to astronomy. They created the world's first practical solar calendar. It demanded the measuring of the positions of the sun on the starry background, i.e. to recognise the zodiac.' There is also the British Egyptologist Richard Wilkinson, who, as we have seen, was among the first in his profession to admit that 'the stellar constellation now known as Leo was also recognised by the Egyptians as being in the form of a recumbent lion' and that this 'constellation was directly associated with the sun god'. To this we can also add the professional views of other scholars such as Yale University Egyptologist Virginia Lee Davis, who, in reference to the star-studded recumbent lion seen in Ramesside astronomical ceilings, asserted that 'the Lion with its outline of stars must be Leo',[46] and American scholar Donald Etz who made the same assertion in an article for the *Journal of the American Research Centre in Egypt*.[47] Even more recently, in 2001, the Spanish astronomer Juan A. Belmonte presented similar cogent evidence to the SEAC 9th Conference in Stockholm, where he informed his colleagues that 'the Analysis of the astronomical data presented in the diagonal Ramesside Clocks has allowed us to prepare a potential list of correlations between the Egyptian stars presented in them and the actual stars in the sky. Some results are very coherent, such as the identification of . . . the Lion with our constellation Leo.' Belmonte also showed that 'the identification of the Lion (in the Ramesside clock) with our Leo and the lion in the ceiling representations' are one and the same. At any rate, we needn't get too entangled in this never-ending scholarly debate about the zodiac. What should really concern us is not whether the whole zodiac concept was known to the ancient Egyptians, but whether they saw in the pattern of the stars that we call Leo the same leonine figure we see, namely a recumbent lion; and, if so, whether or not they called this image Horakhti.

Let us, therefore, now focus our attention on this issue alone.

The Image of 'Horus-of-the-Horizon'

Throughout history the lion has been the symbol of power, nobility and divine kingship. All one needs to do is stroll in any museum or art gallery to be confronted with this blatant fact. In cities such as Paris, London, Rome and Venice, lion symbols abound in squares and piazzas, guarding the entrances of villas and stately buildings, flanking fountains or emblazoned on the walls of churches and palaces. The leonine symbol is also found in heraldry, on coins and even on the old British passport. The archaeologist Selim Hassan gives us his own view of why lion symbolism was used especially in ancient Egypt:

> In the earliest times the lion was the strongest and most imposing animal known to the Egyptians, and as such, it symbolised the king ... the protector of his people; they looked to him to guard them from their enemies, to lead them into battle, to find them fresh hunting-grounds, and to feed them in time of famine. The king and the lion were one in their minds.[48]

Another view is given by I.E.S. Edwards:

> In Egyptian mythology the lion often figures as the guardian of sacred places. How or when this conception first arose is not known, but it probably dates back to remote antiquity. Like so many primitive beliefs it was incorporated by the priests of Heliopolis into the solar creed, the lion being considered the guardian of the Underworld (the Duat).[49]

The lion in Egypt was, as everyone knows, more often than not depicted as a sphinx, that is to say a hybrid creature with the body of a lion and the head of a man or a woman, a ram or even a falcon. The latter, in fact, was very popular in statuary and religious art, and is known as a hierocosphinx ('falcon-sphinx' in Greek). It can be seen on a relief from the pyramid complex of Sahura at Abusir and, more particularly, at the temple at Edfu which was the principal sanctuary of the solar falcon-god Horus.[50] According to archaeologist Paul Jordan, the 'earliest hybridisation of the lion known from archaeological records involves not a human head but the head and wings of a falcon (and) it may well be that the sphinx idea arose in the first (sic) as a lion-bodied transformation of Horus'.[51] There is an inscription also at the temple at Edfu which seems to confirm this alchemical merger of the falcon and lion in the person of the god Horus: 'Horus of Edfu transformed himself into a lion which has the face of a man.'[52]

Sphinxes abound in Egypt, but the most famous of all is, of course, the Great Sphinx of Giza. Who or what did this universally known statue represent? Half-lion, half-man, is it a strange god whose name we have forgotten? Going by the inscriptions and reliefs from Edfu, one would be forgiven for thinking that the Great Sphinx represents Horus. But such obvious cerebral deduction is not how the minds of Egyptologists work when it comes to the identity of the Great Sphinx. Indeed, this is probably the most debated issue in Egyptology. The reason is complex, but its central core revolves around the adamant belief that there are no inscriptions contemporary with the Great Sphinx that speak of it let alone tell us who or what it represented. As the versatile Selim Hassan, who worked at the Sphinx for many years, was at a loss to explain: 'this, in itself, is an enigma'.[53] On the other hand, because the Sphinx is located in front of Khafra's pyramid, many Egyptologists are convinced that it represents Khafra, though this conclusion is not without its dissenters. Eminent Egyptologists such as Rainer Stadelmann and Vassil Dobrev, for example, are equally convinced that the Sphinx is not Khafra but Khufu. There are also others who, in their desire to remain neutral in this debate, are happy to see the Sphinx as representing no one in particular but as a symbol of the sun-god. Mark Lehner, for instance, writes, 'The lion was a solar symbol in more than one ancient Near Eastern culture. It is also a common archetype of royalty. The royal human head on a lion's body symbolises power and might controlled by the intelligence of the pharaoh, guarantor of cosmic order, Maat.'[54]

All Egyptologists do agree, however, that the Sphinx was created during the Fourth Dynasty, and none of them can deny, of course, that it has the body of a lion and the head of a man or king and that it was made to gaze due east at the horizon, where the sun rises at the equinoxes. Not unexpectedly, in the Pyramid Texts the dead king is beseeched to join or become Horakhti in the eastern horizon at sunrise. Accordingly, Selim Hassan concluded that

> Then came the occasion when the Egyptians wished to create an imposing image of their God-king, who after his death was called Horakhti – 'Horus the Dweller in the Horizon' – the Lord of Heaven. How to represent him? The idea of using the form of the lion probably occurred first, but did not quite meet the need, for the lion had come to be associated in their minds with ferocity as well as kingship, and they wished to represent a wise and powerful, but beneficent deity. It is perhaps in this manner that they evolved the form of the Sphinx, which displays the grace and terrific power of the lion and the superior intellectual power of man.

He further explained that

> . . . in the beliefs of the Egyptians, the king was the earthly representation of this god, and we have proof that in the very early period the dead king was especially called Horakhti. When Khafra cut the Great Sphinx, it was made in his likeness, that is to say in the likeness of Horakhti, with whom he was identified.[55]

As far as Hassan was concerned, the equation was simple and straightforward: Horakhti was identified with a lion; Khafra built the Sphinx; the dead Khafra was identified with Horakhti; the Sphinx was the guardian of Khafra's tomb; the Sphinx must be, by all logic, a representation of the dead Khafra as Horakhti. It should be noted that in passages from the Pyramid Texts quoted earlier, we are told that the king joined not just Ra, i.e. the sun, but also Horakhti in the eastern horizon at dawn when the 'Waterway is flooded', i.e. during the summer solstice time of year when the Nile floods. At the epoch of Khafra this was the time of year when the sun was in the constellation of Leo. Leo is a lion constellation. The image of Horakhti is a lion. The Sphinx is a solar symbol. The conclusion must be, by all common sense, that Horakhti is Leo and that the Sphinx of Giza represents the sun-god Ra 'coalesced' with Horakhti in the Fourth Dynasty, which is when Egyptologists such as Wilkinson, as we shall see later on, say this 'coalescing' or synchretisation took place![56] Oddly, however, such straightforward logic does not always work with Egyptologists. As a matter of fact, the idea that the Sphinx might be a symbol of the sun in Leo is one of the most vilified in this profession. But why?

First, as French Egyptologist Christiane Zivie-Coche protests, 'there are no references to the Sphinx in texts from the Old Kingdom', let alone any that remotely suggest that it or Horakhti was a symbol of Leo.[57] As Dr Zivie-Coche argues, the name of the Great Sphinx was Horemakhet, 'Horus-in-the-Horizon', and not Horakhti 'Horus-of-the-Horizon'. *Vive la différence!* But in any case, as she points out, even the name Horemakhet cannot be that of the Sphinx, because it was not given to it by its original builders of the Fourth Dynasty, but a thousand years later by the Eighteenth Dynasty kings who restored it. Therefore this name, she concludes, cannot be taken as the true name of the Sphinx but must be considered as a sort of pharaonic pseudonym. Thus Zivie-Coche sternly warns everyone that it is totally unjustified to speak of Horemakhet when referring to the Old Kingdom. And that's that. This, in a nutshell, is the basic argument put forward by most Egyptologists.

But Zivie-Coche's bold assertion that '*there are no references to the Sphinx in texts from the Old Kingdom*' is in dire need of rephrasing. What she really should have said was that there are no references to Horemakhet in the Old Kingdom, but only in the New Kingdom texts, which is, of course, a very different thing altogether. This is because there are, in fact, plenty of references to the Sphinx in Old Kingdom texts; plenty, that is, if you also accept that the Sphinx was called also Horakhti, as Hassan has shown, in the New Kingdom. Indeed, the Pyramid Texts are full of references to Horakhti, as we have seen. And at Giza, during archaeological digs, Hassan found many votive stelae near the Sphinx on which 'side by side with the name Horemakhet, we find the Great Sphinx also called Horakhti'.[58] This view is echoed by fellow Egyptologist Ahmed Fakhry, who also concluded that 'the stelae and votive figures of sphinxes, lions, and falcons found around the Sphinx reveals the names under which it was known and worshipped. Most commonly it was called Horemakhet,

"Horus-in-the-Horizon", or Horakhti, "Horus-of-the-Horizon" . . . both are appropriate names . . .'[59] Hassan also found a depiction from an Eighteenth Dynasty tomb at Giza that shows a man kneeling in adoration before the Sphinx, with an inscription that reads: 'Adoration to Horakhti, the Great God, the Lord of Heaven . . .'[60]

With all this evidence, it can now be seen why it is perverse for Zivie-Coche and her colleagues to keep on insisting that 'there are no references to the Sphinx in texts from the Old Kingdom'.[61] At the risk of repeating myself, the truth of the matter is that there are *plenty* of references to Horakhti in the Pyramid Texts which date from the Old Kingdom, and it was a name which, along with Horemakhet, was used for the Great Sphinx of Giza in the New Kingdom. Ah, but that's in the New Kingdom and not the Old Kingdom, the critics are quick to reply. And why wouldn't the Egyptians of the New Kingdom know the true name of the Great Sphinx of Giza as given to it in the Old Kingdom? Well, only because Egyptologists say so. This, however, is a circular argument. The Sphinx, like all else in the Pyramid Texts, is referred to in cosmic terms. It is, after all, as Lehner pointed out, the symbol of the pharaoh as guarantor of the cosmic order. The pharaoh, after death, became one with Horakhti. It is, therefore, a symbol of Horakhti, and the latter is, in spite of Zivie-Coche's protestations, profusely mentioned in the Old Kingdom texts.

Heliopolis was the city most sacred to Ra-Horakhti, so much so that Dr Zahi Hawass, the head of antiquities in Egypt, calls it the 'City of Ra-Horakhti'.[62] And for good reason: the high priest of Heliopolis was called 'Chief Seer of Ra-Horakhti',[63] and the object of the veneration was a conical or pyramidal stone called *benben*, which, according to Egyptologist Labib Habachi, 'was sacred to Ra-Horakhti, the rising sun'.[64] There is, too, the obelisk at Heliopolis dedicated to Ra-Horakhti by Senusret I of the Twelfth Dynasty,[65] and the pharaoh Sethi I of the Nineteenth Dynasty designed a temple for Heliopolis which he described as a 'monuments for my father Ra-Horakhti'. Interestingly, Sethi I also called Heliopolis 'the Horizon of Heaven', which is a perfect epithet for its god Ra-Horakhti, i.e. 'Ra-Horus of the Horizon'.[66] On one of the pair of obelisks of the Eighteenth Dynasty pharaoh Thothmoses III which once stood at

Heliopolis is inscribed: 'Thothmoses made as his monument for his father Ra-Horakhti, the erecting for him of two large obelisks with pyramidions of electrum on the third occasion of the Jubilee . . .'[67] It is also a fact that Heliopolis existed before the Giza Pyramids. It is a fact that it was an important centre for calendrical computations from at least the Third Dynasty. And it is a fact that the high priest of Heliopolis bore the title 'Chief of the Astronomers', which, according to I.E.S. Edwards, implies the observation not only of the sun but of the stars:

> Imhotep's title 'Chief of the Observers', which became the regular title of the High Priest of Heliopolis, may itself suggest an occupation connected with astral, rather than solar, observation . . . It is significant that the high priest of the centre of the sun-cult at Heliopolis bore the title 'Chief of the Astronomers' and was represented wearing a mantle adorned with stars.[68]

Any avid stargazer worth his salt, especially one who made it his principal business to observe the rising of the stars at dawn, would have known that the sun journeyed through the year against the fixed background of stars and that during the summer solstice it rose at dawn against the background of a constellation that had the distinct shape of a recumbent lion. Making a giant statue that gazes eternally at the rising sun in the horizon and calling it Horakhti, then saying that the dead pharaoh joined Horakhti in the horizon at dawn when the Nile was in flood, and then dedicating the statue to the pharaoh should leave us with sufficient evidence, if not proof, that the statue was a solar–stellar hybrid of lion and man symbolising the merger of the sun-god, i.e. the sun disc, with Horakhti, i.e. Leo.

Since 1983 I have advocated a stellar symbolism for the Old Kingdom pyramids of the Fourth and Fifth dynasties, though it is evident now that they also belonged to a solar cult. This is because, as the astronomer and historian Alexander Gurshtein bluntly put it: 'the astronomical observations of the sun coordinated its position on the starry background. This is why the elements of the sun-cult were mixed very tightly in the elements of the astral cult.'[69] In my book *The*

Orion Mystery I have shown how the scattering of pyramids on the west side of the Nile was based on a master plan intended to represented the scattering of stars on the west side of the Milky Way. In this plan the three Giza pyramids were, according to my contention, representative of the three stars of Orion's belt.[70] The conclusion, then, was that the ancient pyramid-builders wanted to replicate the starry Duat on their land or, in their parlance, build the 'Duat of Memphis'. Paradoxically, Mark Lehner, who is an opponent of this theory, nonetheless confirms that, 'the word for Netherworld was the Duat, often written with a star in a circle, a reference to Orion, the stellar expression of Osiris, in the Underworld. Osiris was the "Lord of the Duat", which, like the celestial world – and the real Nile Valley – was both a water world and an earthly realm.'[71] Also, according to Egyptologist Natalie Beaux:

> The sign of a 'five-pointed star in a circle', or more simply just the sign of a 'five-pointed star', are those that most frequently are used to describe the Duat. It must be noted that the 'five-pointed star in the circle' found in the Pyramid Texts only refers to the Duat. One passage makes it quite clear what is being referred to: *'Orion is "swallowed" by the Duat, while the Living One (the rising sun) is purified in the Horizon (Akhet); Spd-t (Canis Major) is "swallowed" by the Duat, while the Living One in purified in the Horizon; (Unas) is "swallowed" up by the Duat, while the Living One is purified in the Horizon . . .'*
> . . . The Duat is specifically the region in which the star prepares itself for its apparition – an apparition which is always seen as a 'birth'.[72]

We find that the same idea is discussed by the Egyptologist Selim Hassan, who wrote that

> . . . as the sun rises and purifies himself in the Horizon, the stars Orion and Sothis (Sirius), with whom the King is identified, are enveloped by the Duat. This is a true observation of nature, and it really appears as though the stars are swallowed up each morning in the increasing glow of the dawn. Perhaps the determinative of the word Duat, the star within a circle, illustrates the idea of this enveloping of the star. When

on his way to join the stars, the dead king must first pass by (or through) the Duat which will serve to guide him in the right direction. Thus we see in Utterance 610 [of the Pyramid Texts]: 'The Duat guides your feet to the Dwelling-place of Orion . . . The Duat guides your hand to the Dwelling-place of Orion.'[73]

As we have already seen in Chapter Two, we also have the statement from the Carlsberg Papyrus I (*c.* 1300-1150 BC) which proclaims that,

Orion and Sirius, who are the first of the gods, that is to say they customarily spend 70 days in the Duat [and they rise] again . . . it is in the east that they celebrate their first feast . . . Their burial takes place like those of men . . . that is to say, they are the likeness of the burial-days which are for men today . . . 70 days which they pass in the embalming-house . . . its duration in the Duat indeed takes place. It is the taking place of its duration in the Duat . . . every one of the stars, that is to say 70 days . . . this is what is done by dying. This one which sets is the one which does this . . .'[74]

Notwithstanding the staunch opposition to the Orion Correlation Theory by Egyptologists, to open-minded readers the question is obvious: could all this textual and architectural evidence mean that the vast region that contained the pyramids and temples of the Fourth and Fifth Dynasties be a model, as it were, of the starry Duat?

As Above, So Below

The idea of developing a huge sacred landscape into an earthly model of the starry Duat is certainly mind-boggling, but it is precisely the kind of idea with which the ancient pyramid-builders of Egypt would have challenged themselves. Could the persistent Hermetic claim that 'Egypt was made in the image of heaven' be true after all?

The pyramid-builders were not just interested in Orion per se, but more particularly the 70 days that it spent in the underworld Duat, i.e. from its last setting in the west at dusk (heliacal setting) to its first rising in the east at dawn (heliacal rising). With modern astronomical computers it is a relatively easy matter to demonstrate that in the Pyramid Age those 70 days were bracketed between 21 March and 1 June (Gregorian). During this period Orion was 'invisible' in the Duat, but the sun was not. For the latter was seen travelling through this mysterious region in daytime from a point just below the Pleiades (Right Ascension 24h 00') to a point in front of Leo (Right Ascension 4h 30'). A further three weeks saw the heliacal rising of the star Sirius as it, too, now emerged from the tenebrous region of the underworld Duat. This takes us to 21 June, the summer solstice. The sun had now travelled to a point between the paws of Leo (Right Ascension 6h 00'). The entrance to the Duat can thus be said to be just under the Pleiades, and its exit in the paws of Leo. Let us for the moment accept that the sun temple of Ra-Horakhti at Heliopolis represents the constellation of Leo, the 'house' of the sun at the summer solstice. Let us also hold the thought that the three Giza pyramids may, indeed, be a representation of the three stars of Orion's belt on the ground. Comparing sky and ground maps, we can easily see on the sky map that the sun's position as it enters the region of the Duat is at a point just below the small cluster of stars called the Pleiades, and projecting this on to the ground map shows that it roughly corresponds to the position of the sun temples of Abu Ghorab, just 'below' the small cluster of Fifth Dynasty pyramids at Abusir.[75] If this is correct, then the line of sight between the sun temples of Abu Ghorab and the sun temple of Heliopolis must, by necessity, represent the ecliptic path along which the sun disc has to travel in the Duat from entrance to exit, i.e. from 21 March to 21 June, during that period when both Orion and Sirius reside in the underworld Duat – and in Pyramid Texts parlance, when Isis performs the magical rituals on Osiris (the dead king) to bring him back to life.

Let us now test this hypothesis with facts and figures.

The Gates of the Duat

The site of Abu Ghorab is in the desert fringing the west side of the Nile Valley and some ten kilometres south-east of Giza. You can drive to a spot adjacent to it on a road that runs along an old canal, then carry on on foot through a farm that leads into the desert. Alternatively you can walk to it from the nearby pyramids of Abusir. The site has been closed due to restoration, but since there are no fences it is not too difficult to visit the sun temples off the record, so to speak. Of the two temples that remain, only one, that of Niussera, is really worth seeing. The other is in a pitiful state of ruin, looking more like a builder's dump than a temple. The sun temple of Niussera is basically a large, squat rectangular structure on which once stood a massive obelisk or tower estimated to have been 36 metres high and probably crowned with a polished metal disc to reflect the sunlight. From this slightly elevated vantage point, when there was none of the pollution that plagues the horizon these days, visibility must have been possible to the northern tip of the Muqattam Hills and all the way to Heliopolis beyond. On the eastern side of the rectangular base is a massive alabaster altar whose four sides face the cardinal directions and whose main axis runs east–west. Strewn all around are weird large stone tubs which were probably used to collect the blood of sacrificed animals.[76]

These mysterious sun temples have long intrigued Egyptologists, and according to Miroslav Verner, who excavated there for many years, their significance 'remains disputed . . . (but) they composed an important part of the worship of the dead king and were economically and religiously connected with the pyramid complex'.[77] Each temple had a causeway leading towards the edge of the Nile Valley that linked up to a valley temple complete with a harbour. Since the Nile is several kilometres away, these harbours probably only had a symbolic function. Most interestingly, on the causeway of Niussera's sun temple was found a relief showing the 'stretching of the cord' ceremony, which is indirect evidence that some sort of stellar ritual was probably performed to orientate the causeway and valley temple. Indeed, according to the American astronomer Ronald Wells, both solar and stellar observations were carried out at the sun temples in order to time sacrificial ceremonies at dawn.[78] And although the sun temple's main axis is typically orientated east–west, the causeway deviates sharply towards the north by 46°, which, oddly, is the general direction of Heliopolis. This curious alignment was noted by Richard Wilkinson[79] and also by Mark Lehner.[80] To make things even more mysterious, at the south side of Niussera's sun temple was found a 30-metre-long boat made of mud bricks whose function Lehner describes thus: 'This colossal simulacrum of a ship perhaps signifies the mythical boat in which the sun-god sailed across the ocean of the sky. It also hints that the sun temple, like the pyramid complexes, was seen as a symbolic port to the world of the gods.'[81]

Now, the 'mythical boat in which the sun-god sailed across the ocean of the sky' must, by necessity, have been imagined to sail along the ecliptic path and through the 12 zodiacal constellations in its yearly course. We have seen how, in the Pyramid Age, the sun travelled from the end of March to late June through the starry Duat from a point below the Pleiades all the way to the paws of Leo. If my hypothesis is correct, then this distance in the sky must correspond to the distance on the ground between Abu Ghorab and Heliopolis.

But how can we check this empirically?

A Journey into the Duat

Astronomers measure the apparent distances between stars in degrees known as the 'angular distance'. Using the astronomy programme StarryNight Pro. V.4, it can be determined that the angular distance between the Pleiades and Leo is 90°, which corresponds to the distance that the sun travelled in *c.* 2781 BC (when the Egyptian civil calendar was established and when the master plan was probably conceived) from 21 March to 21 June, being a quarter of the full 360° yearly circuit. Now, using an official map of the region, it can be determined that the distance from Abu Ghorab to Heliopolis is 27,000 metres. In this correlative scheme, this means that 1° angular distance in the sky equals 333 metres on the ground.

Let us now test this.

The distance between the two outermost pyramids at Giza (Khufu and Menkaura), measured between the two extended north-west diagonals, is 928.33 metres. This represents the angular distance of the two outermost stars of Orion's belt, Al Nitak and Mintaka, which is 2.75°. This gives 1° angular distance in the sky for 337 metres on the ground, which is within barely 2 per cent of the value established from

99

the Abu Ghorab to Heliopolis sky–ground distances! With growing excitement I decided to test this further with the distance from the Giza pyramids to the pyramids of Abusir. This is 11,420 metres. Now the angular distance from Orion's belt to the Pleiades is 35°. This gives 1° angular distance in the sky for 326 metres on the ground, a difference of barely 1 per cent of the value for the other sky–ground distances calculated above.[82] In view of the very close consistency of the results, I was now convinced that coincidence should be ruled out. The ancient pyramid-builders were placing their monuments according to a sky map using a 1° = 333 metres scale.[83]

But what was so important about the distance that the sun travelled between the Pleiades and Leo in 2781 BC? The time taken would be about 90 days from 21 March to 21 June (Gregorian), thus from the spring equinox to the summer solstice. We are given a clue in the so-called Carlsberg Papyrus I, which tells us that the star 'which goes to earth (sets) and enters the Duat. It stops in the house of Geb (i.e under the earth) for 70 days . . . It is in the Embalming House . . . it sheds its impurities to the earth. It is pure and it comes into existence (rises) in the (eastern) horizon like Sirius.'[84]

Again using StarryNight Pro. V.4, it can be seen that the days when both Orion's belt and Sirius are 'invisible', i.e. in the Duat, is about 90 days collectively, which corresponds to the 90 days the sun travelled from spring equinox to summer solstice. The astronomer Ed Krupp commented on the Carlsberg Papyrus I that 'this (rebirth) cycle is the essence of Egypt. It is paralleled by the myth. It is played out in the sky.'[85]

It would seem clear that the rebirth of Osiris was played out not in an imaginary sky but in the sacred Memphis–Heliopolis region, which was developed to resemble the Duat, with star pyramids dotted on the western shore of the Milky Way/Nile.

CHAPTER FOUR

As Above, So Below

The cosmos itself is what mattered to our ancestors. Their lives, their beliefs, their destinies – all were part of this bigger pageant. Just as the environment of their temples was made sacred by metaphors of cosmic order, entire cities and great ritual centres were also astronomically aligned and organised. Each sacred capital restated the theme of cosmic order in terms of its builders' own perception of the universe. Principles which the society considered its own – which ordered its life and gave it its character – were borrowed from the sky and built into the plans of the cities.

E.C. Krupp, *Echoes of the Ancient Skies*

It is certainly possible that the religion of historic times in ancient Egypt had its roots this far back in time, and that its gods, as in historic times, were in the sky . . . it is (also) certainly possible that specific members of a group were given the function to observe and remember the positions and movements of the sun, moon, planets, and stars . . .

Jane B. Seller, *The Death of Gods in Ancient Egypt*

Over a period of a thousand years ancient observers could discern . . . the secular shifting of the Great Gyroscope . . . The symmetries of the machine took shape in their minds. And truly it was the time machine, as Plato understands it, the 'moving image of eternity' . . . the Precession took on an overpowering significance. It became the vast impenetrable pattern of fate itself . . .

Giorgio de Santillana and Hertha von Dechend, *Hamlet's Mill*

Looking South

In Egypt you are always aware that the country is sliced in half by the Nile. In ancient Egypt you were said to be either in the east, in the land of the living, where the celestial bodies rise, or you were said to be in the west, in the land of the dead, where the celestial bodies set. East was life and west was death. To cross the Nile from east to west was to enter the world of the dead. To cross from west to east was to be born, or, in the parlance of ancient Egypt, to be 'where the gods are born'.

In ancient times there were no bridges across the Nile. The only way to cross was by ferry. In the royal rebirth rituals of the Pyramid Texts, the dead king is said to 'ferry across' a 'Winding Waterway' when the 'Fields of Rushes are flooded'. This is clearly an allusion to the crossing of the flood plains during the season of inundation in the region of Heliopolis. But in the context of the rebirth rites, the event takes place not on the land but in the starry world of the celestial Duat, which is visible in the east of the sky:

> The Fields of Rushes are flooded and I ferry across on the Winding Waterway; I am ferried over to the eastern side of the horizon, I am ferried over to the eastern side of the sky . . .[1]

> The Winding Waterway is flooded that I may be ferried over thereon to the horizon, to Horakhti . . .[2]

> The Winding Waterway is flooded, that I may be ferried over to the eastern side of the sky, to *the place where the gods were born* . . .[3]

The eastern horizon, then, was that place where 'the gods were born' which, in the context of the rebirth rituals, is where the celestial bodies rise, i.e. are reborn. But the apotheosis of royal rebirth was reached not on any day but at the moment of the heliacal rising of Sirius, which took place during the start of the flood season. This is when Osiris–Orion emerges from the underworld Duat (is reborn), and also when his son, the new Horus-king, succeeds him – an event marked by

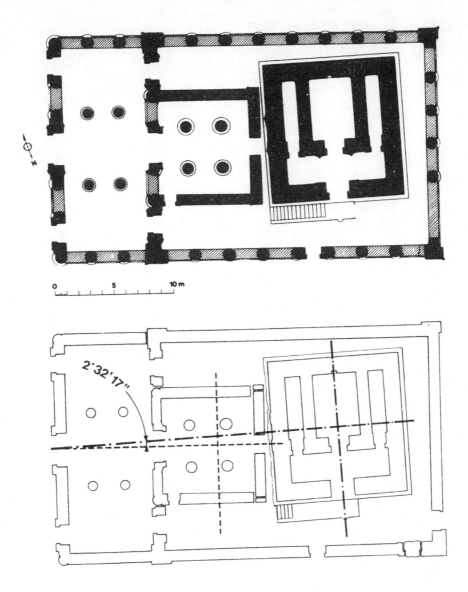

Plan of the 'Birth of Isis' temple at Dendera

the rebirth of the star Sirius, rising heliacally after 70 days in the underworld Duat.

During those crucial 70 days the Nile became swollen like a pregnant sow. And when its waters began to mysteriously turn red (due to the red laterite dust of Central Africa that had dissolved in the water and was carried by the flood all the way to Egypt), it was as if the goddess Isis herself was discharging her birth-waters and placenta when giving birth to Horus in the bulrushes of the Delta. An inscription in the temple known as the Birthplace of Isis at Dendera tells us that the goddess 'loves the colour red', which clearly alludes to the redness of the Nile during the rising of Sirius – a phenomenon that was witnessed by many in modern times, including the distinguished English traveller Lady Duff Gordon, who, in 1867, saw the coming flood and described its waters as 'really red as blood'.[4] Indeed, this phenomenon took place every year around the time of the summer solstice and was only disrupted in 1902 when the first modern dam was built at Aswan. It was finally ended in 1965 with the completion of the High Dam at Aswan. This changed for ever the cycle of the Nile that had kept Egypt in ecological balance. In the perception of an ancient Egyptian, it would have meant that the cosmic order was disrupted and calamity would befall the land. In a dramatic passage of the Hermetic Texts known as the Lament, the god Thoth paints a dark and grim picture of the pollution and chaos that would befall Egypt if its people ceased to respect the Nile and stopped revering the ancient gods and the cosmos. [5]

The economic and social conditions of modern Egypt are perhaps evidence of this ancient prophecy. Today the contamination of the Nile and its canals by toxic and sewage waste constitutes Egypt's worst self-inflicted plague, and the chaos caused by its exponentially growing population (20 million in Cairo today compared with one million 50 years ago) and unchecked fume emissions has made its capital, Cairo, one of the unhealthiest and most polluted cities in the world according to the latest UNESCO figures. No more do the people of Egypt witness the splendour and enchantment that the flood season brought to their countryside. In this respect, the eye-witness account of a nineteenth-century traveller is worth quoting here, as it describes the joy that gripped the whole of Egypt when the flood came in midsummer:

Perhaps there is not in Nature a more exhilarating sight or one more strongly exciting to confidence of God, than the rise of the Nile . . . its bounding waters . . . diffusing life and joy through another desert. There are few impressions I have received upon the remembrance of which I dwell with more pleasure than of seeing the first burst of the Nile . . . All Nature shouts for joy. The men, the children, the buffaloes, gambol in its refreshing waters, the broad waves sparkle with shoals of fish, and fowl of every wing flutter over them in clouds. Nor is this jubilee of Nature confined to the higher orders of creation. The moment the sand becomes moistened by the approach of fertilising waters, it is literally alive with insects innumerable. It is impossible to stand by the side of one of these noble streams, to see it every moment sweeping away some obstruction to its majestic course, and widening as it flows, without feeling in the heart to expand with love and joy and confidence in the great Author of this annual miracle of mercy . . . a scene of fertility and beauty such as will be scarcely found in another country at any season of the year. The vivid green of the springing corn, the groves of pomegranate-trees ablaze with the rich scarlet of their blossom, the fresh breeze laden with the perfume of gardens of roses and orange thickets, every tree and every shrub covered with sweet scented flowers . . . from Alexandria to Assouan . . . it is the same everywhere, only because it would be impossible to make any addition to the sweetness of the colours, the brilliance of the colours, or the exquisite beauty of the many forms of vegetable life . . . It is monotonous, but it is the monotony of Paradise.[6]

This luxurious outburst of new life and abundance of nature was, in the eyes of the ancient Egyptians, a gift from the gods and, more especially, from the goddess Isis, who applied her great magic (as she had done for the dead Osiris) to bring back to life the Nile and induce the flood to rise from the underworld Duat (at Elephantine). And so, for a people who saw their land as 'an image of heaven' and their king as 'the son of Isis', it should not surprise us that they wanted to provide him with a sacred landscape that resembled the Duat in order for him to undergo the same miracle of rebirth with the flood and with Osiris. The apotheosis of the rebirth ritual (prosaically called the 'funeral' by Egyptologists) took place, according to my own thesis, at the temple of Ra-Horakhti in Heliopolis. In my mind I see the cortege bearing the king's embalmed corpse placed on a boat or ferry (a splendid example of such a 'solar' boat is displayed at Giza) and made to travel from the sun temples of Abu Ghorab along the prescribed 'solar' path, then across the Nile and towards the sanctuary of the phoenix at Heliopolis. There the king's mummy would await the '(re)birth of Ra-Horakhti', which took place at dawn on the day of the heliacal rising of Sirius. On that day the starry Duat would be fully visible in the dawn sky, revealing the interrelationship between Orion and the Pleiades, as well as the path of the sun from the latter to Leo on the west and east sides of the Milky Way – as was defined on the land by the Giza and Abusir pyramids, as well as the solar path from the sun temples of Abu Ghorab to Heliopolis. For it is one of those intriguing facts that if you were positioned on a high point at Letopolis-Ausim, where once stood the so-called tower of Eudoxus, looking east at this celestial region containing the Duat, and then imagined that it could be rotated a full 90° clockwise so that it was now in the south, something strange and wonderful would happen: the Milky Way would now 'flow' along the meridian like the Nile on the ground, and the three stars of Orion's belt to its right (i.e., west) would look like the three pyramids of Giza to the west of the Nile. Bringing the sky map and the ground map to an equal scale using the 1° = 333 metres scale ratio (see Chapter Three) we can see that the position of Leo falls right above Heliopolis, and that the small cluster of the Pleiades falls (not quite, but almost) above the small cluster of the Abusir pyramids. Now if we draw an imaginary line mirroring the path of the sun from the Pleiades to Leo, we see that it traces a path from the sun temples at Abu Ghorab to the sun temple at Heliopolis. In this scheme there is an almost perfect sky–ground correlation, or, in the parlance of the ancients, the starry Duat is on the Memphite Duat.[7] As above, so below. Admittedly the match is not mathematically perfect due to the bedrock realities of geography and topography. But the similarity of the sky map with the ground map is so uncanny that coincidence in this case is very difficult to accept. The pieces of the puzzle fit so neatly into the religious beliefs of the pyramid-builders and their clever astronomical alignments and architectural schemes that it is hard to see how all this can be a fluke.

But before we consider this possibility seriously, let us see first if there is evidence that the ancient Egyptians 'rotated' the sky in their minds to have the Milky Way running south–north like the Nile. In other words, did they imagine the Milky Way flowing south-north when in fact it flows east–west? Was east in the sky south on the land?

During my research for this book I made liberal use of the articles published in the 1994 *Hommages à Jean Leclant*. One of these articles particularly caught my attention. It was by the French Egyptologist Arielle Kozloff and was titled 'Star-gazing in Ancient Egypt'.[8] In this article Kozloff proposed that the luminous band of the Milky Way was seen as the celestial counterpart of the Nile, which, as we have seen, was an idea that had crossed the mind of many other researchers including myself. What was intriguing about Kozloff's article, however, was his suggestion that the ancient Egyptians perceived the Milky Way not as running east–west as it actually appears in the sky but running south–north like the Nile! In Kozloff's own words:

Stars, like the sun, appear to move through the sky in an east–west direction. That means that the bright band in the middle of the sky, if one were to think of it in terms of a river, flows from east to west. In considering the Milky Way as a river, the sky must have taken a differential orientation for the ancient Egyptians. We know that in contrast with their own Nile, the Egyptians considered the Euphrates river to flow north by flowing south. Thus, it is likely that they considered the river in the sky to flow north by flowing west. If true-west becomes Nilotic north, then true-north becomes Nilotic east, true-east becomes Nilotic south, and true-south becomes Nilotic west . . . It is probably more than a coincidence that Orion, the constellation with which Osiris, Lord of the West, is traditionally identified, appears in the southern part of the sky, which is to say on the west bank of the celestial river.[9]

What Kozloff is actually saying is that the ancient Egyptians rotated the sky a full 90° in their mind so that the image seen in the eastern sky was projected on to the southern sky, this in order to match the flow of the Milky Way with the flow of the Nile. In other words, celestial east became Nilotic south.[10] Unwittingly, Kozloff's findings had the unsolicited result of corroborating my sky–ground Star Correlation Theory.

There was, however, an ingenious and very original way of looking, quite literally, at the Star Correlation Theory from another viewpoint, which was recently put forward by the researcher Chris Tedder, an amateur Egyptologist and archaeoastronomer living in Finland. Tedder noted that an artery could be drawn from the pyramid of Djedefra at Abu Ruwash, cutting through the pyramid fields of Giza, Zawyet Al Aryan, Abusir and all the way to Saqqara. What drew his attention was that the artery had an orientation of about 52.2° south-of-east, which, curiously enough, was the degree of orientation south-of-west that the pyramids of Giza had. This scheme created a symmetrical geometry that was, at face value, unlikely to be a coincidence. Intrigued by this, Tedder then had the brilliant idea of seeing what happened when Orion's belt was positioned 52.2° south-of-east in the direction of the artery in the year *c.* 2475 BC when the Giza pyramids were built. Being familiar with my Star Correlation Theory, he was struck by the fact that when Orion's belt reached an azimuth of 142.2°, i.e. 52.2° south-of-east, this also became the angle the three stars of Orion's belt made with the horizontal, *thus matching the angle the three pyramids made with the horizontal*. Imagining himself looking south from the vantage of Abu Ruwash, he then realised that something very interesting happened to Orion's belt when it crossed the meridian: the three stars made an angle of 16.2° as seen from Abu Ruwash! At this point Tedder knew he was on to something. For although the sky image was constantly moving round the earth, it could not be a coincidence that when at precisely an orientation of 52.2° south-of-east, it not only aligned with the artery that passed through the pyramid field north of Saqqara, but also formed the same angle that defined the layout plan of the Giza pyramids and, furthermore, formed an angle of 16.2° with the horizontal matching the angle of the three pyramids when viewed from Abu Ruwash.

Egyptologists and sceptics see nothing in this but pure coincidence, and pillory researchers like Chris Tedder, accusing them of being numerologists and fantasists. But others, like Tedder himself, cannot

easily accept that such beautifully interlocking geometry of alignments between sky and ground is merely the result of hazard. To
Tedder it was also self-evident that Abu Ruwash defined a place of
observation that encompassed the whole Memphite region up to
Saqqara. This, on face value, made a lot of sense. Abu Ruwash was,
after all, the highest promontory in the Memphite Necropolis and also
its most northerly point. It would certainly be the ideal place to set up
an observation point. Except for one fact: Abu Ruwash is not along
the meridianal axis of the Giza pyramids but at 52.2° west-of-north
from it. But, as we have seen in Chapter Two, the site of Letopolis-
Ausim is due north of the Giza pyramids. Everything about Giza,
especially the Great Pyramid, attests to a meticulous establishment of
a prime meridian passing through the Great Pyramid. It would thus
also make perfect surveying sense to have an observation point at
Letopolis-Ausim that would define the prime meridian on the ground
for the Memphite Necropolis. And this brings us back to another far
more controversial explanation for the Star Correlation Theory.

Explanation of the Third Kind

Although Tedder's idea to explain the Star Correlation Theory is most
ingenious, there is one nagging problem with it: there is not a shred of
textual evidence to support it. There is, on the other hand, another
explanation which is heavily supported by textual evidence but which
is also the very stuff that fuels accusations of heresy among
Egyptologists. And this is it: what if there had, in fact, been a time
when both the Milky Way and the Nile flowed south–north and that
this time was when both Orion's belt and the Giza pyramids matched
perfectly looking south at the meridian? And what if that time – and
here is the heresy! – was the 'First Time' of *zep tepi* that the ancient
Egyptians mention so often in their religious texts, informing us that
all things began here in the Memphite–Heliopolis region? We should
recall how, by using the Sothic cycle and the first appearance of Sirius
in the Memphite–Heliopolis region, I tentatively dated the 'First
Time' to 11,541 BC. So let us reconstruct the sky for that date and see
how Orion's belt looks when in the southern meridian.

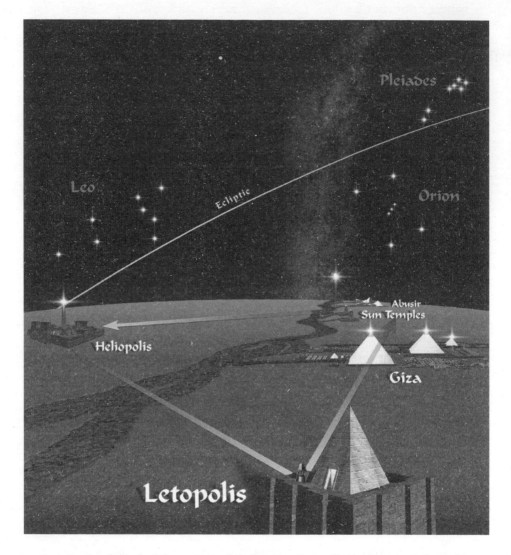

Artist's view from the 'observatory of Eudoxus' at Letopolis (modern Ausim). In this ground-sky map the Milky Way represents the Nile; the three Giza pyramids represent Orion's belt; the Abusir pyramids represent the Pleiades; the sun-temple of Ra-Horakhti at heliopolis represents the sun in Leo. In this ground-sky correlation scheme, the 90 days journey of the sun along that part of the ecliptic from a point below the Pleiades to a point below leo is matched on the ground by the line joining the sun-temples of Abu Ghorab and the sun-temple at Heliopolis.

Looking south at an image of the sky of the 'First Time' from the vantage point of Letopolis-Ausim – and more dramatically from atop an imaginary observation tower[11] – it quickly becomes clear that the Milky Way now seems to link with the Nile in the distant south, as if this sky-river is 'feeding' its celestial waters into the Nile at far-away Elephantine on the southern frontier of Egypt. Looking to the immediate right of the Milky Way we see Orion's belt. Its two brightest stars (Alnitak and Alnilam) make an angle of 43° 20′ with the meridian. On the ground to the right of the Nile is the Giza necropolis, and its two largest pyramids (Khufu's and Khafra's) also make an angle of 43° 20′ with the meridian![12] Slowly, as you pan the map of the Memphite-Heliopolis region looking directly into the southern meridian, it becomes vividly clear that what you see on the ground bears a remarkable resemblance to what you see in the sky also when looking due south. In this astonishing sky–ground correlation, not only does Orion's belt match the Giza pyramids and the Nile the Milky Way, but we can see that the constellation of Leo is directly over the position of Heliopolis. This means that an observer at Letopolis-Ausim at the 'First Time' would have simultaneously been able to see Orion's belt due south and Leo due east, that is at the future location of the Giza pyramids due south and the temple of Heliopolis due east. What I am saying here is this: as amazing as it may seem, the sky image of 11,541 BC seems to correlate with the ground image of *c.* 2500 BC!

How can this be possible? How can we explain the 8,000-year gap between the sky and ground maps? Or, to put it in another way, how could the Egyptians of 2500 BC have known what the sky looked like in 11,541 BC?

A Boring Complication

Whenever I give a conference on ancient Egyptian astronomy, I know that sooner or later I will have to confront my audience with the problematical topic of precession. They are most relieved, however, when I dispose of it in less than 30 seconds. This is because I simply tell them that precession is really nothing more than a very slow wobble of our planet with a cycle of 26,000 years. To visualise it I ask them to think of a spinning top. They very quickly get the general idea. 'Today,' wrote the late Professor Hertha von Deschend, 'the precession is a well-established fact ... (but) it is by now only a boring complication. Whereas once it was the only majestic secular motion that our ancestors could keep in mind when they looked for a great cycle which could affect humanity as a whole. But then our ancestors were astronomers *and* astrologers.'[13] The immediate questions that loom in the mind are: Were the ancient Egyptians aware of precession? And, more importantly, did they track it through the ages and thus know its cycle? From the Egyptologists and most historians of science you will get a resounding no. Others, however, are not so sure. And there is a minority – myself included – that is convinced that it was not the Greeks who discovered precession but the Egyptians long before them.

It was the scholar Anne-Sophie Bomhard who found it necessary to remind Egyptologists that the ancient Egyptians were 'masters of observing Nature' and that they especially observed the motions of the sky. Egyptologists in general do not disagree with her. But they will point out that observing the motions of the sky is one thing, but meticulously studying and recording its various cycles is quite another matter. For that you have to be an astronomer, and it was not until the Greeks came to Egypt in the fourth century BC, Egyptologists insist, that any serious astronomy was performed there. According to one such academic, the Egyptians 'borrowed their knowledge of the Signs of the Zodiac, together with much else, from the Greeks', while another asserts with equal scorn that 'Egypt did not contribute to the history of mathematical astronomy'.[14] Could it be that the entrenched belief that all science and all philosophy stems from Greece is the cause of this disdain for the ancient Egyptian sky-watchers?

Notwithstanding such subjective bias, there is a serious flaw in this reasoning. For while Egyptologists insist that astronomy was taught to the Egyptians by the Greeks, the Greeks themselves insist that it was the other way round. The great Plato, for example, could not stop marvelling at the wisdom of the Egyptian priests and how they 'spent their nights observing the stars'.[15] Strabo wrote how the Egyptians

'excelled in the science of astronomy'.[16] And Diodorus lauded the Egyptian priests and reported how 'Democritus lived with the priests of Egypt for five years and learned many things from them related to astronomy.'[17] Then there is Iambilicus reporting how Pythagoras sojourned 20 years with Egyptian priests, and that 'it was from them that he learnt the science for which, later, he was deemed a genius'.[18] Iambilicus also tells us how 'Pythagoras visited all the temples of Egypt with much ardour . . . (and) he was much admired by the priests with who he lived, learning from them all things with great diligence . . . mostly geometry . . . and astronomy.'[19]

But what of the discovery of precession? Do any of these ancient Greek scholars tell us that it was not one of them but rather the ancient Egyptians who discovered it? There is one at least. For although this discovery is generally attributed to Hipparchus of Rhodes (c. 127 BC), there is the great scholar Proclus Diadochus of Nicea (AD 410-485) who tells us forcefully that this is not true at all, and that the discovery belongs fair and square to the Egyptians. And to boot, Proclus insists that it was the great Plato who had said so. In Proclus's own words:

Let those who, believing in observations, cause the stars to move around the poles of the zodiac by one degree in one hundred years toward the east, as Ptolemy and Hipparchus did before him know . . . that the Egyptians had already taught Plato about the movements of the fixed stars. Because they utilised previous observations which the Chaldeans had made long before them with the same results, having again been instructed by the gods prior to the observations. And they did not speak just a single time, but many times . . . of the advance of the fixed stars.[20]

The Czech Egyptologist Zbynek Zaba, who is well known for his studies in ancient Egyptian astronomy, had this to say about Proclus's commentary:

Until now it has been believed that the Egyptians were not aware of the movement of the fixed stars caused by the precession of the axis of the planet. I believe that the diagrams of the Egyptians of the starry sky tend to prove the contrary. Proclus Diadochus affirms that the Egyptians discovered not only the movement of the fixed stars but also the precession of the equinoxes which is another consequence of the precession of the axis of the planet. To this we have no proof so far, and it is possible that the discovery of the precession of the equinoxes rests entirely with Hipparchus. It is nonetheless more probable, in my opinion, that even this discovery had been made by the ancient Egyptians, and that Proclus was well informed . . .[21]

But how well informed *was* Proclus? First it should be pointed out that he was no dilettante. This was especially true when it came to matters regarding the writings of Plato. So his claim that the Egyptian priests taught Plato the secrets of precession was not something that he plucked from thin air.

Proclus was born in AD 411 in Constantinople (now Istanbul), and for many years he had been a student of the great Neoplatonic philosopher Olympiadorus of Alexandria. Later he also studied under the great Plutarch and Syrianus at the famous academy in Athens which, as is well known, was founded by Plato. Proclus eventually became the head of the Platonic academy and remained an important figure there until his death in AD 485. While at the academy, he specialised in the works of Aristotle and Plato, which were then all available to him. In one of Plato's works the great philosopher had written of 'the beauty and clarity of the skies in Egypt' and how this allowed the Egyptians to see 'all the stars', which they had observed and studied 'for 10,000 years, or an infinity number of years so to speak'. Plato was not alone in attributing great antiquity to the ancient Egyptian sky-watchers. Other scholars, such as Aristotle, Seneca, Diodorus, Simplicius and Strabo, also wrote of how the Egyptian priests had carefully studied the stars for thousands of years.[22] If this is true – and there is no reason to think otherwise – then it is difficult, indeed impossible, to see how the avid Egyptian stargazers would not have noticed over a few generations the apparent movement of the fixed stars caused by the effect of precession.

The possibility that precession was known to the ancient Egyptians was first seriously brought up in the late 1820s by the French astronomer Jean-Baptiste Biot, a member of the prestigious Académie Française. Biot was convinced not only that the ancient Egyptian priests were aware of the precession of the equinoxes, but also that they had tracked its effect through the ages:

> . . . they would have been able, even in the course of a few years, to recognise that the course of the rising and setting points of different stars were changing place on the horizon after a certain period of time, were no longer at the same terrestrial alignment. They would thus have been able to verify the general and progressive displacement of the celestial sphere relative to the meridian line, that is to say the most apparent effect of the precession of the equinoxes.[23]

The next scholar to entertain such views was the British astronomer Sir Norman Lockyer. According to Lockyer:

> The various apparent movements of the heavenly bodies which are produced by the rotation and the revolution of the earth, and the effect of precession, were familiar to the Egyptians, however ignorant they may have been of their causes; they carefully studied what they saw, and attempted to put their knowledge together in the most convenient fashion, associating it with their strange imaginings of their system of worship.[24]

Recently the Russian astronomer Dr Alexander Gurshtein, vice-president of the History of Astronomy of the IAU (International Astronomical Union), used his full academic stature to support the idea that the ancient Egyptians were aware of the shift of the vernal point against the fixed stars and, consequently, were aware of the precession of the equinoxes.[25] Even more recently these same views were expressed by the Italian astronomer Giulio Magli, an associate professor at the Department of Mathematics at Milano Politecnico.[26] Even the usually sceptical American astronomer E.C. Krupp was open to this idea when he wrote that

> . . . circumstantial evidence implies that the awareness of the shifting

equinoxes may be of considerable antiquity, for we find, in Egypt at least, a succession of cults whose iconography and interest focus on duality, the bull, and the ram at appropriate periods for Gemini, Taurus, and Aries in the precessional cycle of the equinoxes.[27]

Krupp added, however, that 'whether the Egyptians were fully aware of precession is one thing; whether they responded to it is another.'[28] Since those words were written, further research has shown that the ancient Egyptians did, in fact, respond to it by changing the axis of many temples that had been aligned to the rising of Sirius. We know at least three such examples where they did this over hundreds of years: the temple of Satis on Elephantine Island; the temple of Isis at Dendera, and the temple of Horus on Thoth Hill near Luxor.

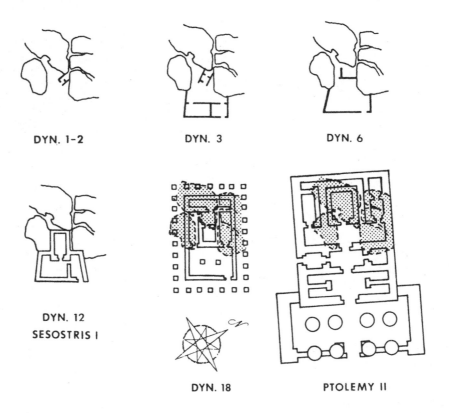

DYN. 1-2   DYN. 3   DYN. 6

DYN. 12
SESOSTRIS I   DYN. 18   PTOLEMY II

Plan of the Evolution of the Satet Temple on Elephantine Island

The Temples of Satis that followed Sirius

Elephantine Island is just a mile or so downriver from the first cataract on the Nile near the modern town of Aswan.[29] The Nile at this point is at its widest and its water is crystal clear with a wonderful deep blue tone. Its banks are lined with tall palm trees and multicoloured bougainvillaea and oleanders. On the west bank rise high sand dunes that catch the pink light of the early morning sun. White egrets fly along the river and water buffaloes float lazily in the shallows, while children swim around and women squat by the water's edge to do their laundry. The gift of the Nile is well appreciated here at Elephantine. Here the river truly excels.

Elephantine was once the capital of the First Nome of Upper Egypt and was sacred to Khnum, the ram-headed creator god who fashioned mankind on his divine potter's wheel. It was also sacred to his elegant consort, the goddess Satet or Satis (in Greek), who was closely identified with the Nile's flood. It is this goddess who predominated here at Elephantine, because throughout ancient times this place was considered the mouth of the netherworld or Duat from where the Nile's flood emerged.[30] Satis was also the guardian of the southern frontier of Egypt, protecting it from invaders with her divine bow and arrow. Not surprisingly, she was later identified with the Greek Artemis, the divine huntress.

Satis's name is first attested on jars found under the Step Pyramid at Saqqara. This should be of particular interest to us, because she was also identified with the star Sirius, the herald of the Nile flood. The reader will recall how in Chapter One we associated the Step Pyramid at Saqqara with the star Sirius, a fact also attested by the name of the pyramid: 'Horus is the Star at the Head of the Sky'. Satis is mentioned in the Pyramid Texts, where she is said to purify the dead king with the divine flood water brought in jars from Elephantine.[31] She is usually shown as a tall, slender woman wearing the white crown of Upper Egypt from which protrude two antelope horns. On the front of the crown is often seen a five-pointed star, which almost certainly represented Sirius, a symbol of the flood. There is also an assortment of epithets attesting to Satis's close connection with the stellar world and implying her cosmic identity as Sirius: 'Lady of Stars'; 'Mistress of the eastern horizon of the sky, at whose sight everyone rejoices'; 'The Great One in the Sky, ruler of the Stars'; 'Satis who brightens the two lands with her beauty' and so on.[32]

Elephantine Island is just two kilometres long and half a kilometre wide. On it were found the remains of several ancient temples, the largest being the temple of Khnum, located on the south side of the island. North of Khnum's temple is the smaller temple of Satis. Archaeological evidence shows that the island has been inhabited since predynastic times, and a team from the German Archaeology Institute of Cairo discovered underneath the temple of Satis evidence of earlier temples going back to the early dynastic period. Indeed, the

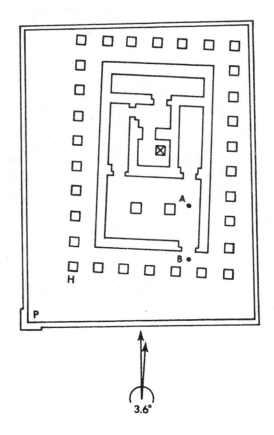

Plan of the Satet temple

peculiarity of the temple of Satis is that it is built on the ruins of several other temples going down in tiers like some giant wedding cake, starting at the bottom with an early dynastic shrine dated to about 2900 BC, then an Old Kingdom shrine dated to 2200 BC, then a Middle Kingdom shrine dated to about 1800 BC, then a New Kingdom shrine, and finally the restored Ptolemaic temple which is seen today and dated to the second century BC.[33]

In 1983 the astronomer Ron Wells from the University of California took an interest in the Satis temple and decided to investigate its alignments.[34] Wells had a hunch that the 2,800-years evolution of this temple, coupled with the fact that Satis was closely associated with the Nile's flood and thus the heliacal rising of Sirius, might yield some interesting astronomical results. Wells knew that the last temple of Satis on this site was built in the Ptolemaic period, and it was obvious to him – even when looking with the naked eye – that its axis was aligned a few degrees further north than the axis of the earlier temple built underneath it. Wells had a hunch that this northerly shift could be explained by the northerly shift of Sirius caused by precession. Making use of the pole star, Polaris (Alpha Ursa Minor), to establish true north, he calculated that the orientation of the Ptolemaic temple was 24.65° south-of-east and that the axis of the earlier New Kingdom temple underneath was 30.60° south-of-east. To his astonishment, he found that this 5.95° difference exactly matched the precessional drift of Sirius during the time between the building of the two temples.[35] Although the axis of the early-dynasty temple further underneath could not be determined with accuracy, it was obvious that it was deviated even more to the south than the earlier temples above it, confirming that the ancient Egyptian surveyors had been aware of the effect of precession on the star Sirius and, more intriguingly, had also tracked it for nearly three millennia.[36]

Tracking Sirius Again: From Rameses II to Augustus Caesar

The same curious tracking of Sirius is also evident at Dendera. This region in northern Upper Egypt is near the modern town of Qena, some 60 kilometres north of Luxor as the crow flies. Known as Iunet or Tentere (Tentyris in Greek) in ancient times, it was the capital of the Sixth Nome of Upper Egypt. Today a visit to Dendera starts at Luxor, where your taxi or coach must join a convoy under the protection of armed policemen. Apart from this amusing inconvenience, the drive along the Nile is marvellous, as this part of Upper Egypt is rich in agricultural land and pretty traditional villages along the way. At Qena you cross the Nile over a modern bridge to the west side where the great temple complex of Hathor stands in glorious isolation at the edge of the western desert.

A goddess whose origin goes back into prehistory, Hathor ranked very high in the Egyptian pantheon. She was the great cow-eared goddess, protector of lovers and dancers, patron of merrymaking and sexuality. Her name literally meant 'House of Horus' (*Hat-Hor*),[37] and as such, she was regarded as the divine nurse (some say mother) of the reigning Horus-king. Hathor was very closely associated with the goddess Isis, wife of Osiris and mother of Horus. Indeed, so close were Hathor and Isis that in Ptolemaic times their names were either fused or interchangeable, as the following inscription at Dendera relating to Hathor clearly shows: 'The beautiful one who appears in heaven, the truth which regulates the world at the head of the sun barge, the queen and mistress of awe, the ruler (of gods and) goddess, Isis the Great, the mother of gods.'[38] In very early times the city of Memphis was an important centre of worship for Hathor, and there she was known as the 'Lady of the Sycamore'. But by the time of the Old Kingdom her cult centre was well established at Dendera.

The great antiquity of Dendera is attested by tombs there that go back to the first dynasties.[39] The temple of Hathor as we see it today was founded by Ptolemy XII Auletes in 54 BC and further developed during the Roman period, but it is known that there existed an older temple at this site dating from the reign of Thothmoses III (*c.* 1450 BC). Also, an inscription on a wall at Dendera mentions the pharaoh Pepi I of the Sixth Dynasty (*c.* 2350 BC), suggestive of an even earlier origin for the temple. There are also inscriptions in one of the crypts that speak of the time of the legendary Shemsu-Hor, or 'Followers of Horus' (although Egyptologists discount them as being 'mythical' ancestors).[40] Indeed, one of the inscriptions claims that the original blueprint of the temple was drawn by the Shemsu-Hor themselves and was preserved on the temple walls by King Pepi I:

> King Tuthmoses III has caused this building to be erected in memory of his mother, the goddess Hathor, the Lady of Dendera, the Eye of the Sun, the Heavenly Queen of the Gods. The ground plan was found in the city of Dendera, in archaic drawing on a leather roll of the time of the Shemsu-Hor (Followers of Horus); it was (also) found in the interior of a brick wall in the south side of the temple in the reign of king Pepi.[41]

The Dendera complex is normally approached through an imposing arch on the north side of the boundary wall that leads into a vast open courtyard. The great temple of Hathor, which is aligned roughly south–north, is reached along a processional road starting from the arch. Upon arriving at its huge gate, you are confronted by six imposing columns whose four-sided capitals are carved with faces of Hathor. These columns support the huge beams that span the north side of the temple's roof. There are a further 18 columns in the first hypostyle hall, and six more in the inner hypostyle hall. Immediately to the west of the open courtyard is a *mammisi*, or 'birth house', built in Roman times. And to the west of the main temple is another of these mysterious *mammisi*, built by Nectanebo I, as well as a sanatorium. Further along the west side of the temple is a sacred lake (now dry, with palm trees growing in it). To the rear of the main temple is a small temple which stands alone and, curiously, has its own monumental entrance in the east side of the boundary wall of the complex. This is also a *mammisi* of sorts with a very special claim: it is said to be the birthplace of Isis, and thus is also known as the temple of Isis. It is the alignment of this particular temple which we shall now examine carefully.

The temple of Isis is unique in that its outer area is aligned west–east while its inner area is aligned south–north and is thus parallel to the axis of the main temple of Hathor. The impression one gets is that something in the eastern horizon was meant to be observed simultaneously with something else seen in the northern horizon. But what?

In 1891, the astronomer Sir Norman Lockyer took particular notice of the temple of Isis when he came across the writings of the French Egyptologist Auguste Mariette, who seemed to have given this little temple a direct connection with the star Sirius. In one of his works Mariette had pointed out that the temple 'is to the south-west of the temple of Hathor, its portal is turned to the east, and the sun shines on its portal when it rises to illuminate the world'. Here is Mariette's own translation of the inscription that implied this cosmic function: '*She (i.e. the star of Isis) shines into her temple on New Year's Day, and she mingles her light with that of her Father Ra on the horizon.*'[42] From this inscription there can be little doubt that the ancient scribe was describing the heliacal rising of Sirius at dawn.[43] For the reader will recall how the heliacal rising of Sirius marked the New Year's Day when the calendar was invented in *c.* 2781 BC (which seems to be the same New Year's Day now celebrated at Dendera). Apparently every New Year's Day an effigy representing the *ba* (star soul) of Hathor-Isis was taken on to the roof of the temple at dawn so that the light of the rising sun could mingle with it. Now, as the astronomer Edwin Krupp pointed out, 'some traditions preserved at Dendera are thousands of years old'.[44] He also agreed that these inscriptions 'describe metaphorically the heliacal rising of Sirius', and quoted one such inscription himself:

> Radiant rises the golden one (Hathor-Isis-Sirius) above the head of her father (near but in advance of the sun) and her mysterious form is at the head of his solar boat . . . As her fellow divinities (the other stars) unite with her father's rays and as they merge with the glittering of his disk, Dendera is joyful . . . There is a festive mood as they behold the Great One, the firmly striding creator of feasts in the holy city, on that beautiful day of the New Year . . .[45]

According to Krupp,

The heliacal rising of Sirius involves only a brief appearance of the star before it is lost in the light of the sun. The event is a union, or marriage, which, when consummated, recreates the world order by celebrating the sun's 'birthday', the New Year. Certainly this astronomical event was watched from the roof of Dendera temple . . .[46]

It was Norman Lockyer, however, who was the first to notice that the east–west axis of the small temple of Isis had an orientation of about 18° 30' south-of-east, which, as we shall soon see, gave it a direct link to very important stellar targets. Typically Egyptologists had not bothered to check the orientation of the temple (or any other temple) because at the time they had assumed (wrongly) that all temples were simply meant to face the Nile without any other meaning to their orientations. In the region of Dendera, however, the Nile takes a sharp turn westwards from its normal northerly flow. From Dendera it thus runs east to west for about 20 kilometres before resuming its south–north flow near the town of Nag Hammadi. Between Dendera and Gebel Law the Nile runs roughly at 18° south-of-west, which means that someone standing at the eastern gate of the Dendera complex and facing the temple of Isis would be looking in its direction of flow. Lockyer had a strong hunch that this unique orientation had something to do with the rising of Sirius at the time the temple was built. Indeed, calculations shows that in 54 BC – the date of the founding of the Ptolemaic temple – Sirius rose at 18° 30' south-of-east and thus was in alignment with the axis of the temple of Isis.[47] Lockyer's conclusion was that 'the temple of Isis at Denderah was built to watch it [Sirius]'.[48]

There are other inscriptions at Dendera that confirm that the axis of the main temple of Hathor was aligned northwards towards the Plough using the traditional 'stretching of the cord' ceremony. Lockyer determined that it was 18° 30' east-of-north, and aligned to the star Dubhe in the Plough.[49] But he was working with an outmoded chronology, so I decided to check for myself this alignment. Using StarryNight Pro. V.4 to reconstruct the sky of 54 BC above Dendera, I could immediately see that the Plough was, as Lockyer had said, east-of-north. But what I found out was that when Sirius was rising in the east, one of the bright stars in the Plough known as Merak (ß Ursa

Major) was positioned at 18° 30′ east-of-north, thus not only marking the rising of Sirius but also forming a right angle with it. Curiously, there exist drawings from the same period that show a figure of a man wearing a hawk-mask clearly representing the Horus-king and using a rod or spear to prod the top of the bull's thigh, which is surrounded by seven bright stars – clearly the Plough – as if he is indicating to someone (Seshat perhaps?) where to aim or align the temple or pyramid. The place to which the tip of the rod is pointing is, interestingly, where the star Merak should be.[50]

It seemed nearly certain that the ancient surveyors had aligned the axes of both temples simultaneously: the temple of Hathor towards Merak in the Plough and the temple of Isis towards Sirius at rising (we should recall that a very similar scheme was applied to the alignment of the Step Pyramid at Saqqara, this time, however, using the star Al Kaid in the Plough to mark the rising of Sirius in the east). Inscriptions at Dendera are very suggestive of such a simultaneous sighting procedure towards east and north:

> The great goddess Seshat brings the writings that relate to your rising, O Hathor (as Sirius), and to the rising of Ra (the sun) . . .[51]

> The king joyously stretches the cord, having cast his gaze towards Meskhetiu (the Plough) and thus establishes the temple in the manner of ancient times.[52]

At any rate, not many Egyptologists paid much attention to all this until 1992, when the French Egyptologist Sylvie Cauville, well known for her extensive work on the inscriptions of Dendera, undertook a detailed study of the astronomical orientation of the little temple of Isis.[53] According to Cauville the temple of Isis at Dendera has been mostly ignored by Egyptologists, and none had paid much attention to the interesting astronomical findings of Lockyer and the commentaries of other astronomers such as Ed Krupp. Realising that this was a mistake on her colleagues' part, Cauville solicited the collaboration of the astronomer Eric Aubourg to examine again the orientation of this temple.

The temple of Isis as we see it today is mainly the work of Augustus Caesar who ordered its construction in *c.* 30 BC on the ruins of a much older temple, whose foundations were two metres lower down. Recent archaeological exploration by a French team has revealed that there had been many interventions throughout the ages at this site. In the foundations of Augustus' temple were found blocks belonging to Nectanebo I (*c.* 350 BC), and it was also revealed that the Ptolemaic kings Ptolemy VI Philometor (*c.* 150 BC) and Ptolemy X Alexander I (*c.* 20 BC) had had a hand in renovation works. But what particularly interested Cauville was the finding of reused blocks dating from the Ramesside period (*c.* 1250 BC) bearing the name of Kha-emouaset, a son of the great Rameses II. Could the original foundation of the temple of Isis be dated to *c.* 1250 BC? Seeing that there was an obvious difference in the orientation of the east–west axis of this original temple with that of Augustus' temple directly above it, Cauville asked Aubourg to find out if it had anything to do with the precessional drift of Sirius. Her hunch proved right. Aubourg first determined that the orientation of Augustus' temple was 18° 40′ south-of-east, which perfectly fit with the orientation of Sirius at its rising in the epoch of Augustus. He then determined the orientation of the original temple lower down and found it to be 21° 11′, which corresponded to the orientation of the rising of Sirius in the epoch of Rameses II. There could be no doubt that here again was proof that the ancient surveyors not only were aware of the precession of Sirius, but also had responded to its effect by changing the orientation of the temple.

The main Hathor temple is, of course, famous for having housed the so-called round zodiac of Dendera (as well as a lesser-known 'rectangular' zodiac that is on the ceiling of the first hypostyle hall). The round zodiac is not so much of a zodiac as it is a planisphere or sky map, that shows the whole celestial landscape from the perspective of having the north celestial pole near its centre. The actual zodiac, which was fixed on the ceiling of a chapel on the upper floor of the temple, is made up of the 12 familiar Babylonian-Greek astrological signs, which are scattered in a rough loop around the celestial pole while in a larger loop are scattered the 36 decans of ancient Egypt that were used for time-keeping and rebirth rites (since they contain Orion and Sirius). It is worth reminding ourselves that the decans were known from at least the Pyramid Age, which suggests, if not proves, that the Dendera planisphere has incorporated in it elements of great antiquity. Here Orion-Osiris is represented by a striding man wearing the royal crown, while Sirius-Isis is shown as a recumbent cow with a five-pointed star above her horns. Interestingly, behind the Isis-Sirius cow is the figure of a woman holding a bow and arrow, almost certainly Satis of Elephantine, who, as we have already seen, was also identified with Sirius (particularly with its heliacal rising and the Nile flood). Very near the centre of the zodiac is the figure of a small jackal on what looks like a hoe. To its left is a large standing hippopotamus that represents the constellation Draconis, and to its right is the familiar bull's thigh that represents the Plough. These last two constellations, as we have already seen, can be traced back to the Pyramid Age, again giving the Dendera planisphere links with the distant past.

The rounded planisphere that is seen today at Dendera is not the original one but a facsimile made in the 1920s. The original was taken to France after the Napoleonic invasion of Egypt in 1798 and is now displayed at the Louvre Museum in Paris. Books and articles abound on the meaning and date of the planisphere of Dendera, and it is well outside the scope of this investigation to review them all. There is little doubt that the planisphere dates from the time the temple was built, i.e. *c.* 54 BC, but it is much less clear whether it represents the sky at that time or, as some have suggested, a much older sky. In other words, is the Dendera planisphere a copy of a much older one into which were incorporated the Babylonian-Greek astrological signs? If that is the case, then there is no question that this artefact is a symbol of the precession of the equinoxes which sees the astrological signs transit the east-west axis of the planisphere in a never-ending cycle of 26,000 years.

The first scholar to suggest that this was the case was the French astronomer Jean-Baptiste Biot (whom we encountered earlier in this chapter), who argued that a careful study of the position of the constellations and planets on the Dendera planisphere indicates a much older sky and, by extension, knowledge of the precession.[54] Such ideas are normally vehemently rejected by Egyptologists and historians of science, but with the recent findings of Cauville and Aubourg at the nearby temple of Isis, Biot's views may very well be vindicated yet. Dendera may indeed have been a religious centre for astronomical observations and records that harked back thousands of years and perhaps even to the time of the legendary Shemsu-Hor, the 'Followers of Horus' (those who tracked Sirius?) across the ages.

Hungarians on Thoth Hill

The third known example of such long-range tracking of Sirius across the ages is found at a temple located at the southern part of the Theban hills on a promontory known as Thoth Hill. This mysterious temple was discovered by George Sweinfurth in 1904 and later studied by Flinders Petrie in 1909. At first it was thought to be the remains of a *heb-sed* chapel for the Eleventh Dynasty king Sankhakare Mentuhotep, but in 1995–8, an extensive investigation was carried out on Thoth Hill by a Hungarian team from Eotvos Lorand University under the leadership of Dr Gyozo Voros which confirmed that the temple, although built in the reign of Sankhakare Mentuhotep, was not a *heb-sed* chapel but a small temple dedicated to Horus. The temple, which is made of bricks, was built on a terraced platform overlooking the eastern horizon, and consisted of an entrance pylon and an inner sanctuary with three small rooms. When the Hungarians excavated there, they soon realised that this Eleventh Dynasty structure was built on top of the ruins of a much older temple dating from the archaic period (*c.* 3000 BC) and which, oddly enough, had a floor plan similar to the temple of Isis at Dendera. Also like at Dendera, the axis of this temple was offset from the axis of the archaic temple by about 2° towards the south. According to Egyptologist Richard Wilkinson:

> The Hungarian team excavating these structures believe this difference may be attributed to the shift in astronomical alignments over the intervening centuries. Their research indicates that the later brick

temple was aligned to Sirius. In the archaic period the same star would have appeared just over 2 degrees further south in the eastern sky – exactly the difference visible in the orientation of the earlier building. Thus, rather than simply follow the physical orientation of the earlier sacred structure, the Middle Kingdom architects had carefully adjusted the temple's orientation in order to align the new building once more precisely to Sirius – which was equated with Horus, the patron deity of the temple.[55]

So here we have it once again: the ancient Egyptians were not only acutely aware of the precession of the fixed stars but also tracked or followed it through the ages by carefully altering the orientation of temples towards the rising of Sirius. The question, then, is not whether they knew about the precession, but *since when did they know of it?* In other words, how far back in time can we assume that precession was common knowledge to the ancient Egyptian astronomer-priests? We have seen how Plato had no difficulty in allocating to them records of the movement of the fixed stars that went back 'for 10,000 years, or an infinity number of years so to speak'. Can Plato have been right in reporting this extraordinary antiquity for the stargazers of ancient Egypt? Is it possible that the ancient Egyptians had observed and recorded the precession from way back in prehistory?

A Cosmic Order Fixed at the Time of Creation

Earlier in this chapter I seriously considered whether the Fourth and Fifth Dynasty pyramids and related sun temples at Abu Ghorab and Heliopolis were positioned according to a master plan. A few years ago, when I proposed this idea in my book *The Orion Mystery*, this was anathema to Egyptologists. Now, with the proposals made by David Jeffreys of an intervisibility between all these sites, the idea does not seem so heretical after all. The gap seems to be narrowing. Contrary to what some critics have said about my theory, I am not claiming that these monuments were built by some lost civilisation of 'Atlanteans', and I wholeheartedly agree with Egyptologists that all the pyramids and sun temples of the Memphite region were built by

Egyptians during a period that spanned from *c.* 2700 to *c.* 2200 BC.[56] But the issue on which we *do* hotly disagree is this: I believe that the master plan executed by the Fourth and Fifth Dynasties is a religious representation of the sky Duat *as it was seen in c. 11,541 BC*, the epoch that I concluded was that mysterious *zep tepi*, or 'First Time', when, in the minds of the ancient Egyptians, creation had taken place in this region.

To put it in another way, I am claiming that in order to position their monuments, the Fourth and Fifth Dynasties used very ancient blueprints which could have been preserved by astronomer-priests over many generations; or, alternatively, that they were able to extrapolate the sky of the twelfth millennium BC by using their knowledge of precession. I believe both scenarios are possible, this in spite of the huge reticence by Egyptologists to seriously consider them.

Towards the end of his life, the Egyptologist Henri Frankfort had come to realise that 'Egypt viewed the universe as essentially static. It held that a cosmic order was once and for all established at the time of creation.'[57] And more recently the American Egyptologist Jane B. Sellers wrote that the cosmic order 'was a form that had been created for gods in the heavens, and how inevitable it was that an imitation of the cosmic order should prevail for men on earth'.[58] I maintain that this mysterious 'cosmic order' was, to the ancient mind, none other than the orderly and majestic cycles of the sky, and more especially, the celestial events that were witnessed in that select area of the starry world that the ancient Egyptians called the Duat. I further maintain that they sought to replicate this sky region on the land around Heliopolis and the Memphite Necropolis. Bringing down the cosmic order to earth 'as established at the time of creation' in the Memphite region is exactly the sort of ambitious scheme that the priests of Heliopolis would have attempted, and their legacy is the colossal star pyramids and sun temples that still survive there. I have applied astronomy to the Pyramid Texts and have extracted from them a calendrical date which might constitute 'the time of creation'. This was done by precessing back the sky to the first appearance of Sirius in that region, and by matching it to the start of a Sothic cycle. The date that emerges from this is 11,541 BC. At this date, when the Milky Way is aligned to the south–north flow of the Nile and Orion transits the south meridian, the Duat region in the sky bears an uncanny resemblance to the Memphite region on the land. The logic and mathematics are sound, bearing in mind, of course, the topographical constraints and the subjugation of astronomical observation to religious needs. I am, of course, acutely aware that the date of 11,541 BC very much disturbs and much displeases Egyptologists and historians of science. I cannot help this. For it would be like telling Copernicus – he was, in fact, actually told! – that his heliocentric theory disturbed and much displeased the bishops of Rome. Truth is not something that is voted for or against by bishops or academics, or that meets with their approval. Truth is truth. And facts are facts. So let us deal with facts, and not votes or opinions.

The Egyptologist David O'Connors was bold enough to state that: 'in my opinion, the only theory that provides a fully comprehensive explanation for the Pyramid Complex . . . is the theory that the complex basically represents – in its entirety and simultaneously – cosmology, cosmic renewal and cosmic governance'.[59] I have demonstrated that the 'cosmic renewal' that most affected the ancient Egyptians was the return of the phoenix, which, in calendrics, was marked by the cyclical return of the heliacal rising of Sirius with the New Year's Day every 1,460 years. It is my firm conviction that the perfect 'cosmic renewal' of c. 2781 BC (when the heliacal rising of Sirius fell on the day of the summer solstice) was the religious impulse that fired the priests of Heliopolis to put into practice a plan to develop the whole Heliopolis–Memphis region into a sort of three-dimensional (almost holographic) model of the Duat as it was established at the time of creation. As we have seen earlier, the Pyramid Texts confirm that the region of Heliopolis-Memphis was where 'creation' had taken place with the appearance of the Primordial Mound upon which the *bennu*-phoenix alighted and set in motion 'time' and the stars and, furthermore, to which it would return every 1,460 years. If this is true, then we should have evidence of such a return around the year 1321 BC, which marked the return of a Sothic cycle (2781 – 1,460 = 1321 BC) within the known historic period some 1,460 years after the Pyramid Age.

So, did anything happen in 1321 BC that could be interpreted as the 'return of the phoenix' to Heliopolis? And if so, then from where was this 'phoenix' returning?

And who was the 'phoenix'?

CHAPTER FIVE

The Return of the Phoenix

Afterwards I went up the river, and made some observations which carried the conviction with them and strengthened the idea in my mind that in the orientation not only of Edfu, but of all the large temples which I examined, there was an astronomical basis.

Sir Norman Lockyer, *The Dawn of Astronomy*

. . . strange to say, the whole number of buildings in stone, as yet known and examined, which were erected on both sides of the river by Egyptians and Ethiopian kings, furnish incontrovertible proof that the long series of temples, cities, sepulchres, and monuments in general, exhibit a distinct chronological order, of which the starting point is found in the pyramids, at the apex of the Delta.

H. Brugsch, *Egypt Under the Pharaohs*

The Kingdoms of Upper and Lower Egypt

In modern European reckoning, when we travel north we use terminology such as 'going up north', while when travelling south we say 'going down south', without quite knowing why exactly. This concept comes, in fact, from the way that seventeenth-century cartographers decided to place north at the top of their maps. But there is no scientific reason for this. The earth is a globe floating, and all directions can be considered as being 'up' depending on how one chooses to perceive them. The decision to place north 'up' is just a choice and not a scientific reality, as all cartographers would agree. There is no good reason why south should not be placed at the top of a map if one wants it so. The ancient Egyptians decided that south rather than north was 'up' through observation of their world. South was 'up' because the Nile flowed *down* from the south, and because the sun reached its highest point at noon in the south. Indeed, the southern part of their country was perceived as 'Upper Egypt' and the northern part 'Lower Egypt'.[1]

Another peculiarity of the Egyptian geography is that it has always been perceived not only as 'upper' and 'lower' but as two distinct lands. According to Egyptologists, the land we now call Egypt was very early divided into two distinct although united kingdoms, one in the north or in 'Lower Egypt' and the other in the south or 'Upper Egypt'. In all guidebooks on Egypt you will be told unequivocally that in 3000 BC or thereabouts, a powerful king of Upper Egypt called Menes (or Narmer or Scorpion) invaded Lower Egypt and united it with Upper Egypt, thus creating the 'Kingdom of the Two Lands', a sort of pharaonic merger of north and south. You will also be told with the same assurance that Menes or Narmer or Scorpion built the capital of this double kingdom at Memphis, 15 kilometres south of modern Cairo. As I.E.S. Edwards, for example, explains:

Menes, at first king of Upper Egypt only, overcame the northern kingdom and united the two former kingdoms under one crown, established himself as ruler over the whole land. Memphis would thus have been the natural place for him to build a strong fortified city . . . In unifying the two kingdoms, Menes performed a military feat that may have been attempted by others before his time, but never with more than temporary success. Menes, however, both achieved the military victory necessary for uniting the two kingdoms and ensured that its effects would be lasting by following it up with an astute policy, on which the greatness of Egypt in the subsequent dynasties was founded. Nevertheless, the historical fact that Egypt had once consisted of two separate kingdoms was never entirely forgotten by its people, for down to the latest times the pharaohs still included among their titles that of 'King of Upper and Lower Egypt'.[2]

Edwards, like many Egyptologists of his generation, seems to have accepted that the 'unification' of Upper and Lower Egypt was an actual historical event. There are, however, some Egyptologists who are not so sure of this, and consider it to have probably been a 'semi-mythical anecdote'. For example, Michael Hoffman, who is an accredited authority on the predynastic history of ancient Egypt, insists that there is precious little contemporary evidence that supports a historical 'unification'. According to Hoffman, the story of the 'unification' event 'is culled from documents that come from hundreds if not thousands of years after the alleged event, by which time Menes, if he ever existed, had been transformed into a culture-hero whose life and accomplishments were embroidered with semi-mythical anecdotes.'[3] This is also the view of the Czech Egyptologist Miroslav Verner, who admits that 'some researchers consider Menes a purely legendary figure',[4] and of the influential Dr Jaromir Malek of the Griffith Institute, who went as far as to suggest that the origin of the idea of two separate kingdoms 'may be a projection of the pervasive dualism of Egyptian ideologies, (and) not a record of a true historical situation'.[5]

But if the 'unification' was not historical, then from where or from what did the ancient Egyptians themselves cull such a dualism for their country?

Unification of Earth and Sky

In the year 1800, during the French occupation of Egypt, a large black stone with rows of hieroglyphic inscriptions on it, was discovered in a field just a few kilometres south of modern Cairo by marauding French soldiers in Napoleon's army. The black stone, which apparently had been used by local farmers to grind wheat, was at first kept in the army barracks at Alexandria, but when the French surrendered to the British forces in 1801, the mysterious stone was taken as spoils of war and promptly dispatched to Earl Spencer in England, who, probably not knowing what to make of it, eventually donated it to Egyptology. Today the black stone is displayed on the south wall of the ground floor of the Egyptian gallery at the British

Museum in London. A rectangular block of granite measuring 92 x 137 cm, it has carved on it 64 lines of hieroglyphic text. Although much of the original inscription has been severely damaged through the ages, enough nonetheless remains to provide us with an invaluable insight into how the ancient Egyptians perceived the origins of their double kingdom of Upper and Lower Egypt and also the genesis of the 'divine' kings who ruled it. The text is known to Egyptologists as the Memphite Theology, and according to Frankfort, it mainly expounds a 'theory of kingship' based on a mythical ancestry.[6] The stone and the inscriptions on it date from about 750 BC during the reign of King Shabaka; hence its occasional name of the Shabaka Stone. But some Egyptologists believe that the text was culled from a much older source, which, in any case, is confirmed by the ancient scribe himself who copied it:

> This writing was copied out anew by his majesty (King Shabaka) in the house of his father Ptah-South-of-his-Wall (Memphis), for his majesty found it to be a work of the ancestors which was worm-eaten so that it could not be understood from beginning to end. His majesty copied it anew so that it became better than it had been before . . .[7]

Egyptologist and philologist Miriam Lichtheim, who studied the writings on the Shabaka Stone, concluded that the 'text is a work of the Old Kingdom but its precise date is not known. The language is archaic and resembles that of the Pyramid Texts.'[8] This view is shared by Frankfort, who was of the opinion that certain doctrines found in the Memphite Theology came from 'traditions of the greatest antiquity'. Also according to Frankfort, 'the text is a cosmology . . . it describe the order of creation and makes Egypt . . . an indissoluble part of the order'.[9]

The first part of the inscriptions narrates how the creation of the land of Egypt had taken place when the primeval waters receded and the 'Mound of Creation' first appeared at Heliopolis. The story then moves quickly to the epic conflict between Horus, the son of Osiris, and his uncle the god Seth, over the legitimate right to rule Egypt. The conflict ends by being resolved by the earth-god Geb, father of

Osiris, nonetheless under the aegis of the Council of Gods or Great Ennead:

> *Geb, Lord of the Gods, commanded that the Nine Gods gather to him. He judged between Horus and Seth; he ended their quarrel. He made Seth king of Upper Egypt in the land of Upper Egypt, up to the place where he was born which is Su (a place near Herakleopolis). And Geb made Horus king of Lower Egypt in the land of Lower Egypt, up to the place in which his father (Osiris) was drowned which is 'Division of the Two Lands'. Thus Horus stood over one region and Seth stood over one region. They made peace over the Two Lands at Ayan (near Memphis). That was the division of the Two Lands. Geb's words to Seth: 'Go to the place in which you were born.' Seth: 'Upper Egypt.' Geb's words to Horus: 'Go to the place in which your father was drowned.' Horus: 'Lower Egypt.' Geb's words to Horus and Seth: 'I have separated you' into Lower and Upper Egypt. Then it seemed wrong to Geb that the portion of Horus was like the portion of Seth. So Geb gave to Horus Seth's inheritance, for he is the son of his first born (Osiris). Geb to the Nine Gods: 'I have appointed Horus, the firstborn.' Geb's words to the Nine Gods: 'Him alone, Horus, the inheritance.' Geb's words to the Nine Gods: 'To this heir, my inheritance.' Geb's words to the Nine Gods: 'To the son of my son, Horus...' Then Horus stood over the land. He is the uniter of this land, proclaimed in the great name: Ta-tenen, South of his Wall, Lord of Eternity. Then sprouted the two great magicians (crowns) upon his head. He is Horus, who arose as king of Upper and Lower Egypt, who united the Two Lands in the nome of the Wall (Memphis), the place in which the Two Lands were united. Reed and Papyrus were placed on the double door of the House of Ptah (a creator god). This means Horus and Seth, pacified and United. They fraternised so as to cease quarrelling in whatever place they might be, being united in the House of Ptah, the 'Balance of the Two Lands' in which Upper and Lower Egypt had been weighed. This is the land (of) the burial of Osiris...* [10]

It does not require much imagination to see that the 'unification' of Upper and Lower Egypt as described in the Memphite Theology has both a mythical and a cosmic ring to it. The land of the 'burial of Osiris' which is the Memphite region is almost certainly also the Duat, the starry underworld containing Orion, which, as we have seen, is the celestial form of Osiris. Bearing this in mind, the words of the Canadian Egyptologist Samuel Mercer have a particular resonance when he informs us that 'the Duat was a kind of duplicate of Egypt. There was an Upper and Lower Duat, and it had a great river running through it.'[11]

This surely raises a question: could the idea of an Upper Egypt and Lower Egypt be rooted in astronomy?

Astronomical Grounds

In 1891 the English astronomer Sir Norman Lockyer developed a deep fascination for ancient Egypt and its mysterious pyramids and temples. He was puzzled as to why a people who so deeply venerated the sun, and who especially observed its rising in the eastern horizon fluctuating throughout the yearly cycle from a point in the north at summer solstice to one in the south at winter solstice, should also have their country similarly disposed with a distinct north and a distinct south concept. After giving much reflection to this geographical peculiarity, as well as to the ancient Egyptians' intense religious focus on the sky, Lockyer began to suspect that 'the double origin of the people thus suggested on astronomical grounds may be the reason for the name of the "double country" used specially in the title of kings'.[12] Almost a century later, in 1992, the very same idea came to the astronomer Ronald Wells, who was more specific than Lockyer when he wrote that

> Monitoring the movements of the sun god must have been one of the earliest of predynastic observations in the Nile Valley; and it would have been natural to interpret the sun's yearly motion along the eastern horizon from the southernmost point at the winter solstice to the northernmost point at the summer solstice and back as journeys or visitations of the god to each of the two kingdoms – the due east point forming at least the heavenly boundary between them.[13]

We have seen how the Egyptians started their calendar in 2781 BC with the summer solstice when the latter coincided with the heliacal rising of Sirius and also with the opening of the flood season (Akhet). Not surprisingly, therefore, this first day of the year, or 'New Year's Day', was referred to as *wp rnpt*, literally 'The Opener of the Year', and was used as an epithet for Sirius.[14] In the civil calendar it was tabulated as I Akhet 1, i.e. first month, season of Akhet, first day. Eventually it was simply called 1 Thoth, which was the first day of the first month of the year, in the same way we call New Year's Day 1 January in our current Gregorian calendar.[15] But another, perhaps even more meaningful, name for the New Year's Day was *ms-wtr*, literally 'The Birth of Ra' or, to be more precise, 'The Birth of Ra-Horakhti' (Ra-Horus-of-the-Horizon). In 1905 the chronologist Eduard Meyer demonstrated that 'The Birth of Ra' had denoted the summer solstice. But this only holds true for the date *c.* 2781 BC when the New Year's Day coincided with the summer solstice. Because the civil calendar was a drifted calendar which displaced the summer solstice by a quarter of a day each year, the same thing happened to the New Year's Day and, by extension, to 'The Birth of Ra'. Simple calculation shows that after 753 years (1506 ÷ 2 = 753 years, half the Great Solar Cycle), the 'Birth of Ra' had drifted to the *winter* solstice and thus a massive 54° to the south of the summer solstice sunrise point. In other words, in the year 2028 BC (2781–753 = 2028) the sun disc rose 28° *south*-of-east at the winter solstice and not, as it had done originally in 2781 BC, 28° *north*-of-east at the summer solstice. Surely this conjunction of 'The Birth of Ra' with the winter solstice, marked by the extreme southerly position of the sun disc on the horizon, must have had immense religious significance to the priests of the solar cult who were based in the southern extreme of Egypt. It must have seemed as if the cosmic order had ordained that now it was their turn to be controllers of the sun religion and that the reigning pharaoh should now also move the capital of the country from its location in the north to a new location in the south.

Is there any indication that this happened? If my hypothesis is correct, then we ought to find in the south of Egypt a major religious centre rising in prominence at around 2028 BC which not only was dedicated to this new vision of the sun-god but, more especially, whose principal sun temple was orientated to the winter solstice sunrise.

The Father of Archaeoastronomy

Amazing as it may seem, it was not until the late 1800s that European scholars began to suspect that the ancient temples of Egypt may have had astronomical alignments. And although it had long been known that the bases of the pyramids were aligned to the astronomical cardinal points, no one as yet had suspected that temples also had anything to do with the rising or setting of the sun or the stars. As we have seen, the consensus among Egyptologists was – and to a certain extent still is – that the temples of Egypt were simply made to face the Nile. But all this began to change – or should have done – one cold November evening in 1890, when the astronomer Sir Norman Lockyer read a carefully structured paper at the Royal School of Mines in London to a small audience of middle-aged gentlemen in white collar and black tie.

That evening Lockyer presented what he thought was a completely new and revolutionary idea: that the ancient temples of Egypt had all probably been aligned to the sun or the stars. He visualised the ancients who designed those temples not merely as superstitious priests but rather as *astronomers* (albeit subjugated to their religion) who had cleverly incorporated their cosmologies and celestial myths into the orientation and symbolism of their religious buildings. It all seemed completely new and very controversial to the learned gentlemen listening to Lockyer – except for one, who, after the lecture, politely informed Locker by letter that a certain Professor Nissen in Germany had beaten him to it by publishing a paper on this topic not long ago. Clearly embarrassed by this news, but being the great gentleman and scholar that he was, Lockyer was later to write in the preface of his famous book, *The Dawn of Astronomy*, the following acknowledgement:

> After my lectures were over, I received a very kind letter from one of my audience, pointing out to me that a friend had informed him that

Professor Nissen, in Germany, had published some papers on the orientation of ancient temples. I at once ordered them. Before I received them I went to Egypt to make some inquiries on the spot with reference to certain points which it was necessary to investigate, for the reason that when the orientations were observed and recorded, it was not known what use would be made of them, and certain data required for my special inquiry were wanting. In Cairo also I worried my archaeological friends. I was told that the question had not been discussed; that, so far as they knew, the idea was new ... One of them, Brugsch Bey, took much interest in the matter, and was good enough to look up some of the old inscriptions, and one day he told me he had found a very interesting one concerning the foundation of the temple at Edfu. From this inscription it was clear that the idea was not new, it was possibly six thousand years old. Afterwards I went up the river, and made some observations which carried conviction with them and strengthened the idea in my mind that for the orientation not only of Edfu, but of all the larger temples which I examined, there was an astronomical basis. I returned to England at the beginning of March, 1891, and within a few days of landing received Professor Nissen's papers. I have thought it right to give this personal narrative, because, while it indicates the relation of my work to Professor Nissen's, it enables me to make the acknowledgment that the credit of having first made the suggestion belongs, so far as I know, solely to him.[16]

In spite of these scholarly niceties, it is Lockyer and not Nissen who has been accredited in the annals of science with the epithet 'Father of Archaeoastronomy' – that relatively new branch of archaeology that makes use of astronomy to study ancient temples and sacred sites.

Joseph Norman Lockyer was born in 1836 to a middle-class family in Rugby. He was educated at private schools in England and various parts of Europe, and as a young man worked at the War Office in London. It was there that he took an interest in astronomy, building a small observatory at his house in the leafy and fashionable suburb of Hampstead. It was thus, in this modest and quaint way, that Lockyer began his distinguished career in astronomy. By 1862 he had been elected a Fellow of the Royal Astronomical Society, and two years later, after purchasing his first spectroscope, he was to direct his sharp brain to the study of solar emissions. In 1868, while working at the College of Chemistry in London, Lockyer observed the bright emissions from the sun during a total eclipse and concluded that they were from an unknown element which he named 'helium' – a quarter of a century before Sir William Ramsay would isolate this gas in his laboratory. In 1885 Lockyer became the world's first professor of astronomical physics.[17] There is another less known 'first' about Lockyer: in 1869 he collaborated with the publishers Macmillan & Company and founded the influential scientific journal *Nature*.[18] For his discovery of helium and his other achievements in science, Lockyer received a knighthood in 1897. An observatory and planetarium which he established at Salcombe Hill in Devonshire in 1912 with his son James still bear their names: 'The Norman Lockyer Observatory and James Lockyer Planetarium'.[19]

It was in the autumn of 1890, at the mature age of 53, that Norman Lockyer began to take a keen interest in the astronomical alignments of ancient Egyptian temples.[20] He delved into the voluminous publications of Napoleon's expedition of 1798 and the work of the Prussian expedition of 1844, but soon realised that neither had 'paid any heed to the possible astronomical ideas of the temple builders'. Lockyer himself strongly suspected that 'there was little doubt that astronomical consideration had a great deal to do with the direction towards which these temples faced'. So, in late November 1890, he decided to go to Egypt and see for himself. Upon his arrival in Cairo he reported to the antiquity authorities, which, at that time, were controlled by the German Egyptologist Emile Brugsch Bey.[21] It so happened that his older brother, the eminent professor Heinrich Brugsch Bey, was the acclaimed authority on the astronomical inscriptions found on ancient temples and tombs, and thus was only too happy to help Lockyer in his investigations.[22] It was from Brugsch's inscriptions that Lockyer became aware of the 'stretching of the cord' ceremony, and he was quick to realise that it was a ritual describing the astronomical orientating of temples. Much encouraged by this, he travelled upriver to Luxor, a journey which in those days took nearly three weeks.

Winter is an excellent time of year to cruise on the Nile, and Lockyer, like all first-time travellers to Egypt, must have felt the mounting excitement as his little Nile steamer, the MS *Mehetmet Ali*, approached ancient Thebes and the great temple of Amun-Ra at Karnak. No modern adjective can do this temple justice. 'Awesome' and 'mind-boggling' do not even get close. To the ancient Egyptians it was *ipet-sut*, 'the most splendid of places'. For me, after the Giza pyramids of course, it is the place that best evokes the splendour and magnificence that once was Egypt. The senses and the emotions run amok here as you walk amid the work of generations of architect-priests who developed Karnak into the greatest and most splendid religious centre of the ancient world. And although there has been much pillage and destruction over the millennia,[23] this amazing temple still manages to dazzle and thrill the modern visitor.

The temple of Amun-Ra at Karnak, as it stands today, is in fact made up of four main sections attached one to the other. First there is the impressive avenue of ram-headed sphinxes that leads to the temple's gates. Past the first pylon, originally 40 metres high, you enter into the vast open court. Beyond this is the great hypostyle hall and, finally, some 200 metres further down, the various inner sanctuaries. The whole temple runs from west to east over a staggering length of about 300 metres. The main entrance is in the west side, but there is also an eastern entrance leading to a smaller temple dedicated to Ra-Horakhti which was built back to back with the main temple of Amun-Ra, the inner sanctuaries of the temple sandwiched between them. There are also seven other minor entrances set in the sides of the huge enclosure that surrounds the whole complex, a sacred lake and several other temples dedicated to 'guest deities' within and also outside the enclosure, notably those of the gods Khonsu and Montu and the goddess Mut. Together all these structures form a huge ensemble that is sprawled over an area of 1,500 × 800 metres. It must be remembered, however, that this vast complex was developed, embellished, added to, modified, rebuilt, and restored several times over a period of nearly 1,300 years. Many things, therefore, are not original. What is certain, however, is that the main axis of the temple has remained unchanged since its origins.

The King and Seshat performing the *Stretching the Cord* ceremony, Temple of Karnak.

Reconstruction of the *Stretching the Cord* ceremony, Hilversum Studios, Holland.

Seshat counting the years on the palm branch,
Temple of Seti I at Abydos.

The *Stretching the Cord*
ceremony, Edfu temple.

Horus figure
marking a
spot in the
Big Dipper
with a spear.

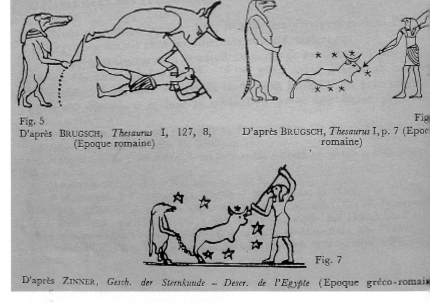

Fig. 5
D'après BRUGSCH, *Thesaurus* I, 127, 8,
(Epoque romaine)

Fig
D'après BRUGSCH, *Thesaurus* I, p. 7 (Epoc
romaine)

Fig. 7

D'après ZINNER, *Gesch. der Sternkunde — Descr. de l'Egypte* (Epoque gréco-romain

The Giza
necropolis
from the east.

The author.
View from
the roof of the
building where
he lives.

Overhead view of
Giza (south at top).

Giza Pyramids
looking south-west.
Note the offset of
the smaller pyramid.

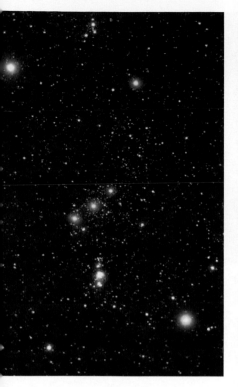

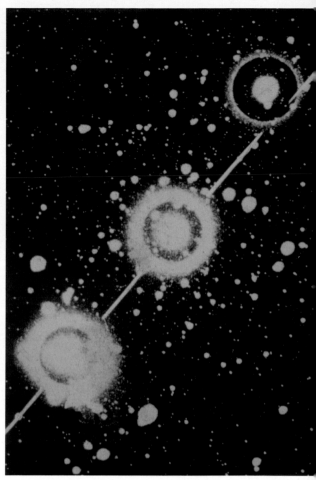

Orion. Note offset of smaller star
(*Mintaka*) in Orion's belt.

Orion's belt showing offset
of smaller star *Mintaka*.

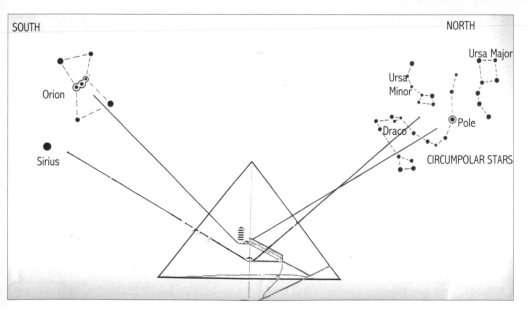

Star-shafts in Great Pyramid.

Angle of Orion's belt at meridian in c. 11,500 BC.

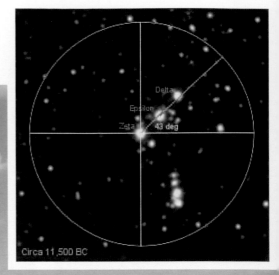

Circa 11,500 BC

Author at Abusir pyramids.

View of the Abusir pyramids from the sun-temple at Abu Ghorab. Note the alabaster sacrificial altar on lower left of plate.

Author at the Temple of Karnak, west entrance.

Sir Norman Lockyer c. 1899.

Elephantine Island at Aswan
in the background. Author
and view from the gardens
of the Old Cataract Hotel.

Sunrise at winter solstice, Temple of Karnak.

When Lockyer visited the temple in 1891, it was not restored or cleared of debris as it is today. He had to clamber over rubble and fallen columns. Yet in spite of the ruined aspect of the temple, Lockyer was stupefied by what he saw. 'This temple of Amen-Ra', he was to write, 'is beyond all question the most majestic ruin in the world . . . one of the most soul-stirring temples which have ever been conceived or built by man.' What specifically captured Lockyer's interest was the long east–west axis of the temple. He estimated that it ran 'something like 500 yards in length' and that the whole point was 'that the axis should be absolutely open, straight and true'. According to Lockyer,

> The axis was direct towards the west hills on the west side of the Nile, in which are the tombs of the kings . . . there were really two temples – the westside one dedicated to Amen-Ra and the eastside one to Ra-Horakhti – in the same line back to back, the chief one facing sunset at the summer solstice, the other probably the sunrise at the winter solstice . . . it is easy to recognise that these arrangements bear out the idea of an astronomical use of the temple . . .[24]

Lockyer described the Karnak temples as 'horizontal telescopes' which, according to him, were designed to be permanently aligned at the eastern end with the rising of the winter solstice sun and at the western end with the setting of the summer solstice sun. Karnak, he thus concluded, was a 'solar temple' *par excellence*.

Summer Solstice Sunset or Winter Solstice Sunrise?

At Karnak's latitude, which is 25° 48′ north, a simple calculation shows that the orientation of the winter solstice sunrise would have been 26° 54′ south-of-east when the temple was founded in around 2050 BC.[25] This is exactly the orientation of the axis of the Karnak temple and, more especially, the eastern part at the rear of the complex that is dedicated to the 'god of the rising sun' Ra-Horakhti. In 1973 the modern astronomer Gerald Hawkins obtained 26° 54′ south-of-east from detailed survey maps from the Franco-Egyptian Research Centre at Karnak.[26] More recently, in 1999, the Egyptologist Luc

Gabolde of the French Mission of the CNRS at Karnak came up with a slightly lower value of 26° 44′ south-of-east, thus only a mere 10 minutes of arc off Hawkins's value.[27] This meant that an observer standing in 2050 BC along the axis of the Karnak temple with his back to the eastern entrance (and thus facing the eastern horizon) would have witnessed the sunrise at winter solstice taking place directly in front of him. Six months later, if that same observer turned a full 180° and faced the western horizon, he would witness the sunset at summer solstice taking place directly in front of him. Because the main entrance of the Karnak temple is facing the west, Lockyer concluded that the temple had been deliberately oriented to face the summer solstice sunset in order to have the sun's rays shine into the temple and illuminate the holy of holies. There was, however, one major problem with Lockyer's conclusion: the Theban Hills, directly in front of the Amun-Ra temple, cause the sun to disappear about five minutes before it actually reaches the horizon and thus the level of the temple's floor. Calculations show that in 2050 BC the sun at summer solstice would have set over the Theban Hills some 1° 25′ west of the spot on the western horizon towards which the temple was oriented. This meant that the sun's rays could not shine into the temple and illuminate the holy of holies. So although Lockyer was not wrong in saying that the axis of the Karnak temple was oriented towards the summer solstice sunset, the Theban Hills made it impossible for the sun's light to shine into the temple. We must remember that Lockyer was at Karnak in February of 1891 and thus did not witness the event *in situ*. Had he been there on 21 June, the day of the summer solstice, he would have realised that the sun disc did not reach the central alignment of the temple but disappeared behind the Theban Hills after it cleared the southern edge of the temple's gate built in the second pylon.[28]

In 1973 the astronomer Gerald Hawkins solved this nagging problem by proposing that the axis of the Karnak temple had not been intended to be towards the sunset at summer solstice but rather towards the sunrise at winter solstice in the opposite direction, *where there were no hills to obstruct the line of sight*.[29] According to Hawkins:

Ipet sut was the name of the earliest temple at Karnak, built about 2000 BC. Ipet sut was *east* of the pylon, in the direction of the *sunrise* . . . Farther along was a temple dedicated to Ra-Horakhti. This composite god title is roughly transliterated as Sun-rising, Sun-Brilliant on the Horizon . . . the Ra-Horakhti temple was on the same long line of the main axis, a line which began at the Nile, ran along the centre of the avenue of the sphinxes, through the opening of the six pylons, and through the altar of the earliest temple, *ipet sut* . . . the statues of pharaohs and gods stood there gazing into the eastern distance with stony eyes. I was sure the line pointed to some sky object. The statues were poised for a celestial happening . . .[30]

The 'celestial happening' that Hawkins was referring to was, of course, the Birth of Ra-Horakhti on the New Year's Day, which, in *c.* 2028 BC, took place at the winter solstice, thus (1506 ÷ 2) = 753 years after 2781 BC (when the New Year's Day had fallen on the day of the summer solstice). This meant that the solar phoenix had come (or returned) south, a potent celestial sign that the sun-god now favoured the south and its new priesthood. New Year's Day was I Akhet 1 (first month, first season, first day), and there are several ancient texts that attest that this day was regarded as the Birth of Ra-Horakhti. For example, according to the chronologist R. Weill, the Gardiner Papyrus (*c.* 1100 BC) states: 'Ramses IX Year 13, Birth of Ra-Horakhti, first month, first day',[31] while in the so-called Calendar of Edfu (100 BC) it is also stated: 'Birth of Ra-Horakhti, first month, first day'.[32] There is, too, a text from the Cairo Calendar[33] that describes the birth of Ra-Horakhti thus: '*I Akhet 1*: The Birth of Ra-Horakhti; ablution throughout the entire land in the water of the beginning of the High Nile which comes forth as fresh Nun.'[34] According to the astronomer Marshall Clagett, 'this latter statement may well reflect the very ancient view that the year was to begin with the sudden rising of the Nile'. The rise of the Nile began at the summer solstice, when the constellation of Leo was 'born', i.e. rose heliacally with the sun. Egyptologist Alan Gardiner also states that the New Year's Day was considered an appropriate date for the coronation of kings, since these were closely identified with Ra-Horakhti.[35] Because of the drift of the

New Year's Day from the true solar year, after 753 years, counting from 2781 BC, the Birth of Ra-Horakhti moved to the winter solstice. Since we know for certain that the Birth of Ra-Horakhti fell on the summer solstice in *c.* 2781 BC, the orientation of the Karnak temple of 26° 54′ south-of-east in *c.* 2028 BC reflects this astronomical fact. In 2003 the Spanish astronomer Juan Belmonte echoed this unarguable fact when he wrote that

There is an early mention in a necropolis report from Deir el Medina of a feast under the name of *mswt re-hr-ahty* (Birth of Ra-Horakhti) celebrated in I Akhet 1 as early as the 20th dynasty . . . We are going to propose the hypothesis that this link can effectively be associated with a moment when I Akhet 1 was at the time of the winter solstice . . . To be precise, because of the wandering of the civil calendar across the seasons, there have been two occasions when I Akhet 1 has fallen at the moment of the winter solstice: . . . 2004 BC and 500 BC respectively. Considering the 19th dynasty (sic.) mention of the feast, we cannot consider 500 BC. This brings us to the year 2004 BC. This was a very interesting moment in Egyptian history. According to most accepted chronologies, Menthuhotep II from Thebes had just re-unified the country and new buildings, on a monumental scale, were constructed for the first time in the very south of the country.[36]

Menthuhotep II belonged to the Eleventh Dynasty, and his reign is dated from 2061 to 2010 BC, smack at the time when the Birth of Ra-Horakhti fell on the winter solstice in 2028 BC. More significantly, he was responsible for moving the capital from Memphis to Thebes and is also believed to have set the original axis of the temple at Karnak which, as we have seen, has its eastern part dedicated to Ra-Horakhti and its axis aligned to the winter solstice sunrise. In moving the capital to Thebes and establishing a new religious centre at Karnak, it was as if Heliopolis or the idea of Heliopolis was itself moved to the south. For the whole of Egypt was now bracketed by two immense religious centres, one in the extreme north founded in *c.* 2781 BC when the Birth of Ra-Horakhti was at the summer solstice (the northern limits of sunrise), and the other in the extreme south founded in *c.* 2028 BC when the Birth of Ra-Horakhti fell at the winter solstice (the southern limit of sunrise). It is not surprising, therefore, that the region of Thebes was known as the 'Heliopolis of the South'. And according to the Egyptologist Cyril Aldred, the term 'Heliopolis of the South' may have referred specifically to Karnak, as attested in the royal title of Akhenaten as the ruler of Thebes.[37] For this title reads: 'Great of Kingship in Karnak; Horus of Gold; he with uplifted diadems in Southern Heliopolis; King of Upper and Lower Egypt.'[38] According to Donald Redford, the city of Thebes was known as the 'Southern City' or the 'Upper Egyptian Heliopolis', which again confirms the idea of a northern and southern Heliopolis.[39]

Egypt, then, was bracketed by two centres sacred to the god of the eastern horizon and sunrise (Ra-Horakhti) which mimicked the north and south limits of the sunrise along the eastern horizon. What seems to clinch this hypothesis is the fact that these two centres were founded in *c.* 2781 BC and *c.* 2028 BC respectively, when the Birth of Ra-Horakhti fell on the summer solstice (2781 BC) and the winter solstice (2028 BC). According to this theory, however, Egypt should have witnessed another more dramatic event change when the 'Birth of Ra-Horakhti' moved again to the summer solstice 753 years later in 1275 BC. According to accepted chronology, this falls in the reign of Egypt's most celebrated pharaoh, Rameses II (*c.* 1290–1224 BC). But to arrive at this date we have made our calculations using the Great Solar Cycle of 1,506 years. Had we used the Sothic cycle of 1,460 years,[40] this would bring us to the year 1321 BC (2781–1,460 = 1321 BC). And 1321 BC, as all chronologists know, brings us tantalisingly close to the reign of Egypt's most infamous pharaoh: Amenhotep IV, better known as Akhenaten (*c.* 1353–1335 BC).

Let us look at these coincidences more closely.

Waiting for the New Age

On the afternoon of 31 December 1999 in Cairo, millennium hysteria was peaking. As midnight approached, people from all walks of life began to gather by the thousands at the Giza pyramids to witness the opening of a new age. Several months earlier, Egypt's Supreme

Council of Antiquities (SCA) had announced that it was going to place a golden capstone on the top of the Great Pyramid to mark the occasion, claiming that this was Egypt's seventh millennium. The world's media prepared itself by sending hundreds of television crews and journalists, all falling over one another for the exclusive rights. Then, at the last minute, the whole thing went pear-shaped. The placing of the golden capstone was cancelled for fear of 'damaging the pyramid', and to make things worse, the smoke from the fireworks mingled with the heavy humidity causing a thick mist that blotted the pyramids from sight. The new age began not with a bang but with a whimper. I happened to be at Giza during this night of madness. In vain I tried to explain to friends that 31 December 1999 of our Gregorian calendar would have meant absolutely nothing to the ancient Egyptians. The Egyptians did not think in millennia but in Sothic cycles, which lasted 1,460 years. The last cycle had started in AD 1599[41] and the next was due in AD 3059. So, strictly speaking, we were 1,059 years early! All this, however, demonstrated to me the strange frenzy that could overcome the populace at the coming of a new astronomical age. One can only imagine the anticipation that must have gripped the Egyptians when the Sothic cycle of 1321 BC was in sight.

In 1995 the astronomer Alexander A. Gurshtein presented a paper to the Academy of Russian Science with the controversial title: 'The Great Pyramids of Egypt as sanctuaries commemorating the origin of the zodiac: An Analysis of astronomical evidence'. In this paper Gurshtein discussed the Sothic cycle of 1,460 years and the foundation of the Egyptian civil calendar in 2781 BC. He then made these intriguing comments:

1460 years after the introduction of the solar calendar in Egypt, its wandering starting point was empirically found to return to its initial position, which correlated with both the heliacal rising of Sirius and the inundation of the Nile. The return fell on 1321 BC. This date is associated with two events: (1) In 1366 BC the Pharaoh Akhenaten moved his capital to *Akhet-Aten* . . .[42]

In an article he published in the British journal *Vista in Astronomy* entitled 'The evolution of the Zodiac in the context of ancient oriental history', Gurshtein further wrote:

> In one of my first publications on the Zodiac, I made a suggestion that the emergence of Amenhotep IV (Akhenaten) as a true Sun believer could be influenced by astronomical motivations . . . In regnal year eight, this heretical pharaoh moved his capital into the middle part of Egypt near the modern site of Tell-el-Amarna . . . Historians do not know Akhenaten's motivations, but it may probably be clarified if we remember that Akhenaten took the crown before the end of the Great (Sothic) Cycle of the Egyptian calendar which, according to Censorinus' information, had happened in 1321 BC – a moment that was potentially within the king's life . . . Let me suggest that the pharaoh Akhenaten knew – as it was his duty to know – the circumstances connecting the establishing of the civil Egyptian calendar . . . his rule began only a short time before the first returning of the New Year's Day to its initial point. Such an event was triumphantly celebrated one and a half millennia later by the Roman Emperor, and of course, it had to be of the utmost significance during Akhenaten's time.[43]

Conflict

When Akhenaten was crowned pharaoh in *c.* 1353 BC the Birth of Ra-Horakhti, i.e. the New Year's Day, or 1 Thoth, now approached the summer solstice. We have seen how seven centuries earlier the Birth of Ra-Horakhti had marked the winter solstice, which may have prompted Menthuhotep II to move the capital to Thebes in the south and, more importantly, to found a new religious centre at Karnak. Now in Akhenaten's time, after seven centuries, the Birth of Ra-Horakhti was edging slowly back towards the summer solstice in the extreme north – and thus symbolically back towards Heliopolis. Could this return to the origins have influenced the young Akhenaten in his desire, as we shall see, to move the religious centre back to Heliopolis? As noted by the Spanish archaeoastronomer Juan Belmonte, the feast of the Birth of Ra-Horakhti was celebrated at the winter solstice at Karnak and Thebes, and, what was more, 'at this precise moment when the actual birth of Ra at winter solstice occurred in I Akhet 1, the feast was frozen at this date for the rest of Egyptian history'.[44] If Belmonte is right in his clever speculation – as I strongly suspect he is – this meant that the priests of Amun-Ra at Karnak were setting themselves in direct conflict with Maat, the cosmic law, which demanded a return of the Birth of Ra-Horakhti to the summer solstice and, by extension, a return of the religious authority to the priests of Heliopolis in the north. Understandably, the priests of the south were in no mood to relinquish their lucrative position of power and wealth to the priests of the north. But to their dismay and horror, the young Akhenaten seemed to support such a transfer, arguing that he was duty-bound to adhere to Maat. The conditions for a religious war were thus in the brewing.

In actual fact the slow process of handing back the religious reins to the priests of Heliopolis had begun much earlier. Indeed, as early as 1420 BC there were signs that such a move was being seriously contemplated by the reigning pharaoh when Amenhotep II, the great-grandfather of Akhenaten, favoured the priests of the north by building a splendid temple near the Great Sphinx of Giza which he dedicated to their god, Ra-Horakhti of Heliopolis. On a stela (a commemorative stone plaque) found near the Great Sphinx is an inscription describing Amenhotep II as 'Divine Ruler of Heliopolis' and 'Offspring [i.e. the son] of Horakhti', a clear indication of this king's devotion and favours towards the ancient sun-god of Heliopolis.[45] Amenhotep II's son, Tothmoses IV, went even further. As a young prince he claimed that Ra-Horakhti had appeared to him in the form of the Great Sphinx and had promised him the throne of Egypt. As Egyptologist Donald Redford put it, 'the king had, by his own admission, been helped to the throne through the agency of the sun god Ra-Horakhti, who had appeared to him as a prince in a dream.'[46] In gratitude to Ra-Horakhti, Tothmoses IV ordered that the Great Sphinx be cleared of the encroaching sand and restored to its former glory.[47] This new-found allegiance to Ra-Horakhti and his priesthood at Heliopolis intensified with Tothmoses IV's son, the great Amenhotep III. All this time, the priests of Karnak brooded in silence. Open conflict was to erupt, however, with the advent of Amenhotep III's dreamy son, Akhenaten.

The Break with Karnak

Akhenaten is known to history for having banned all worship of the gods in Egypt except for Aten, his apparently new sun-god, symbolised by a disc of the sun with golden rays shooting downwards. In other words: one religion, one sun-god, one symbol. Not surprisingly, he is thus often thought of as the precursor of monotheism, and there are even those who claim that he was none other than the real historical patriarch Moses.[48] But whatever Akhenaten was or was not, there is one thing about this mystical king that comes across most strongly in his passionate decrees and proclamations: his absolute and total commitment to the cosmic order, Maat. Over and over the ancient texts emphasise that Akhenaten was *ankh em maat*, 'living in Maat'. As the British Egyptologist Cyril Aldred was to write, 'The king was the personification of Maat, a word which we translate as "truth" or "justice", but has an extended meaning of the proper cosmic order at the time of its establishment by the Creator ... There is in Akhenaten's teaching a constant emphasis upon Maat ... as is not found before or afterwards.'[49]

When Amenhotep IV (the future Akhenaten) first came to the throne in 1353 BC, probably at the age of 16, he was co-regent with his ageing father, Amenhotep III. It is much debated how long this co-regency lasted, but it was probably just a few years. At any rate, Amenhotep IV was quick to introduce his great religious reform by building a temple at Karnak dedicated to Aten, presumably to the annoyance and discontent of the powerful priests of Amun-Ra. But here is the catch. For as Manchester University Egyptologist Rosalie David pointed out,

> Akhenaten probably first envisaged the cult as a development closely associated with the older solar worship; this is indicated in his early inscription in the sandstone quarry at Gebel-el-Silseleh, where he

describes himself as the 'First Prophet of *Re-horakhti*, Rejoicing-in-his-Horizon, in his name of Sunlight which is in Aten'.[50]

British Museum Egyptologist George Hard goes even further. According to him, 'Aten is really the god Ra absorbed under the iconography of the sun disc.'[51] In this he is backed by the German Egyptologist Hermann Schlogl, who stated that in the early years of Akhenaten's reign, 'the sun god Ra-Horakhti . . . was identical with Aten' and that 'Aten's didactic name meant "the living One, Re-Horakhti who rejoices in the Horizon".'[52]

Centuries after the temple of Karnak was founded, and certainly by the time Akhenaten ascended the throne, the priests of Karnak had acquired immense material wealth through taxation and donations, and also from a share in the spoils of war. Evidence shows that they owned vast tracts of land and practically controlled the whole commercial life of Upper Egypt. The priests of Karnak flaunted their sun-god Amun as the most supreme god of Egypt, absorbing the powers and even the names of the older solar gods of Heliopolis, Ra and Horakhti. The symbols, iconography and nomenclature of Amun began to be seen everywhere in preference to those of the older Heliopolitan solar deities, inevitably causing a schism between north and south, as much later in history a deep schism was caused between east and west by the different symbols, iconography and nomenclature of Islam and Christianity, even though they venerated the same unique supreme god.

With such power and wealth the priests began also to pose a political threat to the pharaoh, for as the old saying goes, absolute power corrupts absolutely. It is clear from the many statements attributed to Akhenaten that tension between him and the priests of Karnak ran very high, and that the young king feared for his throne and even his life. Was it this excess of power of the priests of Karnak that prompted Akhenaten to look back to the epoch when the sun religion was in the hands of the more pure and loyal priests of Heliopolis? Or was he mainly prompted by the cosmic order that indicated that the great return of the solar phoenix was imminent and that he, Akhenaten, would oversee this event? Or was it both his fear of the Karnak priests and the dictates of the cosmic order? At any rate, it was during his fourth or fifth year of reign that Amenhotep IV changed his name to Ahkenaten, which means 'Glory of the Aten'. This must have made the priests of Amun-Ra fume, for they surely regarded the name change from *Amun*-Hotep to Akhen-*Aten* as a slap in the face. The crunch came when Akhenaten then announced that the cult of Amun-Ra was banned and that the great temple of Karnak would be officially closed. Along with this unthinkable decision came another, even more devastating blow to the priests of Thebes: Akhenaten declared that he intended to move himself and the whole court to a new city dedicated to the Aten called Akhet-Aten ('Horizon of the Sun Disc') which he intended to have built further north.

Sometime in the early spring of the year 1348 BC,[53] the king and some members of his court visited the site of the future city of Akhet-Aten a few kilometres to the west of the modern town of Tell El Amarna. Riding in a chariot made of electrum and looking as radiant as the sun disc itself, Akhenaten proclaimed that it was 'his father' the Aten who had selected this site for the building of his new and eternal solar city. Apparently the Aten had shown himself to the king at Tell El Amarna and had told him that the place 'shall belong to me as a Horizon of the Sun Disc for ever and ever'.[54]

What cosmic vision influenced Akhenaten to choose this location for his dream city of Akhet-Aten?

Could it have been something to do with the position of the sun there that was somehow vital to the idea of an eternal solar city? And if so, what could that something have been?

What *did* Akhenaten see at Tell el Amarna that totally convinced him that this was the true earthly domain of the sun-god?

CHAPTER SIX

Lord of Jubilees

The benu bird (phoenix) was called 'Lord of Jubilees' . . .
   R.Wilkinson, *The Complete Gods and Goddesses of Ancient Egypt*

Aten: 'Lord of Jubilees'[1] . . .
                  Francis Llewellyn Griffith, 'The Jubilee of Akhenaten'

In Year 6 the Aten was given a new epithet: 'Celebrator of Jubilees'.
                  Ahmed Osman, *Akhenaten and Moses*

*I will make a 'House of Rejoicing' for the Aten, my father, in the island
of 'Aten Distinguished in Jubilees' in Akhet-Aten in this place.*
   Proclamation by Akhenaten at the foundation ceremony of the city of
                                                            Akhet-Aten

*Aten living and great who is in jubilee residing in the temple of Aten at
Akhetaten*
            Amarna inscription, in R. Wilkinson, *The Complete Gods and
                                          Goddess of Ancient Egypt*

A Desolate Place

In November 2002 I made my first visit to Tell El Amarna, a lonely
place on the east bank of the Nile in middle Egypt. I was, however, not
alone but with some 40 rowdy Italians brought to Egypt by my good

friend Adriano Forgione, the editor of *Hera* magazine in Rome. Each year Adriano organises a special tour to Egypt for his readers and often asks me to escort them around. If I am free then I accept willingly, for I very much enjoy these events, which give me the opportunity to meet a sample of my readers face to face and, as often happens as well, make new friends along the way.[2] We had left the Meridian Hotel at Giza with two coaches at sunrise and had taken the new asphalt Fayum road. It was a delightfully warm and bright autumn day and everyone was filled with a sense of adventure. Tell El Amarna had been on my agenda for quite some time, but somehow I had not found the time or opportunity to go there.

Upon reaching the outskirts of the Fayum oasis, our driver turned south-east towards the Nile. We then skirted the river for a few hours and finally reached the busy market town of Al Minya. After a little rest and some refreshments, we drove out of Al Minya to eventually arrive at the small hamlet of Malawi, where we crossed the Nile on a rickety old ferry boat. At this point we left the lush Nile Valley behind and drove into the desert to reach a vast crescent-shaped plain backed by low rocky hills. We were at the fabled site of Tell El Amarna.

But where was the legendary city of the sun?

Sadly, Akhet-Aten has all but disappeared, gone with the wind, to use the popular phrase. Long gone are the sumptuous palaces and splendid sanctuaries that once graced this place. And long gone is the fabulous Great Temple of the Aten. All that remains are the outline of foundations and two broken columns of the so-called Small Temple of the Aten. According to Barry Kemp, leader of the 1977–8 El-Amarna Survey of the Egypt Exploration Society, 'Amarna was never a lost city in the sense that it became invisible, although there may well have been a long period when it was not noticed through lack of interest.'[3] Well, it was quite invisible now. Akhet-Aten, much like my native city of Alexandria, must be seen not with the eyes but with the imagination.

The ruins of Tell el Amarna were first noticed in modern times by the Frenchman Edmé Jomard, a senior member of the 1798–9 Napoleonic expedition, who, on his way back to Cairo down the Nile, was surprised to come across the scant remains of what appeared to be a huge town not shown on any of his maps. 'Most of the constructions are unfortunately demolished, and one can see little more than the foundations', Jomard was to lament. Unwittingly he had stumbled on the lost city of Akhet-Aten, or rather what was left of it after it had been deliberately razed to the ground, stone by stone, by the infuriated priests of Amun-Ra in *c.* 1335 BC. Jomard produced a freehand sketch of the city which served as a rough survey until 1824, when a full archaeological survey was conducted by Sir John Gardner Wilkinson. After him came the Prussian archaeologist Richard Lepsius in the 1840s. It was Sir William Flinders Petrie, however, who started systematic archaeological digs in 1891. From 1917 onwards several detailed surveys were made of Akhet-Aten, the last being by Barry Kemp and Mohamad Abdel Aziz Awad in 1977-8, published in 1993 by the Egypt Exploration Society of London (EES).[4] From all these surveys and especially the latest by Kemp and Awad, a realistic picture can be made of what the city of Akhet-Aten looked like. Today there is a scale model of the city, made by the British architects Ingham Associates of London, displayed at the EES.[5]

As far as ancient cities go, Akhet-Aten was a sprawling metropolis, 12 kilometres long and two kilometres wide. When new, it must have looked like a gleaming jewel along the east bank of the Nile. Its true boundaries extended on both sides of the Nile and included the green fields on the west bank. It is estimated that the city's population grew to about 30,000 within a few years, a huge number for the epoch, which would have made Akhet-Aten a metropolis when compared to primitive cultures elsewhere in the second millennium BC, when people still lived in small settlements and numbers rarely exceeded a thousand souls.

As customary in Egypt, work at Akhet-Aten began with the tombs for the royal family and other nobles. These were cut into the eastern hills behind the city centre. The royal area was called 'Aten Distinguished of Jubilees' and consisted of vast temples with open courts, lavishly designed palaces and villas with gardens and private quays on the Nile, and a variety of auxiliary buildings such as military barracks, workshops, government compounds, record offices, stables and storehouses. There was a splendid avenue that served as a ceremonial route for the king and that ran parallel to the river between the Great Palace and the Great Temple of Aten. The latter was known as *gem-pa-aten*, 'House of the Aten'.[6] This huge temple had an elongated rectangular plan, with its entrance in the west side leading into a closed forecourt known as the 'House of Rejoicing' and then on through a series of six interlocking courts. At the rear of the temple was a slaughterhouse for sacrificial animals, and further still, at the far end of the complex, was the Sanctuary of the Aten, which consisted of a series of open-air courts containing hundreds of offering tables. The whole Great Temple complex measured a staggering 760 metres long and 290 metres wide, and was completely enclosed by a high boundary wall. The King's House, or palace, was immediately south of the Great Temple, and there was a small bridge leading from there to the royal gardens fronting the Nile. South of the King's House was the so-called Small Temple of the Aten, which probably served as a private chapel for the king. The city had two main ports, one for the Great Temple and the other for the royal palace. There was also a large docking wharf with a series of small quays that serviced the various storehouses and the residential areas of the city.

On the surface, all was perfect in Akhet-Aten. Unfortunately, however, it was built in haste – jerry-built according to Donald Redford – in order to satisfy the king's eagerness to quickly move his court out of Karnak. Had it survived, it is unlikely that any building would have remained intact for very long without constant repair and redecoration. As for the location, the king could not have chosen a worse place. This was an inhospitable desert bowl made even more uncomfortable by the eastern hills at the back that would have radiated the sun's heat with ruthless intensity. Summer at Akhet-Aten must have been a scorching nightmare. Unprotected by the lush vegetation of the Nile Valley, the winds would have constantly showered dust from the arid and dry eastern desert. Even today it is a desolate region inhabited only by a few *fellahin* families living in squalor. So why did the king choose this ill-disposed location to build the eternal domain of the sun-god?

According to Egyptologist Cyril Aldred, Akhenaten decided to move his capital from Thebes to Tell el Amarna some time in the fifth year of his reign because he was apparently ordered to do so by the solar god Ra-Horakhti.[7] There is a hint of this in the so-called Earlier Proclamation that Akhenaten made for the city which, 'begins with a sonorous recital of the names and titles of Ra-horakhti-Aten followed by those of the king' and in which the king decreed: 'May the Father live, divine and royal, Ra-horakhti, rejoicing in the Horizon in his aspect of the Light which is in the Aten (sun disc), who lives forever and ever . . .'[8]

Donald Redford, who is regarded as an authority on Akhenaten, drew attention to inscriptions in which apparently 'the king set on record his belief that the gods have somehow failed or "ceased" to be operative; and he describes his newly adopted god as absolutely unique and located in the heavens . . . numerous vignettes make perfectly plain that the god in question is Ra-harakhti, "Ra, the Horizon-Horus", the great sun god of Heliopolis.'[9] He also pointed out that the high priest of the city of Akhet-Aten was known as 'Chief Seer of Ra-Horakhti', which was, according to Redford, 'a title clearly derived from the sun-cult at Heliopolis'.[10] Ra-Horakhti, as we have seen, was the god of the rising sun in the east. Could the vision that inspired Akhenaten to choose Tell El Amarna have had something to do with the rising of the sun over the eastern hills on a particular day that was crucial for the function of the future solar city?

The Great Return

The reign of Akhenaten, which lasted 18 years or so, is generally known as 'the Amarna Period' as it mostly took place in the new city of Akhet-Aten at Tell El Amarna, from the fifth year of the king's reign to his fall in 1335 BC. At first the period represented a return to the much older – and thus purer and more legitimate – solar religion of Heliopolis and its god Ra-Horakhti. For to the Egyptians, as was also indeed the case in many other ancient cultures, it was the past and not the present that served as the perfect model, that golden age when the social order was imbued with lofty moral standards, deep religious convictions and, above all, a strict observance of the cosmic law as clearly attested by the great pyramids and sun temples that had been left behind at Heliopolis. What is also evident in the Amarna Period is the pronounced change in art, a sort of pharaonic renaissance, according to Egyptologist Arthur Weigall: 'Akhenaten's art might thus be said to be a kind of renaissance – a return to the classical period of archaic days; the underlying motive of that return being the desire to lay emphasis upon the king's character as representative of the most ancient of all gods, Ra-horakhti.'[11]

Thus everything suggests that Akhenaten saw himself – or perhaps his departed father, Amenhotep III – as a returning solar god of ancestral Heliopolitan origin,[12] a sort of messiah who would wrench the religious power away from the corrupt priests of Amun-Ra at Karnak and return it to its true keepers, the priests of Ra-Horakhti at Heliopolis. Akhenaten's initial intention is clear enough: to highlight the supremacy of Ra-Horakhti and how this god of Heliopolis had united with the Aten as Ra-Horakhti-Aten. But then why, after such a strong initial display of allegiance to Ra-Horakhti did Akhenaten not return the religious authority to the priests of Heliopolis but instead retained it for himself at Tell El Amarna? This question is even more pertinent when we also recall that his father, grandfather and great-grandfather had begun the process of moving base to Heliopolis.[13] The answer, I believe, lies partly in the political strategy that Akhenaten had adopted to bring about his great plan of religious reform, which is also why, a few years into his reign, he dropped the idea of a combined solar god in favour of a single god, the Aten. For it is very evident that the image of Ra-Horakhti (a falcon-headed man with a solar disc on his head) disappears completely from the religious art at Tell El Amarna. Only the Aten sun disc is allowed to be displayed. It was not as if the king forbade the worship of Ra-Horakhti, for throughout the Amarna Period we find Ra-Horakhti mentioned with much reverence by leading officials and priests of Akhet-Aten. Indeed, the high-priest of Akhet-Aten bore the title 'Chief Seer of Ra-Horakhti'. The most likely reason why the image of Ra-Horakhti is not seen in the latter part of the Amarna Period is probably because Akhenaten had become intolerant of multifarious representations of the sun-god other than that of the Aten as a simple golden disc with energy rays falling down to earth. In other words, the king only allowed representation of the sun-god in the way he actually appeared to everyone in the world. The only hints of extra symbolism were the curious leaf-like hands at the end of the sun's rays (which were probably intended to represent the protective and benevolent warmth and energy of the sun) and the little *ankh*-signs, the symbols of life, that were sometimes attached to the tips of the hands. But that was all. No human or animal figures or any other kind of symbols were allowed anywhere in Egypt.[14]

In a single stroke Akhenaten had removed the diverse iconographies that created the schism between a solar god of the north (Ra-Horakhti, the falcon-headed man crowned with the sun disc) and one of the south (Amun-Ra, the human-headed man crowned with the two divine plumes). All this, however, while it explains the prominence and uniqueness that Akhenaten attributed to the Aten, still does not explain why he chose the site of Tell El Amarna to dedicate to his unique sun-god. Why did he not return the cult to Heliopolis, as would be expected from his early devotion to Ra-Horakhti and the closeness the latter had to the Aten? Could it be that he feared that the move to Heliopolis would precipitate a religious war between north and south? Or could it be that his most coveted epithet, 'living in *Maat*', obliged him to act in conformity with Maat? And is it not possible that he found a way through Maat – which, after all, was all about the balance of the cosmic order in heaven and on earth – to attempt to balance the religious forces that were ripping Egypt apart?

As we have seen earlier, cosmic order or balance seems to have been everything to the ancient Egyptians. Nowhere is it more attested than in the so-called judgement scene when the souls of the dead were weighed on the divine scales of Maat and balanced against her feather of truth and justice. In the natural world this mechanism of balance – which today we call ecology – was manifest in everything, and in Egypt, nowhere more so than in the annual flooding of the Nile and its delicate ecology. We have seen how too weak or strong a flood would spell disaster. The flood had to be just right, which entailed a subtle natural balance between the water level at Elephantine and the time of year. Egypt's survival depended totally on the balance between the forces of nature and the celestial forces that governed time.

Equally, opposing forces between men had to be balanced, as Horus and Seth had been balanced at the time of creation. It was perhaps thus imperative to Akhenaten that north and south should be balanced for the smooth administration of the state. And since the pharaonic state was above all else a religious state, it was the forces of religion that required such balancing.

Since the Eleventh Dynasty onwards, the unbridled rise to power of the priesthood of the south at Karnak had seriously upset the religious balance between north and south. Yet contemplating a handing-over of the religious authority back to the priests of Heliopolis would aggravate matters even more. Tell El Amarna, as it happened, was almost precisely midway between Karnak and Heliopolis, acting as a geographical fulcrum between the 'Heliopolis of the south' and the 'Heliopolis of the north'. Could, therefore, the decision to move to Tell El Amarna be a political act of balance by the king in an ingenious attempt to eliminate once and for all the north and south religious centres in favour of a single one set in the middle of Egypt? As I stood under the starry sky amid the ruins of Akhenaten's dream city of the sun, engulfed in the silence and acutely aware of the great drama that had taken place here more than 3,000 years ago, I asked myself this: Did not the sun disc also have a mid-point (the equinox) that 'balanced' the two extreme points of the summer and winter solstices? And if Egypt was truly made 'in the image of heaven', then should it not, too, have such a religious mid-point or fulcrum in the centre of the country? With growing excitement I began to see that, as such, Egypt would indeed truly become a cosmic kingdom that functioned under the law of Maat, that imperturbable and perpetual cycle of the sun that caused it to alternate between north and south. If this was, in fact, Akhenaten's veiled motive, then his strategy was nothing short of brilliant. For if successful, it would clear thousands of years of religious dichotomy which was now growing into a serious political feud between the north and the south. At the same time, this move would also put everyone under one symbol of the sun-god, the visible sun disc or Aten, whose perfect form represented the sole universal creator and whose only religious centre would be at the very epicentre, the very heart of Egypt.

But like all such dreams inspired by ideologies, Akhenaten's ambitious plan was doomed to failure from the very outset. For he seriously misjudged one thing: human nature. The priests of Amun-Ra at Karnak valued their acquired power and wealth too much to simply hand it on a silver platter for Akhenaten to take to his new capital city at Akhet-Aten, even though Akhenaten was, at least from his own way of seeing things, a solar pharaoh 'living in Maat'. Absolute power corrupts absolutely, and the priesthood of Karnak were beyond redemption. Their iron-fist rule of religious affairs had brought them untold wealth and unchallenged authority. Indeed, when Akhenaten was enthroned they were virtually controlling the royal treasury and all the financial revenues, and probably the levy on every commercial enterprise and the income of every household in the land. Clearly they were not going to let all this go away just because a mystical and probably unhinged 18-year-old king got it into his royal head that he was some sort of solar messiah come to 'monotheise' the ancient religious system of Egypt. And although at first they had not much choice but to tolerate this capricious boy-king, they were eventually forced to strike back. Yet to give the young king his due, it would take the priests of Karnak 17 years to feel confident enough to make their move.

Distinguished in Jubilees

Meanwhile there is something else in Akhenaten's grandiose plan that I believe has escaped attention: the very strong link that the king himself made between the city of Akhet-Aten and the royal jubilees. This, as we have already seen, is made obvious from the name of the city centre, which was known as 'Aten Distinguished in Jubilees'. In Chapter Two we have associated these jubilees with the Sothic cycle and, consequently, with the solar phoenix, who, oddly enough, was sometimes called 'The Lord of Jubilees'.[15] The phoenix was especially sacred to Heliopolis, for it was there that it had alighted at the time of creation – *zep tepi*, the 'First Time' – to set into motion the cycles of the sky and time. Bearing this in mind, it is very significant that Akhenaten described the site of Akhet-Aten as 'The seat of the First

Time, which he [Aten] had made for himself that he might rest in it'.[16]

How many jubilees did Akhenaten celebrate at Akhet-Aten? And for whom? The answers depend on which Egyptologist you want to believe. Donald Redford, for example, allocates only one jubilee to Akhenaten, and not at Akhet-Aten but at Karnak. So does the Egyptian-based Egyptologist Jocelyn Gohary, who is an accredited expert on Akhenaten's jubilee (although unlike Redford, she does leave the question somewhat open).[17] On the other hand others have proposed that there were at least two, and perhaps even three or more, jubilees celebrated by Akhenaten during his 17 years of reign.[18] At any rate, all these scholars seem to at least agree that very early in his reign, probably in the second or third year, Akhenaten decided to proclaim a jubilee not for himself but, oddly enough, for his 'father' the Aten. And this was three years *before* the break with the priests of Amun-Ra at Karnak. It may well be that the king, in his naivety, thought that he could casually impose his new god on the priests of Amun-Ra with such an event. At any rate, Akhenaten's controversial desire to have a jubilee so early in his reign – let alone for the *Aten* – prompted a massive construction programme at Karnak under the very nose of the disgruntled priests of Amun-Ra. Among the many temples built in haste at Karnak, two stand out: the so-called *Gm-(t)-p-itn*, 'The Sun Disc is Found', and the *Hwt-bnbn*, 'The Mansion of the Benben'. These temples, much like all other temples that Akhenaten had built during his reign, were later to be deliberately dismantled stone by stone by the priests of Amun-Ra after the king's death, and the stones used as common hardcore and rubble for new constructions at Karnak.

In the last 50 years archaeologists have discovered vast numbers of small blocks of stones, nearly 45,000 to date, that were once part of the *Gm-(t)-p-itn* and the *Hwt-bnbn*, within the walls of pylons built after Akhenaten's death. These small blocks are known to Egyptologists as *talatat*, apparently a word of uncertain origin.[19] At first some enterprising Egyptologists thought they could reassemble the *talatat* like a gigantic puzzle, but the process was to prove so complex and tedious that hardly any progress was made for many years. In 1965, however, Ray W. Smith, a retired American army officer and a keen amateur student of ancient arts and technologies, proposed to use computer graphic technology to make virtual reconstructions of the various wall panels whence the *talatat* had been removed. He gathered a number of prominent Egyptologists to found the Akhenaten Temple Project under his directorship. In 1972 he was succeeded by the Egyptologist Donald Redford, who established that almost all the *talatat* had come from the *Gm-(t)-p-itn* temple ('The Sun Disc is Found'), which had serviced Akhenaten's jubilee at Karnak. But because there was no similar evidence of a jubilee at Tell El Amarna, Redford concluded that no other jubilee had been celebrated after the second year of the king's reign. But this lack of archaeological evidence – especially in a place which had been dismantled with such ferocity by the armies of Amun-Ra – is largely offset by the circumstantial *textual* evidence, which indicates that Akhenaten had at the very least *intended* to have many jubilees in his new city, not just for himself but also for his 'father', the Aten. Indeed, it is clear that from the very start Akhenaten's intention was that the city of Akhet-Aten should serve as a jubilee centre during his lifetime and, more especially, after his death ad infinitum – very much as the Third Dynasty pharaoh Djoser, I believe, had also intended for his Step Pyramid complex at Saqqara 1,300 years earlier. One of the eulogies that Akhenaten often gave to the Aten is more than sufficient to confirm this intention: 'The great living Aten that is in the jubilee, Lord of Heaven, Lord of Earth, in the midst of "Rejoicing" in Akhet-Aten.'[20] The Aten is several times called by Akhenaten *imy hb(w) sd* and *nb hb(w) sd*,[21] 'Distinguished in Jubilees' and 'Lord of Jubilees',[22] and an inscription on the first boundary stela for the city which the Akhenaten himself had placed makes it clear that 'There shall be made for me (Akhenaten) a sepulchre in the eastern hills; my burial shall be made therein, in the multitude of jubilees which Aten, my Father, has ordained for me.'[23]

The House of Rejoicing

Akhenaten's own father, Amenhotep III, is known to have celebrated at least three jubilees, with the last being in the thirty-seventh year of his reign. According to Egyptologist Francis Griffith, the palace of Amenhotep III in Western Thebes, which was called the 'House of Rejoicing', had included 'a great festival hall for the celebration of the jubilee'. Griffith further noted that

> Two 'Houses of Rejoicing' are named among the buildings designed by Akhenaten to adorn his new capital. In the fourth year of his reign, when he issued the proclamation establishing the city of Akhet-Aten, 'The Horizon of the Sun', at the modern Tell-el Amarna, Akhenaten caused copies of it to be engraved on the eastern cliffs at the north and south limits of the city . . . Herein the king swears by the Aten to build all kinds of monuments in Akhet-Aten and binds himself not to remove elsewhere. Among other things he says: '*I will make a "House of Rejoicing" for the Aten, my father, in the island of "Aten Distinguished in Jubilees" in Akhet-Aten in this place; and I will make a "House of Rejoicing" . . . [for] Aten, my father, in the island of "Aten Distinguished in Jubilees" in Akhet-Aten in this place.*' The gap in the record deprives us of the reason why there should have been two buildings of almost identical name, purpose and situation; perhaps one was a palace, the other a jubilee hall, associated together as in his father's (Amenhotep III) residence.[24]

Griffith seems to have believed that Akhenaten had probably intended to have a *permanent* jubilee temple dedicated to his 'father' the Aten in the new city of Akhet-Aten, to be located somewhere next to his palace. This idea is supported by the fact that Akhenaten's natural father, Amenhotep III, had built a permanent jubilee hall that was attached to his own palace in Western Thebes, and that it was variously known as 'Splendour of Aten' and 'House of Rejoicing'. Archaeological evidence has shown that the 'House of Rejoicing' temple at Akhet-Aten was an integral part of the Great Temple of the Aten, itself called 'House of the Aten'. All this makes it nearly certain that Akhenaten saw the god Aten as the god of jubilees, so much so that, according to George Hart, in the mind of Akhenaten the 'Aten is also thought to celebrate jubilee festivals like the pharaoh himself'.[25] The British Egyptologist Stephen Quirke also proposed that the term 'father' that was often used by Akhenaten when referring to the Aten was because 'Akhenaten seems to have insisted on the survival of his father's presence in the Sun-disc.' According to Quirke, 'These might be the reasons behind the great festivals documented in years 9 and 12, and perhaps the consolidation of the city of Akhet-Aten in year 6. The (heb) sed festivals (jubilees) continued to be celebrated for the Aten, as if the elder king were still alive on earth.'[26] Jocelyn Gohary could not avoid noting that 'in several cases, however, when a wish is expressed that the king may celebrate many sed-festivals (jubilees), it appears to have some connection with time, length of reign, lifetime and so on'. She also noted that the term *and so on* may be, according to some researchers like Flinders Petrie, *a division of the Sothic Cycle*'.[27] We should recall from Chapter Two that it was suggested that the *heb-sed* festivals were based on calendrical computations taking into account various intervals within the Sothic cycle and, furthermore, that some kind of super *heb-sed* was celebrated at the commencement of each 1,460-year cycle. The fact that one such period would have fallen in *c.* 1321 BC and thus well within the expected lifetime of Akhenaten (he would have been 48 years old), may indeed explain the flurry of epithets, feasts and temples that evoked the *heb-sed* in the Amarna Period. The Amarna Period was a Sothic period.

If this is correct, then it is surely relevant that during the elaborate festivities organised for the first jubilee of Amenhotep III for his thirtieth year of his reign, the old king commissioned 730 effigies of the goddess Sekhmet, a solar deity, to be used for the jubilee rituals. This conspicuous number of 730 also crops up in the number of altars that were placed around the Great Temple of Aten at Tell el Amarna, where, according to Donald Redford, 'the continuity of time and the constancy of the calendar depended wholly on the tireless regularity of the Sun-disc, and as if to commemorate the calendric continuum, 365 offering tables flanked Gm-itn on one side and 365 on the other'.[28] This makes a total of 730 offering tables. And 730 is, of course, half the Sothic cycle (1,460 years), equal to the number of years that the sun disc appears to travel from north (summer solstice) to south (winter solstice). Bearing this in mind, Jocelyn Gohary writes that 'with regards to the specific point in the civil calendar at which the (heb) sed-festival took place, the date I prt 1 was considered to be the ideal date for the celebration'.[29] This view was also shared by Alan Gardiner, and by the calendar expert Richard Parker.[30] In the Egyptian civil calendar the date I Prt 1 was the first day of the first month of the second season. It was also known as 1 Tybi (Tybi being the fifth month of the civil calendar). When the calendar was inaugurated in 2781 BC, 1 Tybi fell four months ($4 \times 30 = 120$ days) after the summer solstice, which in our own Gregorian calendar gives us the date 19 October. This date had a particularly strong resonance for me, because it so happened that I had found myself twice on this date at the Great Temple of Rameses II at Abu Simbel and, as all Egyptologists know, this is when the rising sun aligns with the main axis of the temple so that its light shines into the holy of holies, which contains four statues, one of which represents Ra-Horakhti. At this point I knew I was sensing something in all these interlocking clues: something that was going to change for ever my perception of what those great religious centres of Egypt meant.

Jubilee Centres Ad Infinitum

The first time I saw the great rock-cut temple of Rameses II at Abu Simbel was in the spring of 2002, when I was escorting a group of visitors on a tour of Egypt.[31] We had all flown out of Cairo earlier that morning, and after a brief stopover at Aswan airport, the Egyptair jumbo took us another half-hour further south to Abu Simbel.

The thing that one notices first about this dry and hot resort on the southern frontier of Egypt is the clarity and calmness of its weather, which is even more impressive after experiencing the dusty, polluted air of Cairo. On this particular day there was a soft, warm breeze, and the sky seemed dyed a bright cerulean blue, with not a single cloud in sight. At the airport we boarded coaches and after a bumpy ride along the shore of Lake Nasser, we arrived at the Great Temple. After the usual disorganised buying of tickets and security checks, we were led single file along a footpath that sloped down towards the lake. Suddenly the path took a sharp turn and we found ourselves almost face to face with the four seated colossi of Rameses II that dominate the façade of the temple. Even though I had prepared for this confrontation, nonetheless the huge surge in emotion within me almost threw me off balance. I felt dwarfed, humbled, inspired, awed and elated at the same time. I didn't know if I wanted to cry or laugh.

Rameses II, a Nineteenth Dynasty pharaoh who ruled from *c.* 1290 to 1224 BC, has been described as the Napoleon of ancient Egypt. He is, unquestionably, the most universally know pharaoh, who was made even more famous by Hollywood in his role of the super-villain who wanted to prevent Moses and the Jews from crossing the Red Sea into Israel. Whether this is historically true or not is not our debate here. What interests us about Rameses II is that, above all else, he was a compulsive builder who saw things in a big way. Under his reign massive building programmes were implemented all across Egypt, with giant statues of himself flanking the entrances of these gargantuan temples and opulent palaces. At Luxor temple, for example, you will be greeted by a 15-metre-tall effigy of Rameses II seated on a throne. Upon entering the Karnak temple there he is again, this time standing high at the entrance of the second pylon. And at Mit'Rahin (ancient Memphis) you will find him yet again in the form of a huge statue now lying on its back like a sleeping giant under a sheltered area built in the 1960s by the Antiquities Department. But by far the most impressive statuary of Rameses II are those four seated colossi that guard the entrance of the Great Temple at Abu Simbel. Once seen, they will remain in your memory for ever as a reminder that there was once a time when kings were considered giants and gods whose images were made eternal in the stone.

And yet, amazing as this may sound, this very hard-to-miss temple was 'lost' after the Roman occupation of Egypt in 30 BC. It was not until 1813 that it was rediscovered (half engulfed in sand) by the Swiss-German explorer Ludwig Burckhardt when he sailed up the Nile in southern Nubia. But it was the flamboyant Italian Giovanni Belzoni who in 1817 first entered and explored it. It is estimated that the temple took some 30 years to complete, and when one looks at the many features that it incorporates, this comes as no great surprise. The four seated colossi dominating the façade are carved out of the living rock cliff and measure 21 metres in height – by far the tallest statues ever found in Egypt.[32] Above the colossi, and centred on the axis of the temple, was also carved into the rock façade a standing statue of the sun-god Ra-Horakhti in his usual image of a falcon-headed man wearing the sun disc upon his head,[33] which highlights the intense solar nature of this temple. The top fascia of the temple has carved on it a row of 22 cynocephali, a type of male baboon considered sacred to the sun-god. Apparently these creatures were in the habit of gathering at dawn on the shores of the Nile and facing the rising sun with arms upraised while uttering strange cries and yelps. To the Egyptians it seemed as if they were 'speaking' to the sun-god.[34] In ancient Egyptian mythology the sky had many 'gates', with the twelfth gate being the place through which it emerged from the underworld Duat in the east at dawn. According to George Hart, the cynocephali baboons were the guardians of the eleventh gate of the sky who were seen in the 'area directly before dawn' and were referred to as 'baboons of sunrise, gods who carry the blazing light'.[35] Baboons, and particularly the cynocephali type, feature prominently in the decoration of temple façades and the pedestals of obelisks.[36] The god of science and writing, Thoth (the Hermes of the Greeks), was the divine baboon, and in one inscription from the New Kingdom Thoth proudly asserts that 'I am Thoth and I speak the language of Ra as a herald.'[37] Another inscription describes the baboon cynocephali as 'The baboons that announce Ra when this great god is to be born . . . They are at both sides of this god until he rises in the eastern horizon; they dance for him, they jump gaily for him, they sing for him, they sing praise for him, they shout out for him . . . They are those who announce Ra in heaven and on Earth.'[38]

The above texts describe perfectly those 22 baboons that form the frieze of the temple of Rameses II at Abu Simbel, as we shall now see.

A Symphony of Light

When the Dutch Egyptologist Jan van der Haagen headed the UNESCO team in the 1960s to save the temple of Abu Simbel from the rising waters of Lake Nasser, he was quick to notice that each morning the rays of the sun would first light up the row of 22 cynocephali at the top of the temple's façade.[39] As the sun rose a little higher its rays would then light up the solar disc on the head of the statue of Ra-Horakhti carved into the living rock in the upper centre of the façade. Immediately afterwards the sunlight would fall on the four seated colossi of Rameses II, until finally, when the sun reached a height of about 1° over the horizon, the whole façade of the temple would glow in the morning light. But that was just on an ordinary day. Around 19 October, something wonderful would happen at sunrise: a beam of light would shoot into the temple right through the 60-metre axis to light up the four seated statues of Ptah, Amun-Ra, Rameses II and Ra-Horakhti in the holy of holies. The effect – which I have witnessed on two occasions – is truly magical, and for a few minutes (about 24 according to my reckoning) the interior of the temple is like 'a symphony of light'.

Haagen had a hunch that the orientation of the temple's axis was not a coincidence, and that it had deliberately been aligned this way to allow the rays of the rising sun to enter the temple on 19 October. But why that specific date? According to the French Egyptologist Louis Christophe, a colleague of Haagen on the UNESCO project, the various statues of the Abu Simbel temple symbolised the process of deification of Rameses II as the sun-god that took place at his jubilees and which, according to Christophe's reckoning, fell close to 19 October (in the Gregorian calendar). Apparently Rameses II celebrated a total of 14 jubilees in his lifetime, and the dates and locations of some are known with a fair degree of certainty. The fifth and sixth jubilees were celebrated at Memphis, and according to Dr Christophe's calculations they both took place on 22 October. This date was so close to the 19 October that it led him to conclude that the temple at Abu Simbel (which is 1,250 kilometres to the south of Memphis) was probably planned to coincide with the jubilee date when the solar deification ceremonies for the king took place.[40] Haagen agreed in principle with Dr Christophe's conclusion, but nonetheless felt that the three-day difference between the Memphite date of 22 October and the Abu Simbel date of 19 October needed to be reconciled. Thus, in Haagen's own words:

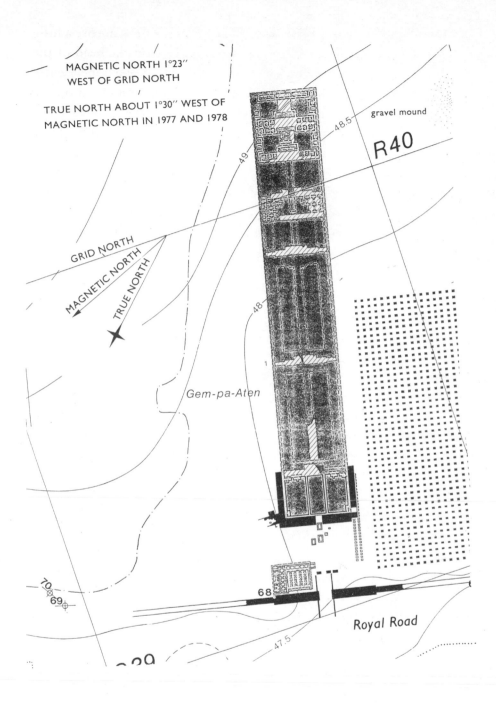

MAGNETIC NORTH 1°23"
WEST OF GRID NORTH

TRUE NORTH ABOUT 1°30" WEST OF
MAGNETIC NORTH IN 1977 AND 1978

gravel mound

R40

49

48.5

GRID NORTH

MAGNETIC NORTH

TRUE NORTH

Gem-pa-Aten

48

70

69

68

Royal Road

47.5

Orientation of the Great Temple of the Aten at Tell El Amarna

Here is my hypothesis. The astronomer of Thebes or Memphis who was responsible for determining the exact position of the sun for 22 October at Abu Simbel may not have had a detailed knowledge of the site: there is, after all, 1250 kilometres between Memphis and Abu Simbel. Also the astronomer may well have used an 'ideal' horizon line fixed at the level of the temple itself. But in reality the sun rises 5 minutes later after the 'ideal' horizon moment because there exists on the east bank of the river, at about 3300 metres distance, a ridge of hills high enough to delay its rising. And since in October at this location the sun's path makes a 66 degrees angle with the horizon, the first segment of the sun's disc appears at a point a little more to the south than that which it had been at the 'ideal' horizon. This problem is also further complicated by the fact that the ridge of the hills is far from being horizontal, and makes a pronounced depression at that specific spot.

An 'ideal' horizon, of course, is only possible in open flat desert regions or at sea. In the context of Abu Simbel, where the view to the true horizon is obstructed by the ridge of hills, sunrise occurs a little later than if it had been observed at 'ideal' horizon conditions, and the position of the sun is, therefore, a little further to the south or to the north depending on the time of year. Haagen was able to calculate that the sun would have risen on 21 October along the temple's axis in 'ideal' horizon conditions. Also taking into account the slightly different obliquity for the epoch 1290 BC, the sun would have been a little further south, thus pushing the date to 22 October. This would imply that the ancient astronomer who determined the orientation of the temple's axis in accordance with the 'jubilee date' had *calculated* the position of the sunrise rather than actually observing it on location. In other words, the ancient astronomer ignored the hills. So although he had the date of 22 October in mind, by ignoring the hills his design produced the date of 19 October. Although Haagen's hypothesis is ingenious, I do not think that this is what happened. There is, in fact, another more likely explanation for the discrepancy in dates.

The pharaoh Rameses II, as we have noted earlier, ruled from 1290 BC to 1224 BC. In the previous chapter we have seen how the return of the New Year's Day to the summer solstice, its point of origin, took place in 1275 BC (2781–1,506 = 1275 i.e., after a Great Solar Cycle). Immediately we can see that this date falls within the reign of Rameses II.[41] This means that the date of 1 Tybi (the 'jubilee date', which is 120 days after the New Year's Day) would have fallen on 19 October (Gregorian).[42] With StarryNight Pro, we can determine the position of sunrise at Abu Simbel for 19 October, which turns out to be close to 11° south-of-east for an 'ideal' horizon. Allowing for the hills across Lake Nasser (and also for the high refraction at that time of year), this value must be adjusted to about 12° 30′ south-of-east. This is also the orientation of the temple's axis. This again cannot be a coincidence, and we must conclude that the ancient astronomer had, in fact, intended the axis of the temple to be directed to sunrise on 1 Tybi (on 19 October) *as actually observed over the distant hills*. In this manner, whether by coincidence or by intention, anyone observing sunrise along the temple's axis on 1 Tybi would, by necessity, be there at the start of a new age or Sothic cycle. This would apply, of course, ad infinitum.[43] And even though it is true that there would be a very small shift of the sun's declination due to the Milokovitch Factor (see Chapter Five, note 25), this would not much affect the solar alignment on 19 October.[44]

The 'Jubilee Date' at Giza

In the middle of winter of the year 1995 I was at the Giza plateau with the author Graham Hancock and the Dutch television producer Roel Oostra. We had come to film the sunrise at Giza on 21 February.[45] I had calculated that on that date the sun would be rising in direct alignment with the ancient causeway that ran alongside the Great Sphinx, and we wanted to film this event for a documentary for the Discovery Channel. For this, we set up the cameras some 100 metres behind the Sphinx and along the axis of the causeway, which is about 13° to 14° south-of-east. We then waited for sunrise. It did not occur to me at the time that we could have equally come here on 19 October, for the sun would also have risen at the same place on the eastern horizon. This, of course, is because the sun will always cross the same point twice at intervals of six months. Had I realised this at the time, and had I also been aware of Haagen's work at Abu Simbel, I would have immediately realised that the 'jubilee date' of 1 Tybi was also locked into the design scheme of the Giza Necropolis. According to accepted chronology, the Great Sphinx and its causeway date from *c.* 2500 BC. This would mean that they were built some 281 years *after* the inauguration of the civil calendar, which was in 2781 BC. In 2500 BC 1 Tybi would not have fallen on 19 October but, because of the drifting calendar, rather on 28 December. The position of the sun at that date would have been about 26° south-of-east and thus way off the alignment of the causeway, which is 14° south-of-east. In other words, for the causeway to align with the sunrise on 1 Tybi, it had to have been aligned in *c.* 2781 BC and not *c.* 2500 BC. But was there any evidence of this?

The British geologist Colin Reader has been involved with the so-called 'Age of the Sphinx Debate' since the late 1990s, and has gained recognition and respect from Egyptologists for his level-headed and professional approach to the problem. In 1997 he investigated the geological conditions around the Sphinx and its enclosure, and at first fully supported the established view that the Sphinx and its temples, as well as the causeway, belonged to the Fourth Dynasty and could thus be dated to *c.* 2500 BC. But as further evidence was uncovered, Reader altered his view, and in 2002 published his revised date in the *Journal of the Ancient Chronology Forum*.[46] The new evidence had forced him to consider that the Sphinx and its causeway could not be attributed to the Fourth Dynasty, but rather must be dated to the early dynastic period. Significantly, one of Reader's arguments involved the alignment of the Sphinx causeway which, when carefully considered in relation to the two adjacent ancient quarries, showed that it 'was established some time before Khufu's work at Giza . . . I conclude that the Sphinx and a number of other related structures must have pre-dated the Fourth Dynasty. Taking into consideration the earliest known use of stone masonry in Egypt I date this Sphinx complex to the Early Dynastic Period.' Reader, however, does not deny that the Fourth Dynasty pharaoh Khafra had a major influence on the Sphinx, 'but not as a builder':

I believe that the unique layout of Khafre's mortuary complex, which includes the Sphinx and the Sphinx temple, developed as a result of that pharaoh's usurpation or re-working of the existing solar-cult complex. How better could the association of the king with the sun-god have been symbolised other than by linking Khafre's 'mansion of eternity' (his pyramid) with a long established site of solar worship and the everlasting circle of birth, death and re-birth manifested in the daily rising and setting of the sun?

The early dynastic period in which Reader places the Sphinx and its causeway falls somewhere between 2920 and 2575 BC, with the First Dynasty falling between 2920 and 2770 BC.[47] This brings us tantalisingly close to the magical date of 2781 BC, when the civil calendar was inaugurated. That the Giza Necropolis as a whole is intensely astronomical – and, therefore, calendrical – needs no further emphasis, as in my previous books *The Orion Mystery* (1994) and *Keeper of Genesis* (1996) the stellar and solar qualities of the monuments have been discussed in great detail. Nowhere else at Giza is the solar connection more evident than at the Sphinx complex. The Sphinx itself, as we have seen, faces the rising sun at the equinoxes, and the calendrical symbolism is clearly attested by the two series of 12 pillars at its temple, which, according to at least one eminent Egyptologist, makes it 'a monument to the circuit of the sun and the hourly and daily cycles of time'.[48] If Reader is correct in his deduction that the Sphinx complex belongs to the early dynastic period, and if we also assume a date near 2781 BC, then this connects the Sphinx complex to the time when the New Year's Day fell on the summer solstice. If this hypothesis is correct, we surely ought to find links between the Sphinx complex and the summer solstice. In a study conducted by Mark Lehner on the astronomical context of the Sphinx complex, he discovered that

a dramatic effect is created at sunset during the summer solstice as viewed, again, from the Sphinx Temple. At this time, and from this vantage, the sun sets almost exactly midway between Khufu's and Khafra's pyramids, that construing the image of the *akhet*, 'horizon', hieroglyph on a scale of acres. The effect is, again, best seen from the Sphinx Temple colonnade, or an equivalent height on the east temple where the sand rises. At this height the image of the Sphinx is merged into the silhouette of Khafre's pyramid. The image is actually to be appreciated from most any vantage point out east of the Sphinx and Khafre Valley Temple.[49]

In view of all this intense solar alignment related to the Sphinx complex, we must also expect that the 14° south-of-east alignment of the causeway had important solar connotations. Already a strong indication of this is that the orientation of 14° south-of-east (or north-of-east) is known in astronomy as the cross-quarter, which is the mid-point of 28°, the orientation of the sunrise of the winter solstice (14° south-of-east) or that of the summer solstice (14° north-of-east) as seen from the latitude of Giza. In *c.* 2781 BC an orientation of 14° south-of-east would have aligned the causeway to sunrise on 19 October (Gregorian), which is, of course, 1 Tybi, or 'jubilee date'. The conclusion that the *heb-sed*, or jubilee, was celebrated at the Giza Necropolis (and other pyramid sites) was also arrived at by Jeremy Naydler in his latest book, *Shamanic Wisdom in the Pyramid Texts*.[50] Dr Naydler, a cultural historian, asked: 'Were the pyramids and their surrounding buildings and ceremonial courts built simply to serve the royal funerary cult, or could they also have served mystical ends? Could they, for example, have been used for the performance of rites such as those of the (Heb) Sed festival, involving the living king?' He then carefully presented a plethora of archaeological and textual evidence that strongly indicated – if not proved – that Fourth, Fifth and Sixth Dynasty kings had celebrated *heb-seds*/jubilees in their pyramid complexes. We have already discussed in earlier chapters the *heb-sed* rites for King Djoser at the Step Pyramid complex at Saqqara. Regarding his immediate successor, King Sneferu of the Fourth Dynasty, there exists a 'stela of king Sneferu from the Bent Pyramid complex, showing him seated on a throne wearing the short tunic of the (heb) sed festival'.[51] His son, the celebrated Khufu, builder of the Great Pyramid at Giza, also seems to have performed a *heb-sed* at his pyramid complex, evidenced by a stone fragment belonging to the northern wall of the causeway of the Great Pyramid that shows him wearing the short tunic typical of the *heb-sed* celebrations.[52] Naydler also demonstrated that virtually all the other pyramid sites in the Memphite Necropolis were probably used for *heb-sed* celebrations.

But what of the Great Temple at the solar city of Akhet-Aten, 'Horizon of the Sun Disc', which seems to have been exclusively dedicated to the Aten, 'Lord of Jubilees' and 'Distinguished in Jubilees'? An inscription quoted by Richard Wilkinson states: 'Aten living and great who is in jubilee residing in the temple of Aten at Akhet-Aten'.[53] Surely, then, it is this particular temple that should, above all others, be aligned towards the sunrise on the 'jubilee date'.

The Hills of Sunrise

We have already seen how the New Year's Day had returned to the summer solstice in 1275 BC during the reign of Rameses II. At the ascension of Akhenaten in *c.* 1352 BC, there were still 77 years left before that event would take place. Because of the calendar's drift at the rate of one day every four years, 1 Tybi would have fallen not 120 days after the summer solstice, on 19 October, but only 101 days after it, on 30 September. Using StarryNight Pro, I worked out that for the location of Tell El Amarna, the sunrise on 1 Tybi would have been at about 3.5° south-of-east. Was this the orientation of the Great Temple of Aten at Tell El Amarna as well?

Obtaining the orientation of this temple was not such an easy task. I contacted the Egypt Exploration Society (EES) in London, who informed me that the information I needed was in the report and maps published by Barry Kemp of Cambridge University, who conducted the latest survey of Tell El Amarna in 1977–8 on behalf of the EES.[54] To avoid delay, I decided to consult the Sackler Library at Oxford, which was closer to my home. To my delight they had a copy of Kemp's publication. I found the information I was looking for in maps marked Sheets 3, 4 and 5. There was an excellent line drawing of the plan of the Great Temple showing its axis and grid north lines R40 and Q40 established during Kemp's survey. I carefully measured the angle of the axis of the Great Temple relative to grid north and found that it was 14° south-of-east. On Sheet 3, however, Barry Kemp gave the necessary angular adjustments: magnetic north was 1° 23′ west of grid north and true north was an extra 1° 30′ west of magnetic north. This meant that the orientation of the temple was 14° + 1°23′ + 1° 30′ = 16° 53′ south-of-east.

The orientation of the temple was thus about 13.38° further south than that of the rising sun on 1 Tybi. The temple, in other words, was *not* aligned to the 'jubilee date' as I had expected it to be. I was puzzled. For here was a temple specifically dedicated to the sunrise and linked to the jubilees. Indeed, many Egyptologists seemed to support the idea that the site for this temple (and the city of Akhet-Aten) had been chosen by Akhenaten himself when he witnessed the sun rise between two hills in the eastern horizon there which defined the hieroglyphic sign for *akhet* ('horizon') – two hills with the sun disc in the middle. Because of all this, I had been certain that I would discover that the Great Temple of the Aten was aligned towards the rising sun on 1 Tybi, the 'jubilee date'. Yet the numbers seemed to indicate otherwise. So why was the temple orientated towards the rising sun at 16° 53′ south-of-east? Checking this 16° 53′ south-of-east orientation with StarryNight Pro gave the date 29 October on the Gregorian calendar. So what happened on 29 October in 1352 BC that prompted the ancient surveyors of Akhet-Aten to align the Great Temple to the rising sun?

Akhenaten, it must be remembered, was a purist who wanted to adhere to the cosmic order as set down by the ancestral religion of Heliopolis. It was the ancestral priest-astronomers of Heliopolis who, in *c.* 2781 BC, had set the New Year's Day, i.e. I Akhet 1, to the heliacal rising of Sirius. This event happened to coincide with the summer solstice at that time.

According to Rolf Krause, there was a festival celebrated at Akhet-Aten on I Akhet 1, the New Year's Day, which was called *mswt-itn*, 'The Birthday of Aten'. But because of the effect of precession, the heliacal rising of Sirius in *c.* 1352 BC had moved to 10 days *after* the summer solstice. So if in Akhenaten's time the New Year's Day was kept linked, as tradition demanded, to the heliacal rising of Sirius, this meant that if one counted the days of the calendar starting 10 days *after* 21 June, i.e. from 1 July, the 'jubilee date' according to the shifting calendar was pushed forward also 10 days, from 19 October to 29 October! This was too much to be coincidence. It seemed to me certain that the Great Temple of the Aten was, in fact, aligned to the 'jubilee date' in accordance with the original Heliopolitan calendar that had fixed the New Year's Day to the heliacal rising of Sirius! Akhenaten was far more of a purist than he had hitherto been given credit for.

In late October 2004 I had the opportunity to visit Tell El Amarna for the second time. My friend Roel Oostra was shooting a television documentary based on my book and wanted to film the sunrise at Tell El Amarna on 29 October. According to my calculations, the sun disc would be seen rising between the two standing columns of the Small Temple of the Aten, which had the same orientation as the Great Temple nearby. As there was not much left of the Great Temple itself Roel felt that the sunrise between the two columns would provide a more dramatic effect for the purpose of television viewing.[55] So on 28 October we drove from Cairo to Al Minya and stayed the night in a small hotel just outside the town. The convoy of armed security police that had escorted us also stayed at the hotel, as this region of Egypt was regarded as a hotbed for religious fanatics who wanted to disrupt the tourist trade by attacking foreigners. Throughout the evening our local guide tried to persuade the convoy's officer to allow us to go to the site of Tell El Amarna before sunrise, but the officer was adamant that this was not possible. So we all went to bed feeling frustrated and tired. Something, however, must have happened during the night to change his mind, because at 5 a.m. our guide excitedly woke us all up with the good news that the officer had agreed to allow the armed convoy to escort us to Tell El Amarna right away. We scrambled out of our rooms, gulped some lukewarm tea and biscuits, and off we went. The armed police in the convoy waved and smiled cheerily at us as we drove towards the city of Akhet-Aten. The gentle 'persuasion', whatever form it had taken during the night, had obviously made them happy.

We arrived at the site of Akhet-Aten some 30 minutes before sunrise, giving us ample time to set up the cameras along the axis of the

Small Temple of the Aten, with its very dramatic view towards the eastern hills between the two standing columns. The gap between the columns acted as a window towards the place of sunrise. Now all that was needed was for the sun to oblige and rise between the columns. I nervously checked my calculations. Sunrise would take place at 7.05 a.m. at about 16° 53′ south-of-east and, hopefully, be in perfect alignment with the axis of the temple. The local inspector of the Supreme Council of Antiquities, a man by the name of Muhamad, was very sceptical. According to him, the sun did not rise there in October but in August. He had worked here for 17 years and he ought to know. I informed him as politely as I could that he was wrong on this. He simply shrugged his shoulders and went to chat with the police officer, who appeared totally uninterested in what was going on.

The eastern horizon began to brighten. The few stars that were still visible quickly faded away as the glow of dawn increased. There was an annoying cloud that hovered over the eastern horizon, threatening to spoil the effect we were hoping to achieve. Then, as if by magic, a gap opened in the cloud allowing the sun disc to be seen in all its glory. And it rose, as I had predicted, smack between the two columns. We were so moved by what we saw that we nearly forgot to turn the cameras on. There was a deathly silence from Muhamad and the smoking policemen as they stared towards the sunrise as if they had seen a ghost. Then Muhamad came to me, smiled, shook my hand, and said: 'You are a clever man! How did you manage to do this?' I explained that I had not done anything and that it was simply the laws of celestial mechanics that were responsible.

Driving back to Cairo, I could not help thinking of the solemn oath that Akhenaten had made and had carved for posterity on the boundary stones of his solar city:

In this place that I have said that I will make a House of Rejoicing for the Aten my father, in the island of 'Aten Distinguished in Jubilees' in Akhet-Aten. And so it is in this place that I have made a House of Rejoicing for the Aten my father, in the island of 'Aten Distinguished in Jubilees' in Akhet-Aten. In this place I do all the works that have to be done for the Aten my father, in Akhet-Aten.

Akhenaten had kept his promise. But the priests of Amun-Ra had shattered his dream with the iron fist of intolerance.

My quest, I knew there and then, was over. I also knew that no one would ever be able to grasp the holy grail of ancient Egypt in their hands. But sometimes it may appear, as it had done on this day, right before your eyes in the glowing light of sunrise, hovering on a distant hill. And all we can really do when this happens is to acknowledge the mystery of our existence on this little lonely planet and rejoice in our resolve to let it be.

CONCLUSION

The 'Code' and the Temple of the Cosmos

Ancient Egypt was subjugated to the law of Maat, the cosmic order, which was believed to have come to earth from the gods at the time of creation, a golden age known as *zep tepi*, the 'First Time'. The Pyramid Texts place the dramatic event of creation and *zep tepi* at Heliopolis, where the cosmic phoenix alighted on the Primeval Mound and set into motion 'time', the cycles of the sun, moon and stars. At Heliopolis in the 'Temple of the Phoenix', the first sunrise took place on the sacred *benben* stone that crowned the Primeval Mound.[1]

After generations of observation and recording the motion of the celestial bodies, the astronomer-priests of Heliopolis had worked out what they believed to be the mechanism or 'code' of the cosmic order, and, more importantly to them, how it could be used to regulate events on earth, especially the yearly flooding of the Nile. They concluded that the universe was governed by six principal cycles, three short-term and three long-term, which involved the motion of the sun and the stars. Measured in either 'days' or 'years', these cycles were as follows:

Short-term Cycles:

1 day:	solar day
365 days:	solar cycle, the solar/tropical year less 0.243 day
365.25 days:	Sothic year; the period between two heliacal risings of Sirius

Long-term Cycles:

1,460 years:	Sothic cycle; return of New Year's Day with the heliacal rising of Sirius
1,506 years	Great Solar Cycle; return of New Year's Day with the summer solstice
26,000 years:	precession cycle or Great Year

To symbolically represent the mechanism of the Egyptian cosmic order, we can draw six concentric circles, so that the image produced will resemble a circular labyrinth or a Copernican diagram whose centre is a point representing the observer himself. More realistically, one should draw a circular star map or planisphere showing the zodiacal belt of constellations which will cater for the three solar cycles, and also showing the principal decanal constellations (such as Orion and Canis Major/Sirius) which will cater for the three stellar cycles, and whose centre is a point representing the north celestial pole. This outer rim of the circular star map can then be divided into four parts representing the two equinoxes and the two solstices and also the four cardinal directions. Such a circular star map would much resemble the circular zodiac of Dendera. But the Egyptian astronomer-priests also observed the rising of the celestial bodies in the east, especially the rising of the sun and certain special constellations such as Orion, Canis Major and Leo. They would thus have registered a cycle for the sun from a point north (summer solstice) to a point south (winter solstice) and back again to north in 365 days. Because they did not take into account the 0.243-day difference with the true solar year, they would also have registered a similar but long-term solar cycle of 1,506 years (Great Solar Cycle) with respect to the summer solstice, and another long-term cycle of 1,460 years with respect to the heliacal rising of Sirius. With regards to the stars, they would also have registered a very slow cycle (precession) moving from south to north.[2] To represent this diagrammatically, we would have to draw an elongated rectangle representing the eastern horizon and marking the two extreme north and south points. With this elongated rectangle constellations would be drawn. Such a diagram would also much resemble the elongated rectangular zodiac of Dendera. The question, then, is: Was the temple of Dendera a centre for recording the various long-term astronomical cycles? Or to use ancient Egyptian parlance, could Dendera be a centre to regulate Maat on earth? An indication of the affirmative lies in the fact that the alignments of the double axes of the temple of Isis (at the rear of the main temple of Dendera) tracked the precession shift of Sirius over at least 1,200 years.

According to the ideas presented in this book, evidence that the ancient astronomer-priests 'followed' the cosmic order should be found in the choice of location and orientations of the various monuments and religious centres built over a 3,000-year span (from 3000 BC to 30 BC) along the shores of the Nile. To be more specific, the changes in the sky (reflected in the three long-term cycles) should match the changes in the location and orientation of monuments and religious centres. Furthermore, evidence of *zep tepi*/First Time ought to be found in the region of Heliopolis, whence 'time' or the long-term cosmic cycles began to be measured.

Zep Tepi and the Memphite Necropolis–Heliopolis region

Throughout the literature of ancient Egypt – from the Pyramid Texts of the Old Kingdom to the Hermetic Texts of the Graeco-Roman period – we hear of the belief that Egypt is made in the image of heaven. Its main geographical feature, the Nile Valley, runs from south to north, and in the context of this belief, would correlate with the main feature of the celestial landscape, the Milky Way. Is it therefore a coincidence that the Milky Way also ran from south to north in the epoch of 11,451 BC, which, as we have seen in Chapter Four, was arrived at by going back in increments of the Sothic cycle, starting from 139 AD and arriving at the 'beginning' of the cycles of Sirius? We have defined this date of 11,451 BC as *zep tepi*, the 'First Time'. Controversial as this may at first seem, we have also seen how, when the sky is precessed to 11,451 BC and the three stars of Orion are aligned along the meridian with the three pyramids of Giza, the image of *zep tepi* in the sky (the triangular region of Orion-Pleiades-Leo) bears an uncanny resemblance to the image of *zep tepi* on the ground (the triangular region of Giza-Memphis-Heliopolis). The celestial region that contained the triangle formed by Orion, the Pleiades and Leo was called the Duat, and it would appear that a copy of it was made in the region of the Memphite Necropolis containing the Step Pyramid, and, more especially, where the three Giza pyramids represented Orion's belt, the Abusir pyramids near Memphis the Pleiades, and Heliopolis the sun in Leo. Were these places, too, centres for regulating the cosmic order on earth?

The Great Solar Cycle and the Sothic Cycle

Testing the 'code' further, we would now expect to find evidence of a north-to-south or vice versa displacement of the solar cultic centres in increments of 730 years (half the Sothic cycle) or 753 years (half the Great Solar Cycle). In Chapter Five we have seen how the great solar centre was developed at Heliopolis in *c.* 2781 BC but was moved some 750 years later to Karnak in the south. We have also seen how Akhenaten, some 750 years after the founding of Karnak, sought to return the solar cult to Heliopolis. We have found specific evidence of the Sothic cycle of 1,460 years in the so-called Jubilee date in the axial alignment of the temple of the Aten at Tell El Amarna. We have also found evidence of the Great Solar Cycle of 1,506 years in the axial alignment of the Great Temple of Rameses II at Abu Simbel and also in the axial alignment of the Khafre causeway at Giza.

The Precession Cycle or Great Year

Evidence of the knowledge of the long-term cycle of precession, especially of the star Sirius, was found at the multi-layered Satis temples on Elephantine from 3000 BC to 100 BC; at the Middle Kingdom temple of Horus on Thoth Hill from 3000 BC to 1900 BC, and also at the temple of Isis at Dendera from 1275 BC to 30 BC.

The Mission of Akhenaten

Egypt, it very much seems, was 'made in the image of heaven', incorporating in its unique geography and in the locations and alignments of its pyramids and temples the various astronomical cycles that were believed to be regulated by the cosmic order or Maat. What is more, by integrating the cosmic order into the very fabric of the religious mythology and rituals, and into the social and legal systems, an ideal state was created that was itself regulated by the natural laws acknowledged by all. Eventually, however, the pure mechanism of the cosmic order was corrupted by the power-driven priesthood and the complex mythology and iconography that they injected into it. It was left to Akhenaten to clean up the mess, to free the old natural religion from the yoke of the priesthood and to strip it of the confusing iconography and mythology by fixing it only to a single god symbol: the disc of the sun, representing the universal god. After trying for 17 years Akhenaten eventually failed, but nonetheless managed to inject the fragile seed of monotheism that would influence the three great Semitic religions of our modern world.

Postscript

Sadly, the three major religions, Christianity, Judaism and Islam, have again fallen into the hands of power-driven priests and, we may also now add, the high priests of politics. Again the great human conflict is made to loom dangerously before us. The only way out of this impending disaster is to restore the natural religion and to instigate in people the sense of a cosmic order that attempts to achieve harmony and balance rather than blindly taking us towards the nuclear Armageddon that surely lies ahead. In other words, to restore a gnosis that is based on the laws of nature and that views man not as its master but as its keeper, who will diligently maintain the delicate balance between social and natural living and safeguard it for the generations to come.

As for the scientific investigation that I have presented in *The Egypt Code*, I hope that it has been cogently demonstrated that there is, at the very least, a dire need for an overhaul of the established consensuses and conclusions established by the last two generations of Egyptologists. I hope that the new generation of Egyptologists will come to see, as I did, that ancient Egypt is not a defunct civilisation to be studied in a dispassionate way, but rather a cultural model that is very much alive and needs to be understood, with, perhaps, some of its principles put again into practice for the benefit of mankind. The very wise and observant priests of ancient Egypt taught not with dogmas and doctrines, nor did they threaten the populace with the fear of their god's wrath; rather they offered a clever and enlightened initiation that would open the mind and sharpen the senses so that nature was seen as the manifestation of the divine principles, and man himself as not only an integral part of nature, but also responsible for keeping it in harmony and balance. Egyptologists, I am well aware, cringe at this sort of talk, which they classify as the 'mumbo-jumbo' of New Age writers, and thus much prefer to ignore it and stick to their own dry scientific and dispassionate approach. But they are wrong in doing so. Ancient Egypt cannot be understood in this way. Ancient Egypt is not a science but an idea. For what is more important: the material legacy of ancient Egypt or its spiritual legacy? What is more important: the ancient stones of pyramids and temples or the ideas and aspirations they represent? When dealing with ancient Egypt, you are dealing with a spiritual civilisation which believed emphatically in eternity and in an afterlife attained by an adherence to the cosmic order. And it must be studied as such.

I have made it as evident as I possibly can that astronomy – or more specifically observational astronomy – should be added to the tool kits of Egyptologists and archaeologists. And although fleeting references to it are made here and there, on the whole it is ignored. Yet if one does not know or understand the basic cycles of the stars and the sun or the effect of precession, then one is merely studying the inert hardware of ancient Egypt's legacy without the benefit of the software that energised and drove it. One is merely looking at the broken 'cosmic' machines without knowing about the engine that powered them. For it is more than evident that the temple priests of ancient Egypt, especially those of Heliopolis, incorporated observational astronomy in their initiatory system of education. Albeit for religious rather than scientific reasons; but this should not lessen its importance to us. This is well attested in their many religious texts, such as the Pyramid Texts, and also in the intense astronomical qualities of the monuments, which, after all, are but the symbolic architectural expression of their beliefs. It is, therefore, imperative that the religious texts and the architecture be married with astronomy, for only then will they react together to reveal their deeper meaning and purpose. All Egyptologists or students of ancient Egypt must, by necessity, be conversant with the rudiments of observational astronomy before being able to properly tackle the ancient religious texts and related monuments.

Modesty aside, I believe that I have been able to make visible an ancient 'code' that can help Egyptology to shed more light on the greatest and most spiritually enlightened civilisation the world has ever known or is likely to know again in the future. Our present civilisation is in dire need of this ancient model of wisdom. For we desperately need to instigate a respect for the natural world and the natural order of things, and to acknowledge that our planet can only thrive when left unhindered and free from our interference. We must stop seeing ourselves as the masters of this planet and start seeing ourselves as merely one existing alongside others. Our planet is not an endless quarry for us to plunder at will, but rather a gift to be protected and nurtured. The ancient Egyptians not only knew this, but had geared their whole religious and social system towards this noble end. It is for this that they turned Egypt into a temple of the cosmos in which all could live in Maat. It is for this that they built on such a massive scale and aligned their star pyramids and sun temples towards the stars and the sun, and then called them 'horizons'.[3] We learn from the Book of What is in the Duat (written around 1400 BC and based on the older Pyramid Texts) that:

Whosoever shall make an exact copy of these forms (constellations in the Duat), and shall know it, shall be a spirit well-equipped both in heaven and in earth, and regularly and eternally . . . Whosoever shall make an exact copy thereof, and shall know it upon earth, it shall act as a magical protector for him both in heaven and in earth, and regularly and eternally.[4]

Who knows, perhaps they were right. Perhaps we need to be constantly reminded that we are an integral part of the cosmos, and that we all are here on this planet as cosmic beings for the same cosmic purpose. In any case, it is a better way than throwing bombs at each other.

Tout passe, tout casse, tout c'efface. All ends, all breaks, all is erased.

APPENDIX 1

Running the Heb-sed

By Greg Reeder

The following article has been published by Greg Reeder and is here reproduced with his kind permission in full and without any alteration. (Published in *KMT*, Vol. 4: 4, Winter 1993–4, pp. 60–71. Photographs and illustrations not included here.)

Egypt's dynastic monarchs periodically underwent death and rebirth, thus magically invigorating their reigns as well as guaranteeing the continued prosperity of the Two Lands and their people.

Kings in ancient Egypt were the embodiment of the 'spirit of Fertility'. They were responsible for the success of the Nile flood and the harvesting of crops. '. . . *Lord of destiny, creating the plenteous harvest; . . . Pillar of the sky; Beam (support) of the earth; Leader who directeth the two banks of the Nile . . . There is a plenteous harvest wherever his sandals may be.*'[1] So said the courtiers of Rameses II.

When in most-ancient times the Nile failed, when the crops then failed, or when the king himself became ill or too enfeebled by age, he was physically sacrificed. Eventually kings circumvented their murders by merely substituting others in their place. 'At last it comes to be realised that the powers within him [the king] being magical, they can be renewed by magic.'[2] In other words, through a ritual of magical birth, the king could not only renew his own life and reign,

but would thereby guarantee the fertility of his land and people. Thus, dimly perceived, were the origins of the festival of renewal known as the *heb-sed*. *Heb* is ancient Egyptian for 'festival', but philologists are divided as to the definition of *sed*. Is the festival perhaps named for the god Set, or for the clothes the king wore during its ceremonies? Is it named for the bull's tail attached to the king's costume as he traversed the field, displaying his vigour? Or is it named for the land itself, reclaimed by the king for Egypt?[3] Cases can be made for all of these possibilities and it is difficult to know just which of these definitions the ancients believed, for they may have thought all were syncretistically acceptable.

It is generally agreed among Egyptologists that the *heb-sed* entailed a rejuvenation of the king and, by proxy, all of Egypt. Just when during a king's reign this festival took place is problematical. It appears that it was ideally celebrated when 30 years of reign had been reached, and then much more frequently thereafter. There are so many apparent exceptions to this, however, that a hard and fast rule cannot be ascertained. It is possible that the health of an individual king – or of the country – at a given time could precipitate a *heb-sed*, since the festival was meant as a rejuvenation for both Egypt and its ruler.

How often was the *heb-sed* celebrated?

Commentators on the subject usually state that the *sed*-festival was ideally held after a king had ruled for 30 years, and at frequent intervals thereafter; yet *heb-seds* were recorded by several rulers (in the Eighteenth Dynasty especially) who reigned something less than three decades – Hatshepsut and Amenhotep II, for example, and even Third Dynasty Djoser, who was king for only 19 years. This suggests at least two explanations. One, that a king could 'advertise' his optimistic intention of celebrating the *heb-sed* in the future, and that representations of him 'running the course' were symbolic rather than records of an actually transpired event. Or, secondly, the *heb-sed* was celebrated regularly on a cyclical basis of 30-year intervals, whenever these fell during a reign. This could be demonstrated by the example of Amenhotep III, who had three *sed*-festivals in years 30, 34 and 37, but who is also represented 'running the course' in one of the very earliest monuments of his long reign, a lintel from the dismantled Thutmose IV portico at Karnak. Could a 30-year cyclical *heb-sed* have been required at the outset of Amenhotep's rule (*c.* 1391 BC), when he was but a boy of 10 or 12? Dating backward 30 years would have the previous *sed*-event occurring in 1421 BC, during the reign of Amenhotep II (*c.* 1427–1401), who is shown 'running the course' and wearing the *sed*-robe in statues. Backing up another three decades to 1451 BC would put a *heb-sed* in the reign of Thutmose III (*c.* 1479–1425), who also had himself depicted in *sed*-activities. Another 30 years and it is 1481 BC, or the reign of Thutmose I (*c.* 1491–1479); and he, also, is shown 'running the course' in Deil El Bahari reliefs and wearing the *sed*-robe in a statue at Aswan. And on back to Amenhotep I (*c.* 1525–1404) in 1511 BC . . . etc. So where does this reckoning leave Hatshepsut, who clearly 'runs the course' in several of her Chapelle Rouge reliefs? An easy answer is that the female pharaoh did things her own way and could have had her *heb-sed* whether it was time for one or not.

Though depictions of the *sed*-festival are recorded on scattered monuments dating back to the archaic period, most information on the event comes from a few major sites: the Step Pyramid complex of Djoser at Saqqara; the sun temple of Niuserra at Abu Gurab; the Temple of Amenhotep III at Soleb in Nubia; and the so-called Festival Hall of Osorkon II at Bubastis. Add to these depictions those on diverse blocks and other isolated scenes,[4] and a picture emerges of the mysterious rites of the *heb-sed*.

Because there is no surviving complete depiction of the festival, there is little agreement among scholars about the sequence and meaning of its rites. Apparently preparations for the *heb-sed* could take years. Shrines were built and statues of the king carved and shipped throughout the land so that they could be set up to proclaim the success of the royal rejuvenation. Memphis, at least in the Old Kingdom, was the principal site of the ritual enactments; but there is reason to believe the festival was also celebrated at Thebes. And it is certain that Amenhotep III built an entire palace-town at Malkata on the Theban west bank for his own jubilee.

Special constructions at these sites included a 'palace' with robing chambers, where the king could rest during the ceremonies and change his attire required for the various rites. There is evidence that a royal funerary and a tomb chamber were included in the *heb-sed* structures and, finally, that 'temporary shrines, called the "Houses of the Sed festival", were erected on the archaic pattern of the reed-hut sanctuaries of prehistoric days.'[5]

The rites themselves included purification, illumination of the thrones and chapels with fire, and processions of the king with dignitaries of the court, statues of the gods and files of priests – including *sem*-priests, magicians, scriptorians from the House of Life and even the 'Opener of the Mouth'.

The king would visit each of the many temporary shrines and offer gifts to the deities housed within; he, in turn, would be visited by these same gods while he sat on his throne in a special pavilion. The king would also visit the Apis Bull, where its shrine was opened and '. . . the bull [was] brought out to be led before the king's throne'.[6]

Some scholars believe that the king also made a visit to his tomb – but more on that later. He also ran a course called the 'dedication of the field'. Dutch Egyptologist Henri Frankfort stated that 'We don't know at what point in the celebration this took place.' But it included the royal celebrant running with the flail-sceptre and carrying also a document or 'will' that gave '. . . authority to the king over the land of Egypt'.[7]

Other *heb-sed* rituals included the raising of the *djed* column by the king, his shooting arrows to the four cardinal points, and four separate enthronements. All of these ceremonies were conducted in the presence of an archaic deity, Upwaut, who was depicted as a wolf perched upon a standard with a most peculiarly shaped 'bag' protruding in front of him. The excavations of the Step Pyramid complex at Saqqara, begun in 1924 by Cecil M. Firth, James E. Quibell and J.-Ph. Lauer, have shed much light on the physical layout of the *sed*-festival activities. Remains of buildings involved with these events were uncovered and several have been reconstructed over the years. These include a double row of facing shrines representing in stone the reed huts of prehistory. The shrines on the west represent Upper Egypt (the south), while those on the east signify Lower Egypt (the north).[8] This double row of structures is called the *itrt*, a word related to the term for river or river channel.[9] These are the 'houses' of the *heb-sed*, the jubilee mansions. Most scholars believe they are 'not the actual buildings used in the *Sed*-festival, but only copies'.[10] They are referred to as 'dummy chapels', to be used only in Djoser's afterlife. The structures are, in fact, merely façades with solid cores. There is a niche in each, where a statue of a deity was placed. The dummy-chapel concept is reinforced by the general belief that the Step Pyramid complex is funereal in nature; thus the shrines were for the use of the dead king. 'No better explanation has been made than that they were intended for celebrations of Sed-festivals in the future life.'[11] A different explanation is offered here.

It is important to remember that the buildings of Djoser's complex are the oldest structures in the world which are made of dressed stone. They were erected under the supervision of the great architect and vizier Imhotep, by artisans skilled in carving statues and stone vessels, but without much experience in stone architecture. This can be shown in the colonnade at the entrance to the complex. Here are imitations in limestone of what were originally columns formed by binding plant material together. Imhotep's craftsmen were so uncertain of the stone medium that none of the columns are free standing, but are joined to the walls. The chapels of the *heb-sed* court gave these Third Dynasty artisans equal difficulties of construction, as they had to render in stone what had been previously been made of wood and matting. Even Firth recognised these ancient construction dilemmas when he stated that 'Everything is built up solid and then carved like a statue'.[12] The *sed* chapels should be thought of more as 'statues' of the archaic shrines they represented, with just the space to hold the portable figure of whichever deity they were meant to house for the renewal festival.

An analogous example is the naos in the Temple of Horus at Edfu. As Barry Kemp has written, '. . . the shrine in the sanctuary [is] carved from a single block of syenite'.[13] This naos has just enough space to hold a statue of Horus. It is not a 'dummy' shrine, however, for it still pays homage to the ideal archetypal form of the reed hut. All other architectural elements are thus erected around this naos-form, whether in the chapels of Djoser's complex or the later great temples with their architectural elaborations of the ideal type. But that still does not answer the question of why Djoser chose to build in stone what had previously been made of perishable materials. Doing so would thus insure a certain permanence, allowing the king to celebrate 'millions' of sed-festivals, or so he doubtless hoped. 'The linking of the gift of millions of years with the gift of Sed-festivals established an interesting connection which suggests the king's desire for a means to increase the length of his life and reign.'[14] Just as the *heb-sed* was a magical event extending the king's longevity, so building in stone would magically make permanent Djoser's temporal reign.

At the southern end of the Step Pyramid *heb-sed* are the remains of a dais, upon which once were double thrones. It was here that Djoser sat to receive the homage of visiting deities. From a later sed-festival there is evidence that a torchlight ceremony took place, during which the two thrones were illuminated. The torch borne by the king was then used to light torches carried by a procession of priests, who carried the flames to the various deity-chapels.[15] This torch-ceremony may explain the small round holes at the top of the central columns of the chapels in Djoser's *heb-sed* court, which have puzzled Egyptologists generally. These holes could very well have been receptacles for the lighted torches used to illuminate the double row of shrines and other buildings of the complex connected with this event of the festival.

Just behind the *heb-sed* court at Saqqara is a curious construction, designated Temple T, which is of particular significance since it is one of the very few 'real' buildings of the Step Pyramid, having a complete interior of rooms and corridors.[16] Firth was the first to link this structure with the 'palace' or robing room used by the king for resting and changing costumes during the festival events.[17] To the west of the *heb-sed* court and beyond Temple T is the great field where Djoser ran around the territorial cairns symbolising the boundaries of the land of Kemet. The Step Pyramid itself borders the northern perimeter of this field, and in subterranean galleries of the pyramid – some panelled with blue-green tiles – were discovered low-relief stelae with representations of the king running, or what Hermann Kees describes as performing an offering dance. Of the three stelae, the southern one shows Djoser running nude except for the White Crown (? – the head is missing), a false beard and a penis sheath. In front of the striding king is a vertical line of enigmatic glyphs which seem to refer to a birth chamber located in the south-west (of an enclosure?).[18] It just so happens that a structure *is* located in the south-west corner of the Djoser complex, a remarkable and mysterious building that has vexed scholars since its discovery. On the surface it is marked by a uraeus-topped wall, and its underground chambers are similar to those beneath the Step Pyramid. Some of these are also decorated with blue-green tiles; and there are three additional stelae of the king, one of which also shows him running all-but-naked, with a vertical band of glyphs likewise mentioning a birth chamber. The purpose of the Great Southern Tomb – as the structure has been designated by scholars – is directly related to this birth chamber. Inscriptions from later *sed*-festivals provide valuable clues for this identification.

From the reliefs recording the *sed*-festival celebrated by Osorkon II in the Twenty-second Dynasty comes evidence that the king entered his tomb – or a building designated as his symbolic tomb – during the events of the festival.[19] Just before Osorkon enters his tomb, priests are depicted, including the Opener of the Mouth, a *sem*-priest and a priest holding a knife and a stick.[20] Eric Uphill, in his seminal article on the *sed*-festival discusses the above scene, as well as parallels from the sun-temple, reliefs at Niuserra and the cenotaph of Seti I at Abydos. In the latter example, the king is shown stretched out prone on a lion couch attired in a robe very much in appearance like that worn by kings during the *heb-sed* enthronement ceremony. Above Seti is the single glyph commanding him to 'awake'.[21]

Back at Saqqara the most prominent deity in the *sed*-festival was the wolf-god, Upwaut, the 'Opener of the Ways'. In all six subterranean stelae of Djoser (three under the Step Pyramid, three under the Great Southern Tomb), Upwaut is depicted atop his forked standard high above the king, with a mysterious 'bag' positioned in front of him. The Upwaut standard accompanies Djoser on his run, and is a key to understanding the purpose of the Great Southern Tomb. Frankfort says of this deity, 'The wolf . . . is lord of the shedshed, a protuberance shown in front of him upon his standard, and the king is said to go to heaven upon this shedshed.'[22] Djoser is depicted on his stelae as running and visiting shrines of the *sed* court, in the company of both the flying falcon-god Horus and the wolf-standard of Upwaut with its shedshed emblem. When he visits shrines, the king is accompanied by an additional 'bag' on a standard, which is probably symbolic of his own 'Royal Placenta'. Frankfort points out that 'the standard of the placenta and the object on the standard of Upwaut are rendered identically, the surface of both cases covered by small dots'. He continues that '. . . the king desired to enter the body of the goddess Nut in order to be reborn by her and there are indications . . . the king entered the body of the mother-goddess by means of sympathetic magic, using an object which has come from her'.[23] Is the shedshed then the skin or bag that symbolised the enveloping placenta from the goddess? By wrapping himself in this skin, could the king magically facilitate ritual death and rebirth? Why – at least in later portrayals of the renewal festival – is the Opener of the Mouth (a funerary priest) shown just before the living king enters his real or symbolic tomb?

In a recent article, American Egyptologist Ann Macy Roth sheds new light on the Opening of the Mouth ceremony, with startling implications for the subject under discussion here.[24] She shows how this funerary ritual had its origin in the birthing process, and that the *pss-kf* (pesesh-kef) knife used to 'open' the mouth of the deceased was the very same instrument employed in severing the umbilical cord of the newborn infant. Roth writes, 'the presentation of the pss-kf can be explained as a ritual gesture that functioned originally as an announcement, but that developed a magical meaning. Until birth a child is nourished by his mother directly through the umbilical cord; when this lifeline is cut he must take a more aggressive role.' Thus, the knife is held up before the face of the baby *to show him that he had been divided from his mother and that he must now begin to take nourishment independently*.[25] Roth points out how the birthing process was mimicked in the Opening of the Mouth ceremony. Spells from the Pyramid Texts indicate that the reborn king suckled, ate and teethed like a newborn baby. There are also references to the suckling of the young king in the *sed*-festival reliefs of Osorkon II. And then there is the apparent iconographic rejuvenation of Amenhotep III following his *heb-sed* celebrated at the site of Malkata. It was this King Amenhotep who sought to perform the festival rituals in the manner of his ancient ancestors, and so appointed the sage of the same name, Amenhotep son of Hapu, to research the most correct forms, he being 'initiated into the god's book [and] skilled among their mysteries'.[26] During Amenhotep III's *sed*-festivities, it was the son of Hapu who ushered the king through the various archaic rites. Apparently the sage's researches on behalf of his king produced some incredible insights into the full intent of the *sed*-rituals, as performed in the days of the predynastic rulers of Kemet.[27] American Egyptologist Raymond Johnson has shown how in the final decade of Amenhotep III's life he was portrayed in statues and reliefs with an 'exaggerated youthfulness' which is 'highly significant when one considers that his last phase must correspond to the time immediately after the celebration of his first jubilee in Year 30'.[28] Johnson believed that Amenhotep III was deified as a direct result of the *sed*-festival, the king being '. . . merged permanently with the creator god'. He states: 'this is probably the whole point of the Sed-festival in the Old Kingdom: the ritual death of the king and his assimilation with the sun after thirty years of rule. In essence, Amenhotep III become a living "dead" king.'[29]

While discussing the role of the *sem*-priest in the Opening of the Mouth ceremony, Wallis Budge pointed out that '. . . before he [the priest] lay down on the bed he wrapped himself in the skin of a bull or a cow, because he intended the deceased to return through that act, and it was believed that by passing through a bull vicariously a man obtained the gift of a new birth, either for himself or for the person he represented'.[30] Of course, in performing this same ritual, the king acted as proxy for all Egypt. That a rebirthing event apparently took place during the *heb-sed* suggests the purpose of the Great Southern Tomb at Saqqara. The ritual death and rebirth of Djoser was probably meant to have taken place in the small 'burial' chamber discovered below the monument. This space is only about 1.6 metres square, too small to accommodate a man lying in prone position, say the scholars.

That this chamber was ever intended to receive a dead body is hard to believe. It would be just possible to get through the hole in the roof but it would not be possible to lay it down full length, the room is too small. What could have been so precious to Zoser as to merit this most expensive tomb, yet not wanted in his pyramid? His placenta? His heart, liver, etc., the usual contents of canopic vases? Or something yet unguessed? . . . We have clear evidence that the pyramid was unfinished when Zoser died, while the south tomb had been closed, its stair carefully blocked and the superstructure built and cased. We saw no reason to suspect that the work had been broken off hurriedly. There is nothing in the contents to indicate that a burial had ever lain here.[31]

Quibell adds that Firth had not found any fragments of bone, cloth or wood in the chamber. Since it was too small to receive an adult in a full prone position, might it have been meant for a man curled into a foetal position, as bodies were buried in the archaic period? What better symbolism could there have been than the living king to have imitated both the ancient burial position and the identical position of the foetus in the womb awaiting birth? It was there then, in this subterranean small chamber in the Great Southern Tomb, that Djoser – perhaps wrapped in the 'skin' (symbolic placenta) of his mother, the cow-goddess – was symbolically entombed and awaited his rebirth.

How much actual time the king would have spent in this cramped space is unknown. There is some idea as to what he was meant to experience during his confinement in the symbolic tomb/womb. Two paired glyphs that look like swinging doors, but are actually the two halves of the sky, are often shown in direct association with the three cairn-shaped glyphs identifying the territorial markers which the king rounded during his run-of-the-field event of the *heb-sed*. Thus, the celebrant not only traversed the field (i.e. Egypt) in a public ceremony, but also traversed the heavens in, understandably, a much less public form. A passage from the Pyramid Texts helps illuminate this concept: 'Teti has gone around the entire two skies, he has circumambulated the two banks.'[32] The king's assimilation with the heavenly Horus – so important for his kingship – is also emphasised: 'O, king, free course is given to you by Horus, you flash as the lone star in the midst of the sky, you have grown wings as a great-breasted falcon, as a hawk seen in the evening traversing the sky. May you cross the firmament by the waterway of Re-Harakti, may Nut put her hand on you.'[33] That this last statement was meant for the living king as opposed to the dead one is assured by philologist Alan Gardiner, who wrote, 'I know of no evidence anywhere among Egyptian texts in which the living pharaoh is assimilated with Osiris, or the dead pharaoh to Horus.'[34]

The Opener of the Mouth priest probably would have assisted the king when it was time for him to emerge from his underground symbolic womb. He would then have made his way to the surface and there begun his run around the territorial cairns, at first clothed only in his penis sheath, almost naked as the day he was born. This course was run four times and in at least one additional costume, a short kilt. Djoser is shown running holding the flail-sceptre in one hand and a document or will in the other. A text from the temple of Edfu explains: 'I have run holding the secret of the "Two Partners" [Horus and Seth], (namely) the Will which my father has given me before Geb. I have passed through the land and touched its four sides; I run through as I desire.'[35] In depictions of their own *sed*-festivals, kings are shown running with other objects as well. Some carry vases of Nile water, some an oar and a curious implement called the *hepet*. Triangular-shaped, this is thought by most scholars to be a navigation instrument of some sort; but clear identification seems elusive. Between the four runs, the king would retire to his 'palace' or robing chamber, to rest and change regalia. It was in this chamber that the celebrant would don the sheath-like knee-length robe worn for the re-enactment of his coronation, the concluding ceremony of the festival. Statues of the king in this *heb-sed* garment would then be unveiled throughout the country, thereby announcing the successful rejuvenation of both ruler and realm. A life-size statue of Djoser in his jubilee attire was discovered in a *serdab* at the north-east corner of the Step Pyramid. This small room is peculiarly tilted toward the northern heavens, with the statue looking through a peephole, as if it was some modern astronaut ready to blast off into space.

Mystery of the *Hepet*

Just what the *hepet* (*hpt*) instrument is has never been satisfactorily explained. It is generally accepted by scholars as a navigational device, but whether this means it was used to steer a boat or to navigate one's way through the desert (as a sighting implement) is not clear. In *heb-sed* reliefs it is shown in connection with an oar, the king carrying both on his run around the field. The hieroglyph is used in the spelling of the name Apis, as in bull, in words for 'hidden' and references to travel by boat (see Worterbuch, Vol. 3, pp. 67–70). Perhaps it is also to be seen in the design of the original entrance to the Pyramid of Khufu, over a horizon symbol. This would give the navigational instrument identification more credibility.

Djoser's pyramid-tomb stands at the northern edge of the field he traversed in his *heb-sed* run, and is more than just the marker of the final resting place of the king, when he did die in actuality. For Djoser it was also 'The solar mountain, the Ben Ben, the obelisk dedicated to the sun. It was the primeval hill which first rose from the flood at the creation of the world . . . The pyramid, this mountain, was loaded with life-forming energy; it was the centre of the earth, the place where the nether and the upper worlds communicated.'[36] What more powerful and magical instrument could the king have constructed to draw down the majesty of heaven and thereby ensure the continuity of life and prosperity for himself and his people?

On the Possible Discovery of Precessional Effects in Ancient Astronomy

Giulio Magli

Dipartimento di Matematica, Politecnico di Milano

P.le Leonardo da Vinci 32, 20133 Milano, Italy.

(NB: The following article has been published on the academic physics archives Website http://arxiv.org/abs/physics/0407108 (revised v.2, 1 August 2004). It is here reproduced with Dr. Magli's permission and approval to correct some of the English text, as the article was originally written in Italian).

1.0 Introduction

The earth rotates around its axis in 24 hours, and the earth's axis rotates around the axis orthogonal to the ecliptic, describing a cone. Thus, the motion of the earth is similar to that of a spin: the earth precedes. The period of this movement of precession is extremely long with respect to human life, since the axis completes a circle in 25,776 years.

Precession has a very important consequence on long-term naked eye astronomy. First of all, the prolongation of the earth's axis on the celestial sphere defines the astronomical north. The direction in which astronomical north points – possibly indicating a star, thereby a pole star – changes therefore continuously in time. Today's pole star (Polaris) will therefore no longer be the pole star in a few centuries, and all the stars which lie close to the circle described by the pole (actually not exactly a closed circle, due to perturbations) may become 'pole stars' during the precessional cycle. For instance, in Palaeolithic times, the north pole crossed the Milky Way and the Pole star in 15,000 BC was Delta Cygnus, thus a northern sky which was completely different from ours (dominated by the two Ursine and Draco constellations) which are probably depicted in a fresco of the famous Lascaux grotto (Rappenglueck 1998).

Although at best visualized with the movement of the north pole (or the south pole, since the choice of north pole is only due to the latitude of the present author at the moment of writing), precessional effects act on all stars. For instance, precession slowly moves the point

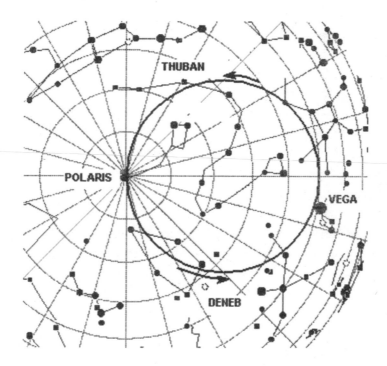

Fig. 1 The circle describing the north celestial pole during a precessional cycle.

of rising on non-circumpolar stars and also their culmination. It follows, that the whole visible sky at any given point and time depends on the precessional moment. As an example, one can consider the group of stars Crux Centaurs in the mediterean sea (the "Southern Cross" was 'isolated' as a constellation only the 16 century AD). The group was quite brilliant and important for people in very ancient times as the research by Michael Hoskin on megalithic "sanctuaries" in Minorca and Majorca and in Malta has shown (we shall come back on this later). However, this asterism became lower and lower over the horizon during the centuries, and today it culminates below the south horizon due to precession and is, therefore, invisible (it will be visible again only in 12,000 AD).

The question now arises, when was the discovery of precession actually achieved. Standard scientific point of view states the following:

1) Precession was first discovered in 117 BC by Hipparchus of Rhodes.
2) Precession was never discovered in pre-Columbian cultures. In other words it was not known in any place in the Americas before Columbus.

In spite of this, the very opposite idea that *all* archaic civilizations discovered precession very early has been around for a long time and was stated in an authoritative way by Giorgio de Santillana and Hertha Von Dechend in their famous book *Hamlet's Mill* (1983). Although an extremely interesting book, and worth reading, *Hamlet's Mill*, however, cannot be of any help when discussing the *basic* issue of the discovery of precession, since all the 'proofs' recorded in the book cannot be considered as true scientific proofs. Indeed the authors report an (albeit impressive) amount of occurrences of similar images, same numbers, similar situations in a great number of cosmological myths around the world. Although it is well known that myths have actually been used to sometimes convey a technical language, without independent verification of assertions in contextual environment it is impossible to accept 'images' and 'numbers' as 'proofs'.

The aim of the present paper is, therefore, to discuss which hints do we have about discovery of precession before Hipparchus in ancient cultures in order to stimulate further research in this field.

2.0 Astronomical Data

It would have been nearly impossible, even for a very experienced naked-eye astronomer in ancient times, to discover precession in the course of his own life using only his own observations, due to the extremely slow nature of the phenomenon with respect to the length of a human life. It is, however, sufficient to have astronomical data collected during, say, two or three centuries, like the height of transit of a bright star, and *to trust in them,* to become aware that 'something is happening' in the sky with a very low, but measurable, velocity (this is exactly what happened to Hipparchus: he collected a great quantity of astronomical data over more than 800 celestial objects coming from the Alexandria observatory and based his discovery on such data). I shall thus, of course, be concerned here with what I have called the discovery that 'something is happening'. This means that I am not speaking about the possible discovery of the actual mechanism and/or of the length of the precessional cycle (although this discovery is not *a priori* excluded) but rather of the observation of a discrepancy of specific visual data which, from now on, I will call *precessional effects.* Typical examples may include the observation of the 'Precessional Era', namely the fact that the sun at the spring equinox rises in different places within a constellation and finally changes constellation every 2000 years, or the observation of the change in the declination of heliacal rising of a star.

2.1 Babylonian culture
There are many examples of ancient cultures that kept written track of astronomical data for centuries. First of all, of course, the Mesopotamian cultures (usually referred to, collectively, as Babylonian). We have astronomical data collected by Babylonian astronomers on clay tablets which contain observations which are more precise than one minute of arc. Since it is nearly impossible to

obtain such an accuracy with the naked eye, it was probably obtained with the first spyglasses ever invented (Pettinato 1998). One example of a Babylonian star catalogue is the famous *Mul-apin*. Probably written around 1000 BC, it contains astronomical data which can be traced back in time up to 2048 BC. The content includes:

1) A list of 71 celestial objects (constellations, single stars and the five planets) divided in three "courses" (Enlil, Anu and Ea).
2) A list of heliacal rising of many stars.
3) A list of simultaneous rising/settings of couples of stars.
4) A list of time delays between the rising of the same stars.
5) A list of simultaneous transit/rising of some other couples of stars.

It is difficult to believe that astronomers possessing data so accurately did not notice the effect of precession, for instance on heliacal risings. However, no written record citing the phenomenon explicitly has been discovered so far.

2.2 The Indo-Savrastati Culture

The history of the Indian civilization has been plagued until twenty years ago or so by the foolish and anti-historical idea of the so called Arian invasion. The basis of this idea was that civilization was brought to India by indo-European people, the Arians, around 1000 BC. After the discovery of the 2500 BC towns of Harappa and Moenjo-daro, the Arians started to be considered warriors and invaders, but the idea remained that the fundamental books of the Hindu religion, the Vedas, were conceived after this invasion. Today we finally know that the Arians simply never existed and that the Indian civilization (traditionally associated with the sites of Harappa and Moenjo-daro, but actually much more spread than the area individuated by these two cities) developed between two rivers, the Indo and the Savrastati rivers (Feuerstein, Kak, and Frawley 1995). The Veda contains explicit reference to the latter river, which was however dry at about 1900 BC, and thus the books (actually memo-books learned by memory by Brahmins) are at least as old as that period.

Together with this new approach to the Veda, in recent years a new approach to what we can now call Vedic astronomy emerged (Kak 2000).

In Vedic astronomy a fundamental role is played by the five visible planets, the sun and the moon, identified with seven fundamental deities. However, to keep track of their motions, 27 astronomical objects were used, the *naksatras*, asterisms/constellations used to divide the ecliptic in equal parts, in each one the sun "resting" about 13 and ⅓ days. *Naksatras* occur in ordered lists. For instance, one can identify (using modern names) the Pleiades, *alfa-tauri* (Aldebaran), *beta-tauri, gamma-gemini, beta-gemini* (Pollux), *delta-cancri*, Hydra, Regulus, and so on. Interestingly enough, lists of *naksatras* belonging to different periods contain the same objects but begin at different points. The starting point is individuated by the sun at the spring equinox, and this means that Vedic astronomers were almost certainly aware that the Sun was 'changing naksatra' with a velocity of more than one naksatra per roughly one millennium (25,776 ÷ 27).

2.3 Egypt: Middle and New Kingdom Astronomical Data

The study of ancient astronomy in Egypt has been plagued for many years by the influence of the most important scholar in the field, Otto Neugebauer, who stated in several occasions view such as 'Egypt did not contribute to the history of mathematical astronomy' (Neugebauer 1969, 1976). But it just suffices to read the information contained in the monumental books by Otto Neugebauer himself and by Richard Parker on ancient Egyptian astronomical texts (1964) to realise how such an assertion is far from being true. Another serious problem generated by the negative influence of Neugebauer is the idea that astronomy was not present in the Pyramid Age (Old Kingdom). In fact the Neugebauer-Parker book begins with the Middle Kingdom (we shall see later that also this assertion is clearly false).

Much of the confusion arises from the fact that we do not have any Egyptian text of explicit astronomical nature, a thing that, in my opinion, is probably due to the fact that papyri were simply not part of the funerary items, and almost only such items are being recovered. In any case, it is obvious that Egyptian astronomers did actually keep track of many astronomical data. This is readable from those "astronomical texts" which were used in funerary contexts and are written in Middle Kingdom sarcophagi and in many New Kingdom tombs, such as the famous tomb of Semnut, architect of the Queen Hatshepsut, and many of the Ramesside tombs of the King Valley.

In the Middle Kingdom, the so-called decanal lists were used. Decans were 36 stars (or groups of stars) whose heliacal rising (the day of the first rising before dawn after a period of conjunction with the sun, i.e. invisibility) occurred in subsequent "weeks" (the Egyptian week was made out of 10 days). In this way, the calendar was divided into decans (36 × 10) plus 5 epagomenal days associated to special decans as well (the calendar I am speaking about is the so-called religious or Sothic one, based on heliacal rising of Sirius which therefore was the first of the decans).

It was shown by Neugebauer and Parker that possible decans must lie in a band south of the ecliptic (decanal band) but they considered explicit identification of decans to be impossible. This is untrue and, in fact, today we do have a quite clear picture of which stars the decans represented (Belmonte 2001a,b). Decans were used to keep track of time during the night as well. This is proved by the so called Star Clocks in which hours during the night are counted associating the last hour of the first day with the decan which has heliacal rise in that day. After one "week" the rising of this decan shifted back in time to signal the previous hour, and another decan signals the last hour, and so on 12 times. Of course each hour had a non–fixed length. One can say that for us one hour has a fixed length and that the night has a variable length in the course of the year, but for the Egyptian it was the opposite (our 24 hour division of the day comes from the 12+12 Egyptian division added to the fixed length Babylonian division of hours).

In the New Kingdom the decans were observed at the meridian transit rather than at rising, but the way of keeping track of stellar events was similar. This is evident in the so called Ramesside star clocks. In a Ramesside star clock a man (an assistant of the astronomer, or perhaps a statue) is seen behind a list of 9 columns and 13 levels. Levels are associated with hours of the night, columns with parts of 'the reference man', and spots signal the transit or position of stars

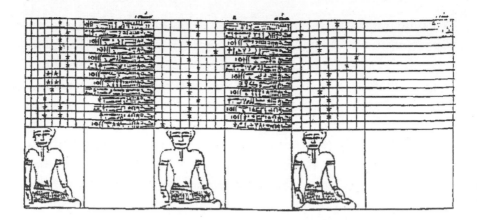

Fig. 2 Examples of Ramesside star clocks.

during the night. The framework was changed each 15 days. I will not enter into further details on the problems of interpretations of such texts. The point I want to stress here is, that such astronomical devices, although depicted in the tombs (as 'guides to the soul during the night') were almost certainly copied from scientific sources (the reader can, if he likes to, add quotation marks to the word 'scientific' but I will not do so). In fact, already in the Middle Kingdom Egyptian astronomers were able to keep accurate track of 36 stellar objects taking into account their motion (hour of rising, period of invisibility and so on) and therefore they should have selected such properties from a huge amount of observational data. It is absolutely certain that one can discover a precessional effect in the heliacal rising of a star with data accurate to ½ of degree in, say, three centuries. This led Pogo (1930) and Zaba (1953) to propose that precession was probably discovered very early in Egypt. It is, in addition, worth mentioning that several authors have proposed, in order to explain the curious arrangements of the constellations in the famous round picture of the sky known as the Dendera Zodiac, that it could contain a reference to the precessional movement of the north pole (see for example Trevisan). The Zodiac is however dated to the first half of the last century BC, and therefore after Hipparchus' discovery. Again, we do not have any explicit records which can be associated unambiguously to the discovery of a precessional effect.

2.4 Mesoamerica

As is well known, the Maya kept track of astronomical data in a written and extremely accurate way (Aveni 2001). Unfortunately, only four Maya 'codices' survived the *auto da fe* during which the bishop of Yucatan, Diego de Landa, condemned all the heretic books. Such codices contain data about eclipses, Venus and Mercury. The Data is so precise (for instance, the Venus table in the Dresda codex is based on tens of years of observations) that the ability of the Maya astronomers in taking extremely accurate measures is beyond any doubt. However one cannot discover precession using the motion of the sun, of the planets and of the moon, and we do not possess any record of star observations by the Maya (the unique exception possibly being in the so called Paris codex, which is still not fully understood).

3.0 Astronomical Alignments

So far, we have discussed possible textual evidences. There is, however, another possibility to keep track of celestial motions and to leave astronomical data to successors as a heritage, namely the construction of stellar alignments. Following their accuracy during a few centuries one can easy discover precessional effects (I am using here an abuse of notation calling 'stellar' the alignments pointing to stars different from the sun).

3.1 Egypt: Orientation of Temples

The pioneer in the studies of the astronomical orientation of temples in Egypt was Norman Lockyer (1894). In his book he studied the orientation of many temples, but I shall discuss in details here only the case of the two main Theban temples, Karnak and Luxor, because it suffices for our purposes.

These two temples have a millenary history and were embellished and enlarged several times. In particular, different pharaohs in different epochs added further galleries in the direction of the main axis of both temples. If one looks at the plan of the Karnak temple, it is clearly seen that the temple was always enlarged maintaining strictly the original direction of the main axis. It was shown by Lockyer that this direction is that of the setting sun of the summer solstice. The work of Lockyer was criticised because hills at the horizon would have prevented the light of the setting sun from penetrating the gallery, and today we actually know that observations were performed at the other end of the temple in a chapel which – being on an axis parallel with the temple - is obviously oriented to the winter solstice sunrise (Krupp 1983, 1988). In any case, solstice alignment of the temple is certain, and of course, since precession does not effect the apparent motion of the sun, so any enlargement was added in the same direction.

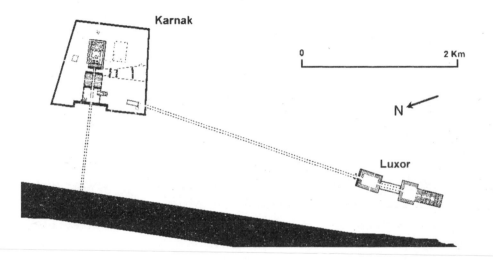

Fig. 3 Plan of Karnak and Luxor temples.

The other main temple of Thebes, today called Luxor temple, is instead aligned to the stars. This is pretty clear because the axis was *slightly* deviated no less than four times, every time on the occasion of a subsequent enlargement which took place over the centuries. Unfortunately, although we do have several descriptions of the alignment ceremony of temples to the stars, called by the Egyptians *Stretching of the Cord*, we do not have a clear picture of how the ceremony actually took place. For instance, in many cases it is said that the alignment occurred towards the *Mes* constellation, i.e. the Big Dipper/Plough which the Egyptian saw as a Bull's Foreleg, but we do not know exactly to which star it was made. It is as yet unclear therefore to which star or asterism the Luxor temple was aligned (Lockier proposal, *alfa-lyrae* or Canopus, is, as far as I know, still to be confirmed). In any case, the slight deviations in the temple axis clearly point to the discovery of a precessional effect.

3.2 Egypt: orientation of pyramids

It is very well known that the main pyramids of the fourth dynasty (the main three at Giza and the two Snefru pyramids at Dashur) were oriented to face the cardinal points with a high degree of precision. The deviation of the east side from true north is in fact the following:

Meidum –20′ ± 1.0′; Bent Pyramid –17.3′ ± 0.2′; Red Pyramid –8.7′ ± 0.2′; Giza 1 (Khufu) –3.4′ ± 0.2′; Giza 2 (Khafre) –6.0′ ± 0.2′; Giza 3 (Menkaure) +12.4′ ± 1.0′.

The precision achieved by the pyramid builders was so high that it is absolutely certain that the orientation method used was based on stars and not on the measurement of shadows (recently, the French mission directed by M. Valloggia has determined the orientation of the pyramid at Abu Roash [Mathieu 2001], probably constructed by Djedefre who ruled between Khufu and Khafre, to be – 48.7′, but this error is so out of stream with respect to the others that it points to a different, perhaps solar, orientation ceremony).

The stellar methods which have been proposed in the past, e.g. the observation of rising and setting of a bright star on an artificial horizon, are not affected by precession. However, as already noticed by Haack (1984), the data strongly point to the existence of a time-dependent font cause of systematic error and this font is certainly precession. This problem induced Kate Spence (2000) to propose a method of orientation – "the simultaneous transit" – which consists in observing the cord connecting two circumpolar stars, namely Kochab (b UMi) and Mizar (z UMa) when it is orthogonal to the horizon. Due to the precessional motion of the earth axis the cord does not always identify the true north: it has a slow movement which brought it from the left to the right of the pole in the 25th century BC. Plotting the deviation from north against time, Spence shows that the corresponding straight line fits well with the deviation of the pyramids i.e. to true north if the date of 'orientation ceremony' occurred for the Giza 1 pyramid in 2467 BC ±5y (although no written evidence of orientation ceremony exists for the old kingdom pyramids, the 'Stretching of the Cord' foundation ceremony is actually already present in the Old Kingdom stele called 'The Palermo Stone'). If one, in turn, accepts the method as the one effectively used, the graph plotted can be used to calibrate the dates of construction of all the fourth dynasty pyramids, which turn out to be around 80 years later than usually accepted.

Further to Spence work, Belmonte (2001c) proposed that the method actually used consisted in measuring alignments between two stars (as Spence proposed) but using a couple of stars – probably Megrez (d UMa) and Phecda (g UMa) – which are not each other opposite to the pole. The pole is thus obtained by elongation of a cord lying below or over it. This looks more natural (at least for modern naked-eye sky-watchers) and reconciles the astronomical chronology with the usually accepted one. However, it should be noted that the astronomical dating of the so called air shafts of the Giza 1 pyramid (Trimble 1964, Badawy 1964, Bauval 1993) support Spence's earlier chronology.

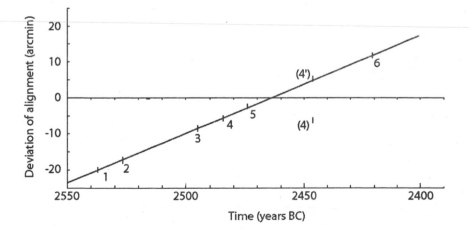

Fig. 4

The solution proposed by Spence for the orientation of the Giza 2 pyramid fits in the calibration line if and only if the corresponding point is 'lifted up' vertically in the positive region. To solve this problem, Spence speculates that the orientation of the second pyramid was carried out in the opposite season (summer instead of winter) with respect to the others (also in the Belmonte proposal the problem arises and has to be solved by assuming a special procedure for the orientation of the Giza 2 pyramid). I tend rather to think that a ceremony of religious nature, such as the orientation of a giant king's tomb, could not occur scattered in time but rather in a fixed, precise time dictated by astronomical counting, such as those rituals connected with the Sirius cycle, and I have, therefore, proposed that the error in the orientation of the 'second pyramid' actually shows that it was constructed before Giza 1 or, more precisely, that the two projects were conceived together (it can be shown that this idea is not in contrast with any indubitable archaeological evidence: see Magli (2003) for details).

In any case, what is really interesting for us here is that the orientation errors of the pyramids form a set of experimental data from which a precessional effect can be deduced. Whatever the reason, the effect is absolutely transferable exactly in the case of the most huge and perfectly built pyramids, namely Giza 1 and Giza 2. However one can speculate, for instance, that the relative orientation of the Giza 3 pyramid could have been compared with that of Giza 2 and therefore the precessional effect leading to a deviation of 18,4′ i.e. about ⅓ of a degree, be observed. In any case, I want to stress that the astronomically anchored data coming from Giza (orientation of air-shafts and pyramids) as well as the many astronomical references present in the Pyramid Texts do show beyond any possible doubt that astronomy was present in the Old Kingdom as a fundamental part of thinking (religion and knowledge).

3.2 Malta

Strangely enough, the Mediterranean archipelago of Malta (composed of the isles Malta, Gozo and Comino) has a short history which, according to all sources, begins only in the fifth millennium BC when

Malta was first colonized by humans (Trump 1991, 2002). However, after only 1500 years, with the beginning of the so called Temples Period (about 3500–2500 BC) Malta's civilization became the first to construct megalithic buildings (only a few megalithic tombs are dated before this period, like Kintraw in Britain, while the first stone phases of Stonehenge and of other megalithic monuments – i.e. not tombs – belong to the first half of the third millennium).

In the megalithic phase more than 40 temples were constructed. Actually the world 'temple' should be put in quotation marks because it is far from being clear which was the real function of the buildings. However traces of a worship for a "mother goddess" deity are evident. The temples are composed of buildings (up to three, corresponding to subsequent phases and numerated accordingly) which all have an external masonry of ovoid shape while the internal plan is composed of a subsequent series of 'lobes' constructed along the same axis and ending with an 'apse'. The internal 'lobes' probably define the shape of the "Mother Goddess".

The best preserved temples are *Ggantija*, the place of the giants, in Gozo, and *Hagar Qim*, *Mnajdra* and *Tarxien* in Malta. The temples show a clear interest of the builders for celestial phenomena. This interest is absolutely evident in Mnajdra II, which is a solar calendar built in stone: the axis is aligned to due east, and the 'altar' stones are put in such a way that one can keep track of the yearly movement of the sun from the far left to the far right of the 'apse'. All other Malta temples have axes oriented to the south, and the orientation is to the south of all directions related to sun and moon (i.e. winter solstice sunrise and southern moon major standstill). Due to the work by Michael Hoskin and collaborators and by Klaus Albrecht however, today we have a quite clear picture of the astronomical orientation of Malta temples. As a key example, I will discuss Ggantjia.

The two temples of Ggantjia correspond to two subsequent phases, and the second one is oriented further south with respect to the first. Both exhibit a solar orientation in the left altar, which is oriented to winter solstice sunrise (Albrecht 2001) and both exhibit a stellar orientation in the main axis, which is oriented towards the asterism composed by the Southern Cross and the two bright stars of

Centaurus (remember that it is only in the last few centuries that the Southern Cross has been identified formally as a constellation, and that ancient constellation by no means should coincide with ours. In any case, ours belongs to the mesopotamic-greek tradition) (Hoskin 2001).

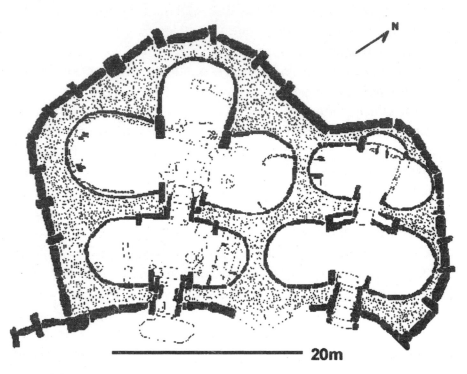

Fig. 5 Plan of the Ggantija temples

Although the discoverer of the solar orientation, Albrecht, states that the stellar hypothesis is not viable, I do instead think that this is a quite clear example in which *both* solar and stellar orientations were realized. The problem was, of course, that while the solar one was to remain accurate for centuries and centuries, the stellar one was changing due to precession. It is therefore strongly tempting to conclude that they were *obliged* to construct the second temple to match the movement due south of the raising of the Crux-Centaurus asterism.

3.3 Majorca

The Balearic isles of Minorca and Majorca were, about one thousand years after Malta and thus during the Bronze Age, inhabited by megalithic sky-watchers. The so called sanctuaries of the two islands, including the famous Minorcan *Taulas,* megalithic structures composed by two monoliths disposed as a giant 'T', were oriented due south to the same asterisms mentioned before, composed by the Southern Cross and the two bright stars of Centaurus (Hoskin 2001).

We are interested here especially in one of the sanctuaries, called *Son Mas*, in Majorca.

When the Hoskin group studied the site, it became clear that it was oriented to the low arc in the southern sky that the asterism Crux-Centaurus was following at the end of a valley, in about 2000 BC However the lower part of this asterism would have become invisible due to precession in about 1700 BC. Therefore, if the site was really connected with astronomical observations, it should have been abandoned around that date. Hoskin was not, at that time, aware that a team headed by Mark Van Strydonck of the Belgian Royal Institute of Cultural Heritage was carbon-dating samples from the same site, and was actually wondering why the site was abandoned exactly in that period!

This is thus a very interesting example of the way in which Archaeo-astronomy can act as a predictive science. What is especially interesting for us here is, of course, that it is clear that an astronomical alignment showed that 'something was happening' in the southern sky in Majorca and induced the people to abandon the site.

3.4 The Medicine wheels

The so called *Medicine Wheels* are stone monuments composed of a central cairn of stones connected by radial rows to an external circle and other cairns. Most wheels can be found in Alberta, Canada, but the most famous of them, the Big Horn wheel, lies near the Medicine Mountain in Wyoming and the name of the family comes from this wheel.

There are several typologies of wheels, but some of them have been indubitably linked to astronomical observations. The first wheel to be identified with an astronomical observatory is the Big Horn one. A solar physicist, John Eddy, recognised that the small cairns which are distributed on the external circle of the wheel serve as astronomical outpost for many alignments. The alignments recognised by Eddy are at the summer solstice and at the heliacal rising of Aldebaran, Rigel and Sirius (Eddy 1974, 1977). The window of validity of such alignments (which is of the order of three centuries due to precession) holds for the last three centuries, and indeed independent archaeological data give to the Big Horn an age of 250 years.

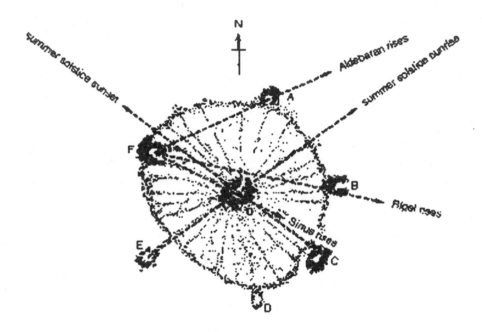

Fig. 6 The astronomical alignments of the Big Horn Medicine Wheel discovered by Eddy.

Eddy's interpretation received a wonderful confirmation after the archaeological study of another wheel, the Moose Mountain Medicine wheel. This wheel in fact has alignments towards the same targets, but the window of validity is completely different, and lies around the last centuries BC. When archaeologists Tom and Alice Kecoe obtained C-14 datable samples from the site, they were able to confirm the 'astronomically predicted' age of the monument, showing a constant interest of the (at yet unknown) wheel builders for the same astronomical objects in the courses of two millennia: another wonderful example of Archaeoastronomy as a predictive science (actually the wheels astronomical tradition is much older than this: the Majorville Wheel in Alberta was used for solar observations already in 2500 BC).

What is especially interesting for us here is the missing "D" alignment, which was later individuated by Robinson (1980) both at Big Horn and at Moose Mountain. Robinson discovered this direction to be aligned with the rising of Fomalhaut, a star of the constellation Pisces Australis (not to be confused with the zodiacal constellation Pisces). The window of validity of this alignment is however *shifted in time* by some centuries with respect to Eddy's estimates for Moose Mountain. This looks strange, but the radial line of stones is curved along its length. It looks as if the line was originally pointing more westerly and was then curved *in order to follow the precessional shift of the point of rising of the star.* A similar deviation is shown by the cairn pointing to Sirius, another southerly star more quickly affected by the precessional cycle than Aldebaran and Rigel.

Thus the Moose Mountain Medicine Wheel strongly candidates as a place where tenacious astronomers discovered a precessional effect.

3.5 Teutihuacan and the "17 degree" family

While, as we have seen, we have a very clear picture of the way in which the Maya recorded their astronomical observations, the same cannot be said of other Mesoamerica cultures. We practically do not know anything about the astronomy of the so called mother culture of Mesoamerica, the Olmecs, and we do not have written records coming from the most important culture of the Mexico valley, which flourished during the pre-classic Maya period, roughly between the second and the sixth century BC, and which influenced all subsequent civilization in central Mexico, including the Toltecs and, finally, the Aztecs. I am speaking, of course, of the place which the Aztecs themselves considered as the city of the gods, Teutihuacan.

Teutihuacan lies not far from Mexico city, and is still today a huge town which, at the moment of maximum urbanization, should have reached more than 125,000 inhabitants. The city was planned under a rigid project which aimed to *replicate* the landscape. This is evident from the fact that the main two buildings of the town, the so called Sun pyramid and Moon pyramid (these are late denominations, as no connection with the sun and moon has ever been proved) are disposed in such a way to be a 'copy' an image of the two mountains which lie respectively behind, the Cerro Gordo and the Cerro Patlachique.

The town was planned and constructed on a 'cardinal grid' based on two axes, a 'T-north' axis oriented 15.5 degree east of north, and a 'T-east' axis oriented 16.5 degrees south of east. This was by no means due to geomorphologic reasons (it suffices indeed to think that the river crossing the town was canalised to conform to the grid). Teutihuacan 'cardinal directions' are thus rotated with respect to the 'true' cardinal directions and tilted one further degree from each other for symbolic reasons. Astronomy plays here a fundamental role, since the most reasonable explanation is the following:

The T-east orientation is a solar orientation. It is too close to east to signal any special event in the motion of the sun at the horizon (solstice and days of zenit passage) however the sun sets at T-west on 13 August and 29 April, and these two dates are separated by 260 days. It is well known that the so called sacred calendar of Mesoamerica (well documented by the Maya, but probably coming from the very early civilization and codified around 4 BC) was composed of 260 days. The origin should be the passage of the sun at zenith, which of course depends on latitude and occurred in those two dates at the latitude of the pre-classic site of Izapa (see Aveni 2001 for a complete discussion). Thus, the T-east orientation was probably a reminder for the sacred calendar of solar origin. What is especially interesting for us here is however the T-north orientation, because it is almost certainly a stellar one.

The axis orthogonal to T-north (which, just as a reminder, is *not* parallel to T-east) is individuated by an accurate alignment between two so called pecked crosses, pecked symbols incised on the ground, one on a hill at the west horizon and the other one in the centre of the town. This alignment points to the setting of the Pleiades around 1-4

AD, and this asterism had heliacal rising approximately on the same day of the zenith passage of the sun (18 May) and were culminating near the zenith as well (Dow 1967).

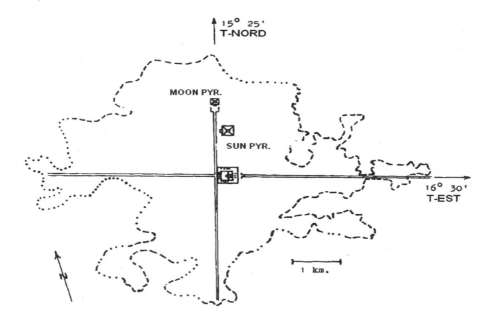

Fig. 7 Map of Teutihuacan

Teutihuacan collapsed a couple of centuries thereafter, and it is therefore unlikely that Teutihuacan astronomers were able to realise that the alignment was not accurate any more due to precession. What is especially interesting for us here is rather what has been called after Aveni and Gibbs *The 17 Degree Family* (Aveni and Gibbs 1976).

The family comprises several archaeological sites in central Mexico. All such sites exhibit – *during the course of several centuries up to 1000 AD* – the same (or very near to) T-north orientation (for instance, the first phase of the giant Cholula pyramid, the toltec temple of Tula, the pyramids of Tenayuca and Tepotzteco). The family thus comprises buildings which have been constructed several centuries after 400 AD, and therefore the T-north orientation did not have the meaning of indicating the rising of the Pleiades any more. The question obviously arises, if the architects were aware that they were orienting buildings to a stellar direction which was no more effective for some reasons, and in this case, if they asked themselves the reasons or simply if were doing so 'in memory' of the past glory of Teutihuacan without even knowing which was the original meaning of the direction.

4.0 Post-discovery hints

4.1 The cult of Mithras

The facts which I have exposed point, in my view, towards showing that precessional effects were actually discovered. However, the problem arises why we do not have explicit mention of such effects anywhere. Being a physicist, I like enigmas (i.e. solvable problems) and I do not believe in 'mysteries'. Since it is very tempting to think that the discovery was not explicitly stated because it was considered a thing to be kept secret, or at least reserved to a group of initiated people, it is natural to investigate whether traces of the discovery can be found in cults of this kind at least in historical times. Actually, it is so.

As is well known, the cults which were reserved to initiates are called in historic literature Mystery Cults, one famous example being the so called Elysian Mysteries in Greece and another being the Mithras Mysteries in the first three centuries AD in the Roman empire. Interestingly enough, an extremely intriguing hint pointing to the discovery of precession in ancient times comes exactly from such cults.

Hipparchus discovers precession about 127 BC, working on Rhodes island but using data from the Alexandria observatory in Egypt. About 50 years *later*, Pompey fights with the Phrygian pirates, and his legionnaires come into contact with a religion which will rapidly spread in the whole Roman empire in the subsequent two centuries, and will be destroyed by the Christianisation of the empire: the Mithras cult.

In the Mithras cult the rituals were kept secret to non-adepts and we do not have any written records describing them. However, several underground 'shrines' have been unearthed and studied by the archaeologists, perhaps the most famous of them being the one present in the St. Clement catacombs in Rome. Thus, the iconography of the

The Temple of Satis (Satet)
on Elephantine Island.

The goddess Satis (left)
with the ram-headed god
Kknum, Temple of Satis
on Elephantine Island.

The Temple of Hathor
at Dendera.

The Temple of the *Birth of Isis* at Dendera. View from the roof of the Hathor temple, looking south.

Author in the Osiris chapel of the Temple of Hathor at Dendera.

Dawn at the Great Temple of Rameses II at Abu Simbel during the sun festival in late October.

Great Temple of Rameses II at Abu Simbel. The holy of holies illuminated by the sun's ray on 19th October.

Great Temple of Rameses II at Abu Simbel. Sunrise on 19th October.

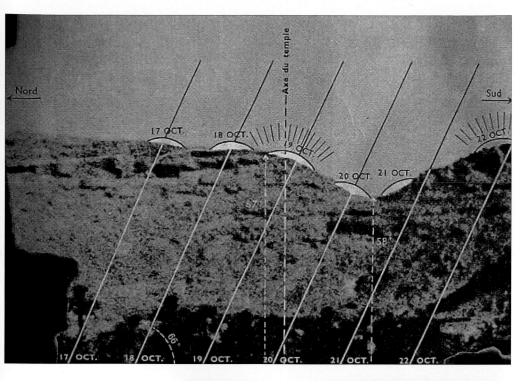

Nord ←   Axe du temple   → Sud

17 OCT.   18 OCT.   19 OCT.   20 OCT.   21 OCT.   22 OCT.

57   58   66°

17 OCT.   18 OCT.   19 OCT.   20 OCT.   21 OCT.   22 OCT.

Photo-montage by Jan van der Haagen of UNESCO (1961) of the various sunrise points between 17th and 22nd October *before* the temple was moved to a higher location. It can be seen that the alignment of the axis was directed to the sunrise on the 19th October when the disc appeared over the distant hill on the east side of the Nile.

Akhenaten, Cairo Museum.

Akhenaten making offerings to the Aten sun-disc.

The remains of the Small Temple of Aten, at Tell El Amarna.

Author at sunrise on 30th October
at Tell El Amarna.

Heb Sed (jubilee) scene,
Step Pyramid at Saqqara.

Heb Sed (jubilee) scene, Karnak temple. Note the King racing with the sacred bull.

Heb Sed (jubilee) scenes from the Abu Ghorab sun-temples.

cult, always the same, is very well known and represented, sculpted or painted, in the ending 'chapel' of the shrine. We see the god, Mithras, represented as a young man, killing a bull with a sword. The god does not look at the bull. Under the bull, a scorpion strikes at the genitals of the bull, and the figures of a dog, a serpent, a crow, a lion and a vessel also are seen. From the bull's tail some ears of grain sprout. Frequently, the zodiacal signs and planets are represented as well.

The history of modern Mithraic studies is very instructive and almost unbelievable. In 1896 the Belgian scholar Franz Cumont formulated a theory in which the cult was interpreted as an adaptation of an ancient Iranian cult of a deity called *Mithra*. Although many clear aspects of the Mithras cult were not recognizable in the Mithra cult and, in particular, in the Mithra cult there was no sign of the killing of a bull, the authority of Cumont was so strong that his curious ways of deriving Mithras from the Iranian Mithra (for instance, recovering the bull from another Iranian myth in which Ahriman, a devil god, kills a bull and Mithra does not appear) was accepted *up to 1970!*

This "Cumont dogma" is a wonderful example of the risks to which scientists present themselves with authority of 'giants' (or perhaps supposed giants) and that they are accepted outright by others.

In any case, finally in 1971 some persons began to take these dogmas to task, and it became immediately clear that Mithraic studies had to be re-started from the very beginning and that the natural point to start with was astronomy. Actually already in 1869 the German scholar K. B. Stark had noticed strong and clear connections of the iconography with constellations. However Cumont went out to say that although astronomy could admittedly have played a role in the lower degrees of initiation, the main stream of the high degrees was the Iranic tradition on the origin and the end of the world.

Since the main personages in the scene are Mithras and the Bull, it is clear that the bull has to be identified with Taurus but it is not clear with which constellation Mithras is to be identified. All the astronomical interpretations which have been proposed since 1970 e.g. heliacal rising of Taurus, have had a serious problem with the identification of Mithras. For instance, one could think Orion, but Orion is under, and not above, the Bull.

Fig. 8 The Mithras iconography.

Finally, the solution of the puzzle has been given by David Ulansey (Ulansey 1989). Ulansey observed that *over* Taurus there is Perseus, a constellation identified with a Phyigian warrior already in the 5 century BC. But why the Scorpion? If we fix the sky back in time up to the end of the Taurus era, about 2000 BC, we discover that the other equinoctial constellation was Scorpio. The celestial equator crossed at that time Taurus, Canis Major, Hydra (i.e. a serpent), Vessel, Crow and Scorpion (besides a small part of Orion's sword). There remains the Lion which, however, was the summer solstice constellation at the same epoch. The grain ears from the tail of the Bull give the association with spring equinox. This is what concerns the interpretation of the Mithras cult: a god who is so strong as to be able to change the cosmic order of the motion of the sun with respect to the stars. This is a very convincing interpretation. However, the interest for us arises from the way in which Ulansey explains the origin of the Mithras cult. According to Ulansey, what happened is (in brief) the following. In

128 BC Hipparchus discover precession. The discovery rapidly permeates and fits into the symbolic scheme of the stoic philosophy school at Tarsus. Since for stoic philosophers, natural forces were manifestations of deities, so it was natural for them to introduce a new god responsible for the new movement of the cosmos: a god so strong as to be able to move the 'fixed' stars. Since Perseus was already venerated at Tarsus, the identification followed naturally. Regarding the missing link with the pirates, which are the first Mithras adepts historically documented, Ulansey remarks that they had 'contacts with intellectuals' and were used to the stars being sailors.

I should say immediately that I do not believe in Ulansey's ingenious interpretation of the Mithras cult and that I am unable to believe in his ingenious explanation for its origin. The reason is very simple. Although doing the best of my efforts, I cannot find even one example in history in which a scientific discovery became a religion. It could eventually have become a myth within a religious framework, as in *Hamlet's Mill* viewpoint, but not the foundation of a cult of a new god. There is also a technical reason for which I cannot believe in Ulansey's interpretation. Let us suppose that a scientific discovery of a mechanism becomes a religion. A religion is usually associated with eschatological thought: we expect an event, the future advent of a god, for instance. Therefore, I would rather think that the new religion will be based on the end of the present era (Aries to Fish) rather than on the end of the previous one occurring 2000 years (I repeat, 2000 years) before. Based on slight different motivation, this objection has already been raised, and Ulansey's answer is based on the fact that Hipparchus estimation of the precessional velocity was too low (about one degree for one century). As a consequence, this led to an estimate of the future change of the precessional era after many centuries (about 800 years) and not at the time it really occurred, actually in the first century AD more or less.

While I consider this as a possible explanation of the decline of the Mithras cult (I am not aware of any other scholars making this observation, but it looks natural to me) I do not consider this as a good explanation for the point, because 'time of religion is the time of gods' so there is usually no urge for eschatological events to occur.

All in all, I think that the origin of Mithras precessional iconography can be much older than Hipparchus discovery. Once again, these are only speculative statements however. Hopefully new epigraphic or archaeological discoveries might be of help in assessing this interesting point, but at least one archaeological finding already exists.

4.2 The Gundestrup Cauldron

The so-called *Gundestrup Cauldron* is a huge vessel made out of silver plates. Found in Denmark in 1880, it is exposed in the Copenhagen National Museum and it is the most renowned masterpiece of Celtic art, dated to the first century BC (dating is however only approximate since no physical method is known to date such kind of objects).

The Gundestrup is magnificently decorated with enigmatic images. It undoubtedly shows peculiarities of Celtic art, e.g. the god called Cermnumon, but it also shows clear 'oriental' influxes (also elephants are represented on it). There is still debate about the meaning of the scenes, and what is most debated is the meaning of the central plate representation. It shows, at the centre, a dying bull with, forming a circle contour to the animal, a warrior, a lizard and a dog. A bear seems also to be present, and a tree branch with leaves.

One can easily solve the exercise of foreseeing which interpretations have been proposed for this image. Of course we have 'ritual sacrifice', 'ritual fighting with bulls', 'ritual fighting between bulls and dogs' and so on (actually the *Corrida* is missing). Finally, the French scholar Paul Verdier (2000) proposed what would seem the obvious idea that the symbolism of the cauldron has an astronomical content. For instance, one of the lateral plaques contains two bands separated by a branch. The upper band shows four riders (the solstices) the lower band twelve warriors (the months of the Celtic lunar calendar) while the tree branch is the Milky Way. The central plaque is probably a representation of the death of the Taurus Era, as in the Mithras main iconography, and in fact if we take a look to the sky in 2000 BC, we can actually see in clockwise direction Lacerta, the lizard, Canis Major, the dog, Orion, the warrior, and Taurus, the bull, while the two Ursae 'overlook' the scene from the north celestial pole. In my opinion, the warrior in the scene might well be Perseus, and not Orion, since moving in clockwise *spiralling* towards Taurus one actually encounters Perseus, as exemplified in the figure. In this case the analogy with the Mithra cult would become striking. In *any* case the astronomical interpretation of the scene is clear.

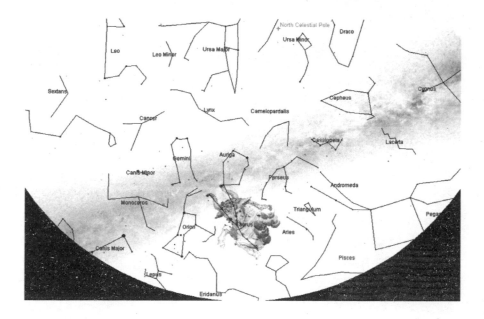

Fig. 9 Portion of the sky at the latitude of Copenhagen, in 2000 BC.

Unfortunately, we do not know the level of astronomical knowledge of the Celtic astronomers, because most of the information we have on them comes from secondary sources, especially (curiously indeed) from the stoic Hellenistic writer Posidonio, besides the Roman sources like Caesar's writings. However, some primary information is available, like e.g. the *Coligny Calendar*, a lunar calendar written in Roman characters but in the Gallic language. In addition, the lore of astronomy in Bronze Age in North Europe has still to reveal his secrets, as shows the recent discovery of the so called Nebra Disk, a 16th century BC Bronze disk showing 32 stars, a crescent and the sun and probably representing a particular sky on a particular day.

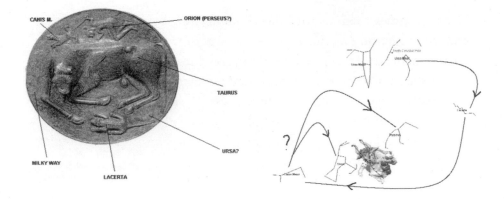

Fig. 10 The central plaque of the Gundestrup cauldron and the corresponding astronomical interpretation. The picture on the right is the same as that in Fig. 9, with only the relevant constellations shown. Reading in clockwise direction in a spiral from the pole (Ursa) we find Lacerta, Canis Major, Orion (actually Perseus if one has to proceed on the spiral) and Taurus.

In any case, it is again difficult to believe (at least to me) that also the Celts did rapidly filtrate the discovery by Hipparchus, in such a way that an artist of the first century BC decided to represent a precessional event occurring 2000 years before in his masterpiece.

5 Concluding Remarks

All in all, there is *no* clear, absolute evidence of the discovery of precession before Hellenistic times or in pre-Columbian culture. There is, however, at least in my view, a clear evidence that simple astronomical phenomena, such as heliacal rising of bright stars or the movement of the equinoctial point through zodiacal constellations were traced for a sufficient amount of time and with a sufficient precision to lead many ancient astronomers to the discovery that 'something was happening' with a very slow velocity with respect to human life.

More research focussed on this issue is certainly needed, first of all in Egypt. In fact, the problem of the stellar alignment of Egyptian temples should be reconsidered taking into account that the chronology of Egypt is much more clear and accurate than it was in

Lockyer times, and controlling the assertions of Lockyer from a *quantitative* point of view (for instance following the subsequent enlargements of the Luxor temple in terms of precessional movement of the stars). Theoretical research is also needed to relate in a secure way decanal lists coming from different centuries.

The need for further research holds true also in Malta, and in all the places which show an interest of the builders for alignments changing in time due to precession.

References

Albrecht, K. (2001), *Maltas Tempel: Zwischen Religion und Astronomie*, Naether-Verlag, Potsdam.

Aveni, A. F. (2001), *Skywatchers: A Revised and Updated Version of Skywatchers of Ancient Mexico*, University of Texas Press, Austin.

Aveni, A. F and Gibbs, S. L. (1976), 'On the orientation of pre-Columbian buildings in central Mexico', *American Antiquity* , Vol. 41, pp. 510–17.

Badawy, A. (1964), 'The stellar destiny of pharaoh and the so called air shafts in Cheops pyramid', *M.I.O.A.W.B.* Band 10, p.189.

Bauval, R. (1993), 'Cheop's pyramid: a new dating using the latest astronomical data', *Discussions in Egyptology*. Vol. 26, p.5.

Belmonte, J.A. (2001a), 'The Ramesside star clocks and the ancient egyptian constellations', *SEAC* Conference on Symbols, calendars and orientations, Stockholm.

Belmonte, J.A. (2001b), 'The decans and the ancient Egyptian skylore: an astronomer's approach', *INSAP III Meeting*, Palermo.

Belmonte, J.A. (2001c), 'On the orientation of Old Kingdom Egyptian Pyramids', *Archaeoastronomy* 26, 2001, S1.

De Santillana, G.,Von Dechend, E.(1983), *Hamlet's Mill*, Dover Publications.

Dow, J. (1967), 'Astronomical orientations at Teotihuacan; A case study in astroarchaeology', *American Antiquity*, Vol. 32, pp. 326–34.

Feuerstein, G., Kak, S., and Frawley, D. (1995), *In search of the cradle of civilization*, Wheaton, Quest Books.

Eddy, J. A. (1974), 'Astronomical alignment of the Big Horn Medicine Wheel', *Science.* Vol 18, p.1035.

Eddy, J. A. (1977), 'Medicine wheels and plains Indian astronomy'. In Aveni, A. (ed.), *Native American Astronomy*, University of Texas Press, Austin, pp. 147–70.

Haack, S. (1984), 'The astronomical orientation of the Egyptian pyramids', *Archeoastronomy*, Vol. 7, S119.

Hoskin, M. (2001), *Tombs, temples and their orientations,* Ocarina books.

Kak, S. (2000), 'Birth and Early Development of Indian Astronomy'. In *Astronomy Across Cultures: The History of Non-Western Astronomy*, Helaine Selin (ed), Kluwer, pp. 303-40.

Krupp, E. C. (1983), *Echoes of the Ancient Skies*, Harper, New York.

Krupp, E.C. (1988), 'The light in the temples'. In Ruggles C.L.N. (ed.) *Records In Stone: Papers In Memory Of Alexander Thom*, Cambridge: Cambridge University Press.

Lockyer, N. (1894), *The Dawn of Astronomy*.

Magli, G. (2003), *On the astronomical orientation of the IV dynasty Egyptian pyramids and the dating of the second Giza pyramid* (pre-print)

Mathieu, B. (2001), 'Travaux de l'Institut Francais d'Archeologie Orientale en 2-2001', BIFAO, p. 101.

Neugebauer, O. (1976), *A History of ancient mathematical astronomy*, Springer-Verlag.

Neugebauer, O (1969), *The exact sciences in antiquity* Dover Publications, New York .

Neugebauer, O, Parker, R.A.(1964), *Egyptian Astronomical Texts*, Lund Humphries, London.

Pettinato, G. (1998), *La scrittura celeste*, Milano, Mondadori.

Pogo, A. (1930), The astronomical ceiling decoration of the tomb of Semnut, *ISIS*, Vol. 14, p. 301.

Rappenglueck, M. (1998), 'Palaeolithic Shamanistic Cosmography: How is the Famous Rock Picture in the Shaft of the Lascaux Grotto to be Decoded?', XVI Valcamonica Symposium Arte Preistorica e Tribale, Sciamanismo e Mito.

Robinson, J.H.(1980). 'Fomalhaut and Cairn D at the Big Horn and

Moose Mountain Medicine Wheels', *Archaeaoastronomy: Bull. Center for Archaeoastr.*, pp.15-9.

Spence, K. (1999), 'Ancient Egyptian chronology and the astronomical orientation of pyramids', *Nature*, Vol. 408, p.320.

Trimble,V. (1964), *'Astronomical investigations concerning the so called air shafts of Cheops pyramid'*, *M.I.O.A.W.B.*, Band 10, p. 183.

Trump, D. H. (1991), *Malta: An Archaeological Guide*, Progress Press Co. Ltd.

Trump, D.H. (2002), *Malta: Prehistory and Temples*, Midsea Books.

Ulansey, D. (1989), *The Origins of the Mithraic Mysteries*, Oxford University Press, Oxford.

Verdier, P. (2000) L'Astronomie celtique : l'énigme du chaudron de Gun-destrup, Archéologue 6.

Zaba, Z. (1953), *L'orientation astronomique dans l'ancienne Egypte et la precession de l'axe du monde*, Prague, 1953.

APPENDIX 3

An Overview of the Orion Correlation Theory (OCT): Was the angle of observation 52.2 degrees south of east?

By Chris Tedder

The following article has been published by Chris Tedder and is here reproduced with his kind permission in full and without any alteration.

Background

In 1983, Robert Bauval noticed the similarity between the three-star asterism in Orion, and the site layout of the three pyramid complexes on the Giza plateau. This observation became the core idea of the Orion Correlation Theory (OCT). Following a recommendation by Dr Edwards, Robert Bauval's paper, 'A Master Plan for the Three Pyramids of Giza Based on the Configuration of the Three Stars of the Belt of Orion', was published in the journal, *Discussions in Egyptology*, Vol. 13, 1989.

A wider thematic vision?

No plans or documents have survived in the archaeological record that can shed light on the rationale behind the revolutionary design of the true plane-sided pyramid – the central component of the royal funerary complex, or that can provide textual evidence for a possible thematic vision for the Giza group, or links with other pyramid fields along the western escarpment. This lack of textual evidence limits our ability to interpret the archaeological remains of this exciting period of innovative architectural developments. However, various clues found in the layout of the three complexes, in the ancient Egyptian sky and in the earliest surviving royal funerary texts inscribed within pyramids from the end of the Fifth Dynasty, might suggest a wider thematic vision for the Giza group. These texts provide the ideological background for the idea of an overall thematic vision inspired by the large striking constellation of Orion, or more specifically, the distinctive three-star asterism in Orion commonly known as Orion's Belt.

The angle of observation

The Giza pyramids are aligned to the cardinal points, and it seems only natural that if an attempt were made to represent Orion's distinctive three-star asterism in the site layout, a match should occur when the asterism was due south. However, no match occurred during the Old Kingdom (c. 2686–c. 2160 BC) – the era when the Giza pyramids were built. The angle from the centre of Khufu's pyramid to the centre of Menkaura's pyramid is 52.2 degrees south of west, but when the asterism was due south, the angle between the corresponding stars Alnitak and Mintaka was only 16.2 degrees. As a N/S meridian match with the Giza layout did not occur in the Old Kingdom, Orion was precessed nearly 8,000 years back in time, to c. 10,500 BC, when Orion was at its lowest in the precessional cycle. However, even going this far back in time is not enough for the asterism to match the Giza layout – Orion needs to be precessed a further 1,000 years for a close match. It seems highly unlikely the ancient Egyptians in the Old Kingdom were aware of precession and its effect on Orion over long periods, and could visualize how Orion appeared at its lowest point in the precessional cycle and represent this it at Giza. It also seems unlikely the layout was conceived by a civilization nine millennia further back in time from the Fourth Dynasty. However, going so far back in time to find a close match is unnecessary, as one *can* be found in the Fourth Dynasty, although not due south as might be expected. At some point in the south-eastern sky as Orion was rising, Alnitak and Saiph aligned vertically, a useful aid and reference line if the relative positions of the three stars within the asterism needed to be roughly determined. When Alnitak and Saiph aligned vertically (52.2 degrees south of east), the asterism in Orion closely matched the Giza layout. Interestingly, this mirrored the angle between Khufu and Menkaura's pyramids, which is 52.2 degrees west of south. According to the Pyramid Texts, the 'Field of Offerings' where the 'Imperishable Stars' are found was founded by means of a plumb-line (Pyramid Texts, 1,196). This may be an allusion to vertical alignments of stars in the sky that may have been an aid in 'founding' the royal funerary complexes.

This link between the Giza layout and Orion in the south-eastern sky is also highlighted by another interesting clue that involves all the pyramid fields between Saqqara in the south and Abu Rawash in the north. Looking south-east from Djedefra's pyramid at Abu Rawash, 8.5 km north-west from the Giza pyramids, the pyramid fields along the western escarpment overlooking the Nile valley as far as Saqqara lie on, or are either side of a straight line, beginning with the pyramid of Djedefra (son of Khufu) at the extreme northern end, and ending with the pyramid of Userkaf (son of Menkaura and great-grandson of Khufu) in the south. Userkaf's complex was built right up against the north-east corner of Netjerikhet's (Djoser) 13ha funerary complex that dominated the Saqqara necropolis. When Orion's three-star asterism was above Userkaf's and Netjerikhet's complexes, viewed from anywhere along this line of pyramid fields, it closely matched the Giza layout when viewed from north of the Giza site looking south. Interestingly, the appearance of the asterism in the sky due south, closely matched the Giza layout when viewed from the north-west looking south-east along the 52.2 degree line that highlighted the asterism in the south-eastern sky when it closely matched the Giza layout. A direct line between Djedefra and Userkaf/Netjerikhet has a bearing of 52.2 degrees south of east, and runs past the two important pyramid fields of Giza and Abusir. Both these pyramid fields extend away from the line to the north-east towards the edge of the escarpment, and are roughly oriented towards the important religious centre of Iunu. Clearly, the general south-east direction of the escarpment dictated the line-up of these pyramid fields, but not exactly, as not all follow the edge of the escarpment. The two Zawyet el-Aryan pyramids are near the edge, but Djedefra's funerary complex is about 2 km, and Menkaura's about 1 km from the edge. The preferred site for these funerary complexes was usually high ground where they could be clearly seen over long distances – they were certainly not hiding their tombs as in later times.

Pyramids as 'stars'?

The pyramids are distinctive landmarks, and in their pristine state, with their white polished limestone casings that reflected the sun, moon and starlight, meant the pyramids shone brightly in a sea of sand during the day, and shone with an ethereal gleam at night. As the sun rose over the eastern horizon, the first rays of sunlight lit up the apexes of the pyramids causing them to shine like stars in an otherwise dark landscape – an awe-inspiring line of beacons/'stars' along the western escarpment. The same effect happened when the last rays of sunlight lit the apexes as the sun set in the west, when all else was in shadow.

At the southern end of the line of pyramid fields, the name of Netjerikhet's Third Dynasty funerary complex at Saqqara, was 'Horus is the Star at the Head of the Sky' (Quirke/Helck), or 'Star of Horus, Foremost of the Sky' (in the Pyramid Texts, Horus was called the 'Morning Star'). At the northern end, the name of Djedefra's (Radjedef) pyramid was sHdw Dd=f ra, 'Radjedef's Star' (J. P. Allen). One of the two pyramids at Zawyet el-Aryan, roughly midway between Abu Rawash and Saqqara, was named 'Nebka is a Star' (Edwards).

The true meaning and implications of these explicit stellar names, only become apparent in the earliest surviving royal funerary texts inscribed within pyramids from the end of the Fifth Dynasty. Unas the king (the first king to have 'son of Ra' included in his cartouche), purified himself with the cool water of the stars and bathed in the starry firmament (Pyramid Texts, 138), the 'Imperishable Stars' raised Unas aloft (Pyramid Texts, 139), and Unas guided the 'Imperishable Stars' (Pyramid Texts, 373). Unas was born as a star, and he appeared as a star (Pyramid Texts, 262). Unas opened his place in the sky among the stars of the sky, for he was the 'Lone or Unique Star' (Pyramid Texts, 251). Atum, the 'father' of Unas, assigned Unas to the excellent and wise gods, the 'Imperishable Stars' (Pyramid Texts, 380). He was a son of Sopdet (personification of Sirius, the brightest star in their sky) (Pyramid Texts, 458), and was given a warrant as Great Power by Sah (Orion), 'father of the gods' (Pyramid Texts, 408).

This text, from Utterance 273-4, is regarded as one of the oldest of the corpus of texts found within Fifth–Seventh Dynasty pyramids. Referring to Utterance 273-4, Badawy states: 'At least one of the pyramid spells mentioning Orion belongs to the older stock since it occurs in the context of the so-called Cannibal Hymn' (Badawy 1964: p. 199).

The 'warrant' granted by Sah to the king, may be an allusion to a celestial, 'afterlife' version of a title deed, held in the king's hand when he performed the ceremonial *heb-sed* run, and thought to be a legal document legitimizing the king's right to rule the unified land of Upper and Lower Egypt, or as Lehner states: '. . . the household deed to the whole of Egypt' (Lehner 1997: 92).

Beneath the Third Dynasty Step Pyramid and its 'South Tomb', depictions of Netjerikhet performing the ceremonial *heb-sed* run and holding the 'title deed' are found. 'The step pyramid includes numerous architectural elements designed to perpetuate the role of the king in the afterlife. Symbolic components of the royal palace complex from which the king could rule for eternity. Elements associated with the celebration of the heb-sed (festival of rejuvenation of the kingship) express the desire to maintain the king's ruleship in the netherworld' (Wegner 2002: p.72).

From the Fifth Dynasty pyramid of Unas: 'Sah (Orion) is encircled by the Duat, pure and living in the horizon. Sopdet (Sirius) is encircled by the Duat, pure and living in the horizon. I am (the king) encircled by the Duat, pure and living in the horizon. It is well with me and with them. It is pleasant for me and for them, within the arms of my father, within the arms of Atum' (Pyramid Texts, 151).

The ideogram for Duat (N15) is a five-pointed star in a circle – an encircled star – just as the dead king who appeared as a star was encircled by the Duat. Like the classic ancient Egyptian five-pointed star motif that 'decorated' the royal funerary complexes, the pyramid has five points that define its form – the four corner points and the apex. Three early pyramids had names that were explicitly stellar. Evidence from the end of the Fifth–Sixth Dynasty, shows that the pyramid itself was believed to be the body of the king, and the king after his death was reborn as a star, and appeared as a star – 'O Atum, set your arms about the king, about this construction, and about this pyramid as the arms of a Ka-symbol, that the King's essence may be in it, enduring forever' (Pyramid Texts, 1653).

Piankoff noted: 'The pyramids were personified (C. Wilke, 'Zur Personifikation von Pyramiden', ZÄS, LXX [1934], 56–83), and the title of the queens of Dyn.VI shows that the name of the royal pyramid stood for the name of the deceased himself. Thus the daughter of Unas is the royal daughter of the body of the (the pyramid) 'Perfect are the Places of Unas'; see P. Montet, 'Reines et Pyramides,' Kemi, XIV (1957), 92–101) (from 'The Pyramid of Unas', Piankoff 1968: p.4).

The names of the pyramids, 'Djedefra's Star' and 'Nebka is a Star', suggests the royal funerary ideology was significantly influenced by the starry sky in the Fourth Dynasty. Ra the sun god was becoming popular with royalty at this time, and the name of the sun god, the brightest celestial body in their sky was incorporated into the name of Khufu's son, Djedefra. However the explicitly stellar name of his pyramid shows that the royal funerary beliefs also had an important stellar content. The king appeared as a star – a brilliant star, who travelled far, and daily brought products from far away to Ra (Pyramid Texts, 263).

A simulation of the night sky over Giza in the Fouth Dynasty, shows the three-star asterism in Orion closely matched the layout of the three pyramids at Giza when the asterism was 52.2 degs south-of-east. The line up of pyramid fields along the western escarpment highlighted the asterism as the line from Djedefra in the north to Userkaf/Netjerikhet in the south was also 52.2 degs south of east, which mirrored the angle of the Giza layout. This meant that Sah (Orion) the 'father of the gods' was 'standing upright' – 'alive' after rising from lying 'dead' on his side in the east – a metaphor used by the Egyptians to illustrate the king rising up, from being dead on his side, to standing up, alive in his celestial realm.

The main deities attested at Giza are Horus, Hathor (lit. House of Horus) Seth, Thoth and Anubis. The name of the god Khnum was incorporated into the full name of Khnum Khufu, which shows he was also an important deity. The name of the sun god Ra, was incorporated into the names of Khufu's sons and grandson, Djedefra, Khafra, and Menkaura, and the epithet 'son of Ra' first appears with Djedefra, which shows Ra was a major player at this time also, although the cult of Ra found a fuller expression with the building of sun temples during the Fifth Dynasty. From the later Pyramid Texts, Ra was the brother of both Sah (Orion) and Sopdet (Sirius) (Pyramid Texts, 2126). Sah, Sopdet and the northern 'Imperishable Stars' played a significant role in the royal funerary beliefs, and when the explicit stellar names of at least three pyramids from the Third and Fourth Dynasties are considered, it seems a reasonable assumption that these stars were also included in the royal funerary beliefs then. If the upper southern shaft in Khufu's pyramid linked to Sah (Orion) and the layout of the Giza group was a realization of a thematic vision for the Giza site that involved Sah, this reflected only one aspect of their multi layered belief system.

The so-called 'star-shafts'

Robert Bauval is not alone in noticing a possible link between the Giza pyramids and Sah (Orion). In 1954, Egyptologist Dr Alexander Badawy, proposed that a link between Khufu's pyramid and the Orion constellation was incorporated into the design of the pyramid. He theorized that the upper shafts in Khufu's pyramid should be '. . . considered as open ways for the king's soul to reach the circumpolar stars to the North and the Orion constellation, to the South'

(Badawy, 1954, p.138). Badawy provided the ancient Egyptian religious/funerary rationale behind these stellar links in his 1964 paper 'The Stellar Destiny of Pharoah and the So-Called Air-Shafts of Cheops' Pyramid', and in her accompanying article, 'Astronomical investigation concerning the so-called air-shafts of Cheop's pyramid', the astronomer Virginia Trimble, showed how the three-star asterism in Orion, '. . . passed once each day, at culmination directly over the southern shaft of the Great Pyramid at the time it was built'.

Dr I.E.S. Edwards, who was Emeritus Keeper of Egyptian Antiquities in the British Museum, and one of the leading authorities on the pyramids: 'Symbolism was one of the most important features in Egyptian funerary and temple architecture. Its interpretation is often difficult, either because too little is known about the source of its inspiration or because elements have become stylized and their original hard to recognize. Dr Badawy devoted a number of articles to various aspects of this subject; they show that he had a deep understanding of the mentality of the ancient Egyptians and of the conventions which they observed. His articles on the so-called air shafts of the Great Pyramid paved the way to the final elucidation of these features – so long a puzzle to students.'

If, as Badawy proposed, the upper shafts connected to the sarcophagus chamber, linked to Orion in the south, and the circumpolar stars in the north, they can in principle be astronomically dated, as astronomer Virginia Trimble showed. If the three-star asterism in Orion and the Pole or North Star, Thuban, were the 'targets', then using survey data from the top ends of the shafts, the astronomically derived date for both shafts is *c.* 2570 BC ± 10 years, which is well within the estimated time for Khufu's reign (*c.* 2590–2550 BC ± 50 years).

You have your tomb, O King, which belongs to the heart of Him whose seats are hidden; he opens for you the doors of the sky, he throws open for you the doors of the firmament(?), he makes a road for you that you may ascend by means of it into the company of the gods, you being alive in your bird shape. (Pyramid Texts, 1,943)

These small architectural components within the royal funerary complex may have linked to Sah (Orion) the 'father of the gods' and with the northern 'Imperishable Stars' (*ixm.w-sk*, lit. 'those who do not know destruction'), who were described in the royal funerary texts as *akhs* (spirits) and gods. The Old Kingdom Pyramid Texts describe how the king ascended to the sky among the Imperishable Stars, his sister was Sopdet (Sirius), his guide was the Morning Star (Horus) and they grasped his hand at the 'Field of Offerings' (Pyramid Texts, 1,123b). Horus of the Duat, the 'Morning Star' (Pyramid Texts, 1,207), set the king to be a magistrate among the akhs (spirits), the 'Imperishable Stars' in the north of the sky . . . (Pyramid Texts, 1,220).

A stairway to the sky was set up for the king among the 'Imperishable stars' (Pyramid Texts, 1,941), and he went to the northern gods the 'Imperishable Stars' (Pyramid Texts, 818c). The king guided the 'Imperishable Stars' (Pyramid Texts, 373), and was the head of the akhs (spirits), the 'Imperishable Stars' (Pyramid Texts, 656c). The king became an 'Imperishable Star', son of the sky goddess who dwelt in the 'Mansion of Selket' (Pyramid Texts, 1,469a). On later 'astronomical' ceilings, Selket was depicted in the northern sky near Meskhetiu, the Plough/Big Dipper asterism, also an 'Imperishable' (Pyramid Texts, 458).

Sah (Orion) in the southern sky was one of at least two distinctive star patterns the ancient Egyptians recognised and incorporated into their funerary ideology. In the earliest surviving royal funerary texts inscribed within the pyramids from the end of the Fifth Dynasty, Sah was the 'father of the gods' – the gods referred to were probably the *akhs* (spirits) of the dead kings, who became 'Imperishable Stars' or gods/great ones. The king was a great star, the companion of Sah (Orion), who traversed the sky with Sah, who navigated the Duat with Wsir. The king ascended from the east of the sky, and was renewed at his due season and rejuvenated at his due time, and the sky bore the king with Sah (Pyramid Texts, 882–3).

The ancient Egyptians observed celestial cycles and used them to decide the date of their festivals and the correct timing of rituals. A fragment of a relief assigned to chamber A, from the chapel of Kawab's *mastaba* (Fourth Dyn), shows the crescent moon (N11) placed horizontally over the five-pointed star (N14) that when combined was the ideogram for 'month'. According to Gardiner, this showed 'time as indicated by stars'. This suggests observations of celestial cycles were a vital part of the temple work that determined the right or potent time for ritual practices and keep track of their sacred calendar. Pyramid Text, 269, may be an allusion to observations of timekeeping stars, 'O you who are over the hours, who are before Ra . . .' The stars accompanied Ra the sun god as he traversed the sky, but the light of the rising sun completely overwhelmed the light of these stars. From the cenotaph of Sety I: 'As he (Ra) sails inside the dusk, these stars are behind him . . . these sailing stars enter after him, and come forth from him.'

'The end of the year was equated with death and burial, and the new year was equated with resurrection. The Wag festival was the great festival of the dead. On those occasions, ceremonies and processions took place in the temples and in the necropolis' (Englund, 2002: 282). The important Wag festival is attested in the Fourth Dynasty, and mentioned in the Pyramid Texts (716) – 'cows in suck' were slaughtered for the king, and Sah (Orion) was 'Lord of Wine' in this festival. The king was conceived with Sah by the sky – the dawn light bore the king with Sah. The king regularly ascended with Sah from the eastern region of the sky, and regularly descended with Sah into the western region of the sky – Sopdet (Sirius) guided the king on the goodly roads which are in the sky in the Field of Rushes.

Realising a thematic vision at the Giza site

To make effective use of the Giza site, three suitable building plots may have been marked out on the Giza plateau, leaving the design of the separate funerary complexes up to the architects responsible for each design – a simple ordered planning of the site that takes into account the constraints of the terrain, potential quarries etc., and a possible thematic vision that reflected an aspect of the royal funerary ideology. This would ensure that each individual project could begin with the minimum of fuss. The people responsible for designing and building the royal funerary complex and for realizing a possible thematic vision for the site, were the architects/master builders, overseers of the stone masons, overseers of the quarry men, transportation etc. involved in the building of each complex, whose main concern was that each individual project should progress as quickly and efficiently as possible. Often they were unable to finish the royal funerary complex according to the original specifications, as the kings sometimes died before the complex was completed. However, they ensured the royal cult complex could function, and the king could be buried securely within his pyramid. Key officials responsible for the royal building works, were involved in more than one project, as there are examples of high officials in the Old Kingdom, responsible for the royal building works, and served more than one king.

Some part of each complex may have been marked out when the Giza plateau was chosen as a suitable site, for example the centres of the pyramids, centres of the eastern baselines where the royal cult complexes were built, or the centres of the northern baselines where, for example, the entrance to Menkaura's pyramid is located. The detailed design of the complex was left up to the architects responsible for an individual king's complex. A coherent overall plan could have been achieved gradually as each architect followed similar design rules that considered or dictated the positional relationships between pyramids built at the same site. This still allows freedom for individual complexes to express aspects of the royal funerary ideology in their own distinctive way, and also allows for an overall thematic vision for the site, but this only meant that each king built his complex at a predetermined location that satisfied practical and ideological concerns.

The king planned his complex in any case, and he was free to design it how he wished. Building it at a location that had the additional 'magic' of being part of a wider thematic idea might have seemed very attractive, similar to Userkaf building his complex right up next to the north-east corner of Netjerikhet's Third Dynasty enclosure wall. It seems he wanted to associate his 'house of eternity' with this huge sacred site that dominated the Saqqara necropolis, as if something of the 'magic' of the place might rub off on his.

It has been argued that if a thematic idea was envisaged for Giza, why did successive kings not build at Giza? Dr Jaromir Malek gave some possible explanations why it was not usual for successive kings to build next to each other:

One can, in fact, find only one case where the pyramids of two successive kings were built in relative proximity, those of Sahure and Neferirkare. The inescapable conclusion is that a new pyramid was built at some distance from that of the preceding king, often at a different 'site' (the division of the Memphite necropolis into 'sites' is modern). The following were the most probable reasons:

1. *In the case of the predecessor's unexpected death, the site was so encumbered with the remnants of the building activities, in particular massive building ramps, that the planning, site survey and building work on the new pyramid could not have started until this situation was resolved.*
2. *If the predecessor's pyramid was complete at the time of his death, the surrounding area would have already been at least partly occupied by the tombs of priests and officials. The proximity of quarries, easy transport and access to the prospective building site would have been of great importance but, in view of the enormous ideological significance of the pyramids, it is impossible to reduce the decision-making to these considerations. Other explanations offered in the past, such as feuding within the royal family or the location of the royal palaces, are even less convincing. The idea that the distribution of the pyramids is governed by definable ideological (religious, astronomical, or similar) considerations is attractive . . . (Orion and the Giza pyramids by Jaromir Malek, Discussions in Egyptology 30, 1994, pp 101–114)*

One objection to the idea of a wider thematic scheme for the Giza group, is that kings were only concerned with the design of their own complex and gave little thought to other complexes nearby. It is true that each funerary complex was independent, and self-contained, and the architectural components that made up these complexes expressed some aspect of the royal funerary ideology – the entrance on the northern side for example, was perhaps a link with the northern 'Imperishable Stars', and/or the cooling north wind.

Each component of the royal funerary complex had either a practical function, and/or satisfied ideological concerns, but the overall site layout may also have been an expression of one aspect of the royal funerary ideology that appears to have been an intricate mesh of traditional and new ideas, sometimes apparently contradictory ideas as the priests were kept busy rearranging the order of heaven to adapt to developments in the king's beliefs in the afterlife. Primarily, ideas both traditional and new were centred around night and day celestial phenomena, and to understand and explain the architectural rationale behind the designs, the sky with all its fascinating aspects, needs to be factored in.

If an association with Sah (Orion) was intended for the Giza layout, then what was seen in the sky – three points of light – two in line and one slightly offset, with the outer stars almost equidistant from the middle star – were simply drawn by eye, and given to the surveyors for scaling up to fit an appropriate site. No accurate measurements of the asterism were necessary, as simply drawing by eye would have sufficed. The oldest graphic representation of Orion's three-star asterism is thought to be depicted on the New Kingdom ceiling of Sennemut's tomb at Deir el-Bahri. Here the slight offset of the end star is 3 degrees. The actual offset in the asterism in the sky is 7 degrees, and at Giza, the centre of Menkaura's pyramid is offset from the others by 11.5 degrees or 6.6 degrees if the centre of the eastern baselines where the royal cult complexes were built, are compared.

It has also been argued that if the Giza layout was designed to be a symbolic representation of the asterism, then the north/south directions are reversed – north in the sky is south on the ground – in effect, 'turning Egypt upside down', invalidating the idea of a symbolic representation of the asterism, at Giza. However, if the correct directionality is preserved, an 'unnatural' mirror image of the asterism is created, and a mirror image is not a symbolic or natural representation of what is seen in the sky.

When representing the natural world, the ancient Egyptians took each individual element and represented it as clearly and naturally as possible despite inconsistencies. In a painting of a pond from a tomb in Thebes, the pond is depicted in plan view, as if it were seen from above, but the fish, geese and trees are painted as seen from the side. Does this mean that the ancient Egyptian thought that fish swam on their sides or that trees grew horizontally along the ground? Of course not. It could be said that they 'cannot have it both ways', either they needed to change the view of the pond to conform with the rest of the scene, or the fish, geese and trees needed to be changed to conform to the overhead view of the pond.

Their design conventions however dictated that each individual element in the scene was depicted as it appeared most natural, despite the obvious contradictions. A relief portrait of Hesira, carved into the wooden door of his tomb (c. 2650 BC) also gives valuable insights into how the mind of an ancient Egyptian artisan worked, and the stylistic conventions or rules they were using. Everything had to be represented from its most characteristic angle. The head was most easily seen in profile so they drew it sideways. But if we think of the human eye we think of it as seen from the front. Accordingly, a full face eye was planted into the side view of the face. The top half of the body, the shoulders and chest, are best seen from the front, for then we see how the arms are hinged to the body. But arms and feet in movement are much more clearly seen sideways. That is the reason Egyptians in these pictures look flat and contorted. Moreover, the Egyptian artists found it hard to visualize either foot seen from the outside. They preferred the clear outline from the big toe upwards. So both feet are seen from the inside, and Hesira on the relief looks as if he had two left feet.

Even an architect today, given the task of representing the three-star asterism on the ground as three pyramids, would probably arrive at the same solution as can be seen at Giza. If the ancient Egyptians represented the three stars as three pyramids, and linked to the stars using shafts or 'model' passageways directed up at the sky from the main chambers in Khufu's pyramid, then the way they did it was 'right' and natural according to their way of looking at things, though modern astronomers might complain about Egypt being turned upside down and 'logical inconsistencies' in the design.

Astronomical ceilings

Sopdet (Sirius) and Sah (Orion) with the decans of the Sah group are depicted in the New Kingdom tomb of Senenmut, on the southern part of the ceiling and in the centre of the upper register. Some decan stars belonging to Sah are described as in the upper part or above Sah and in the lower part or under Sah. If the creators of this 'astronomical' ceiling thought that 'up' or 'over' was north they would have described the decan stars as in the northern part or north of Sah. They did not describe it this way however, which suggests their descriptions of 'upper'/'over' or 'lower'/'under' was the natural way they understood celestial directions in this context. This is not all this 'astronomical' ceiling can tell us about how the ancient Egyptians thought about celestial directions and the way they depicted the sky. The flat ceiling is divided into a southern and northern half. The upper part of Sah (Orion) in the southern half of the ceiling, is further away from the northern half of the ceiling than the lower part of Sah. Modern-day astronomy purists could complain that the artisans had 'turned Egypt upside down' – to depict the sky correctly the scene in the southern half of the ceiling should be flipped over. Only by doing this will the upper stars in Sah (Orion) be nearer to the northern part of the sky.

As evidenced by this New Kingdom 'astronomical' ceiling, the ancient Egyptians did not in this case, describe stars that were higher in the sky or lower down near the horizon as north or south of lower or higher stars, and did not seem too concerned or were even aware that they had inadvertently turned Egypt upside down in this picture.

The tomb of Sety I (1294–1279), built 180 years after Senenmut's tomb, has a similar 'astronomical' ceiling divided into two halves. However, some interesting differences are immediately apparent – the ceiling is not flat but has a shallow 'elliptical' curved profile, and the corresponding part of the ceiling to where Sopdet (Sirius) and Sah (Orion) are depicted is oriented correctly compared with the other half of the ceiling. The upper parts of each picture meet at the centre of the ceiling, whereas in the two pictures in Senenmut's tomb, the upper part of the northern half of the ceiling meets with the lower part of the picture on the southern half of the ceiling.

The ceiling in the tomb of Rameses VI (1143 –1136) is similar to Sety I, but the ceiling of the temple of Rameses II (1279–1213) in Luxor, has an arrangement similar to Senenmut's ceiling with the upper part of Sah (Orion) further away from the upper part of the northern group. The scenes are laid out in 'strips' one on top of another that is very similar to a surviving water clock from Karnak dated to Amenhotep III (1390–1352), where similar 'astronomical' scenes are arranged in three strips one on top of another that circle around the water container.

These 'astronomical' ceilings, are not maps of the sky, and whatever conclusions that can be drawn from these should be treated with caution. 'The survival of material specifically related to funerary practices dominates what we think we know about ancient Egyptian capabilities.' Funerary art found in tombs and inside coffins that depict sky scenes, met religious/funerary requirements – ritual magic etc, and probably do not give a true picture of their 'technical' knowledge of the sky that was needed for calendar development, time keeping, navigation in the desert, and the surveying techniques needed for the orientation of sacred buildings. However these examples clearly reveal something of the mind set of the artisans.

The so-called 'Giza diagonal'

Egyptologist Mark Lehner has spent years studying the Giza Necropolis, and although he has not found any evidence for an overall plan for the necropolis, has investigated the evidence for various alignments that may have partly determined the location of successive pyramids relative to each other and to other features within and outside the necropolis. 'When it came time to build Khafre's Pyramid, the alignments with Khufu's Pyramid may have been consciously and carefully chosen as the layout lines were surveyed. At the same time, the design of the necropolis, from one complex to the next, was not so much a premeditated pattern laid down from the very beginning of Khufu's reign, as an organic development in which some thematic considerations may have been accommodated to certain geological and topographical constraints' (Lehner, 1985)

The Giza 'diagonal', has been noted by Lehner. A line connecting the SE corners of Menkaura and Khufu's pyramids is parallel with a line connecting the centres of Khafra and Khufu's pyramids. The NE direction of the Giza 'diagonal' is about 43.3 degs east of north, which means that if this 'diagonal' is extended to the north-east it will be heading in the general direction of Iunu. This bearing is interesting as it has the same angle as the slope of the corner edge of Khafra's pyramid, and it closely approximates the angle of incline of the upper part of Sneferu's southern pyramid at Dahshur, which suggests the master builders/architects, were designing the complexes according to common design rules. Egyptologists (including Lehner), who have studied and worked at the Giza and Abusir pyramid fields, have supported the idea that both these pyramid fields were aligned with the great religious centre of Iunu across the river to the north-east. If this is true, then all the architects involved in these more than half a dozen royal funerary complexes, were following the same alignment strategy that persisted through many generations. This same idea influenced the location of the royal funerary complex in relation to the other complexes in the same group – in other words there may have been constraints other than the purely practical that determined the location of an individual complex in relation to others in the same group. Ideological considerations, the positional relationships between complexes close to each other, and with other groups further away, and/or to an important sacred site outside the necropolis, apart from practical concerns, may also have influenced the overall process of designing and building a royal funerary complex.

In a sometimes frustratingly complex world we try to keep things simple, and 'the constraints of topography' argument, with other practical considerations, is seen as a simple, practical explanation that can logically explain most of we need to know about the Giza layout, but this emphasis on the purely practical can divert attention from other important design considerations that are not so immediately obvious. The constraints of the terrain were taken into account, and the need for the sides of the pyramid to have clear views to the cardinal directions was probably important. The presence of quarries also placed constraints on the decision making process, but as Malek has suggested: 'The proximity of quarries, easy transport and access to the prospective building site would have been of great importance but, in view of the enormous ideological significance of the pyramids, it is impossible to reduce the decision-making to these considerations.'

If a wider thematic vision was envisaged for the Giza site, then this would of course mean that close cooperation between the people in charge of the three individual projects was necessary to ensure that they all conformed to the wider plan that integrated the separate complexes into a coherent whole. The people in charge of the royal building works were often closely related members of the same extended royal family, sometimes father and son. From Sneferu through to Menkaura, the 'overseers' of the king's grandiose funerary projects were probably a close-knit fraternity, with a common aim and purpose. They were working together in the development of a revolutionary and exciting design for the royal tomb involving new architectural and structural innovations, probably influenced by developments in the royal funerary ideology. Some high officials served more than one king, and their knowledge, experience and a possible thematic vision was passed on to the next generation of architects/builders.

The royal funerary complexes were built for the extended family of Khufu, in the same extended necropolis along the west bank of the river between 'The White Wall' and Iunu, and if evidence of possible common alignment strategies that linked these complexes together or with the great religious centre at Iunu are noticed, it should come as no surprise. The team of architects/master builders and overseers may also have realized a thematic vision for Giza, inspired by an aspect of the royal funerary ideology that looked to the sky – the sun, moon, planets and the stars for the king's hopes of an eternal afterlife.

The Cosmic Order, the Egyptian Calendar and Christianity

At least 5,000 years separate us from the origin of the pharaonic civilisation. Two thousand years separate us from its final demise. But thanks to the prowess of its ancient builders in raising massive monuments in stone, the obsession of its people with the afterlife and the preservation of the corpse in the tomb, and the use of stone by its scribes to inscribe hieroglyphs, we know more about this ancient civilisation than we know of the alleged biblical civilisation. In contrast to the prolific archaeological evidence for the pharaonic civilisation (there is so much of it that it has even filled museums outside Egypt), there is not one shred of archaeological evidence to buttress the written history of the Old Testament. In view of this glaring reality, some authors have started to claim that biblical narratives are nothing but a pseudo-mythical history probably culled in part from the real history of ancient Egypt.[1]

Until the late eighteenth century of our era, pharaonic Egypt remained a blurred memory, almost a dream. In Europe during the Dark Ages and the Renaissance the Western psyche was befuddled by rumours and inaccurate reports brought back by lone travellers, and it was not until Napoleon's invasion of Egypt in 1798 that the pharaonic civilisation was reawakened in its historical reality. Fortunately, Napoleon had brought along with him a group of scientists and artists who began to systematically record the ancient monuments along the Nile and who started the orderly collection of ancient artefacts. Part of the legacy left by these early Egyptologists was the Institut Français in Cairo, the scientific embryo that would eventually serve as the role model for the various foreign archaeological institutes that would sprout in Egypt and, more importantly, for the future Egyptian Antiquities Department that would be founded in 1856 by the intrepid Frenchman Auguste Mariette Pasha (and which in 1994 was renamed the Supreme Council of Antiquities, or SCA).

By the time Naopoleon's scientists rediscovered ancient Egypt, the country had suffered several centuries of foreign occupation and experienced many internal wars, and its ancient monuments and tombs had endured many centuries of ruthless plunder. The Persians were the first to come, in 525 BC and occupied the country till 380 BC (and a second time from 365 to 332 BC). It was during these two Persian occupations that so much damage was done to the pharaonic legacy, not only materially but also spiritually. The Persians were finally ousted in 332 BC by Alexander the Great, whose leading general, Ptolemy son of Lagos, founded the so-called Ptolemaic dynasty at Alexandria in 305 BC. The Ptolemies, in contrast to the Persians, were enlightened masters who, rather than destroy and plunder, restored the ancient temples and built many new ones along the Nile. At Alexandria they founded a new capital which, with its celebrated library, university and museum, became the principal source of scientific and philosophical enlightenment for many centuries.

All this, however, was rudely interrupted by the arrival of the Roman legions under Augustus Caesar in 30 BC. Egypt became a Roman province and the pharaonic civilisation was no more. It was mostly under the Romans, and especially later under the Christians, that the legacy of pharaonic Egypt suffered the most. Temples were deliberately destroyed or converted into churches, and in AD 491 the few that still practised the old religion were officially closed and their priests and priestesses killed or banished. The last stand was at the temple of Isis on the island of Philae which, in AD 550, was ransacked by Christian monks and turned into a basilica. Within a few decades the old religion had been forgotten, and even the hieroglyphs could no longer be understood by their own people. The country had totally converted to the new faith of Christianity, with the Christianised Egyptians becoming known as the Copts. Ironically, it was the Copts, more than the foreigners, who turned against their 'pagan' origins with venom. Yet, even more ironically, the 3,000 years of the old religion was too deeply entrenched both on the land itself and also in the collective unconscious of the people. The old religion, refusing simply to die, entered into the bloated body of Roman Christianity and there lay dormant like a virus, occasionally releasing its subtle and subliminal influence. There is no doubt that a great deal of the iconography and mythology of Christianity was borrowed from that of ancient Egypt. Isis and the child Horus become the Virgin and the child Jesus, and even the passion of the dying and resurrected man-god Osiris served as a model for the passion of the Christ.[2] But another, perhaps less well-known legacy of ancient Egypt that affects our daily life even today is its calendar.

The origin of the Egyptian calendar is fraught with controversy and uncertainty. Egyptologists are constantly split as to when it was invented and even whether there existed more than one calendar running at the same time. The subject is so vast and so controversial that it is well outside the scope of this book to do it full justice here. Only a cursory view is possible. We have already dealt in Chapter Two with the debate regarding the origin of the Egyptian civil calendar, so we will leave that issue aside. Suffice here to say that the consensus is that the civil calendar was put into practice – if not actually invented – in 2781 BC, when the heliacal rising of Sirius coincided by fluke with the summer solstice and the start of a Sothic cycle. The Egyptian calendar – indeed as all other ancient calendars – was not intended for pedestrian usage such as the public administration of agriculture or tax levies, as is often claimed, but for purely religious purposes, and above all to keep track of the many annual feasts and ceremonies that were associated with the cycles of the sun, moon and the constellations. At first most Egyptologists were convinced that the ancient Egyptians had three calendars operating side by side: an old lunar-Sothic calendar that was regulated with the heliacal rising of Sirius; and a 365-day civil calendar regulated probably by the annual solar cycle but left to drift or 'glide' through the season at the rate of ¼ day per year, and a second lunar-civil calendar that was attached to the 365-day civil calendar. Even though the Egyptologists themselves readily admit that there is precious little evidence to support this three-calendar hypothesis, they nonetheless argue that if only the civil calendar was operational then it would have been impossible to fix dates for all those religious feasts linked to seasonal events, such as the feasts related to the inundation of the Nile. Whereas by assuming the existence of an old lunar-Sothic calendar that kept in line with the seasons, the problem was solved.

The originator of the three-calendar hypothesis was the chronologist Richard Parker, who published his finding in 1950. In Parker's own words:

> Exactly when the second lunar calendar was introduced remains uncertain, but it was probably not too long after the divergence of the two forms of year (civil and lunar) became apparent. A good guess might be to put it in the neighbourhood of 2500 BC. From that date the Egyptians had three calendar years, all of which continued in use to the very end of pagan Egypt.[3]

In recent years, however, several chronologists have challenged Parker's three-calendars hypothesis. The Spanish astronomer Juan A. Belmonte Aviles even went as far as to claim that only one calendar was operational throughout Egyptian history, and that was the civil calendar of 365 days.[4] It is not, however, my objective here to discuss the merits or faults of the many calendar theories regarding ancient Egypt. We can all agree that the civil calendar had existed since at least 2781 BC, and also, in my opinion, that an older lunar-Sothic calendar was also used for the purpose of keeping the date of religious feasts in line with the seasons. I think that the argument I have presented in Chapter Six regarding the 'jubilee date', strongly supports (if not proves) the hypothesis that such a lunar-Sothic calendar was in use by temple priests for their religious needs.

At any rate, it is known for certain that the civil calendar was operational in Egypt from *c.* 2781 BC until Roman times. Legend has it that in October 48 BC the young and beautiful queen Cleopatra VII introduced herself to Julius Caesar by rolling out of a carpet totally naked. Caesar was then a ripe 52, she a tender 22. The Roman poet Lucan (AD 39–65) claims that it was love at first sight between Caesar and Cleopatra, and that the couple made love that very night. A few weeks later Cleopatra threw a sumptuous party in honour of Caesar, where she dazzled everyone with her beauty by wearing a dress made of Sidon fabric that revealed 'her white breasts' and her hair decorated with garlands of roses. It was during this opulent Alexandrine soirée that Caesar was told about the Egyptian civil calendar by the scholar Acoreus. According to David Ewing Duncan, author of the bestselling book *The Calendar*: 'It was during this conversation that Caesar heard about Egypt's reliance on the sun for its year – measured by the annual rise of Sirius in the eastern sky and by the flooding of the Nile, which, the Alexandrian sage (Acoreus) said, "did not arouse its water before the shining of the Dog-star (Sirius)."'[5] Caesar then asked the court astronomer, Sosigenes, to create a new calendar for Rome based on the Egyptian civil calendar.

Sosigenes was the author of several books about the stars (all now lost) and was thus well-aware of the ¼-day difference between the true solar year and the civil calendar. But he also knew that the Egyptian priests had always refused to tamper with the calendar because of the sacred oath they had taken. In spite of this, he advised Caesar to add an extra day every four years (the 'leap year') in order to keep the calendar in line with the solar cycle and the seasons. This produced the so-called Julian calendar, which was in use in Rome and throughout Europe until the late sixteenth century. In 1582, however, it became obvious that the calendar had again slipped away from the seasons by about 10 days. This was because the true solar year is 365.2423 days and not, as Sosigenes had assumed, 365.25 days. The Julian calendar had thus increased by 11 minutes each year so that by the sixteenth century it was 10 days ahead of the seasons. Under Pope Gregory XIII the Julian calendar was reformed, and this produced the Gregorian calendar we are still using today. The Gregorian calendar is basically the same as the Julian calendar except that every so often a fine-tuning is needed in order to keep it in line with the seasons.[6]

Contemporary texts make it certain that in Cleopatra's time the 'New Year's Day' was celebrated at the heliacal rising of Sirius.[7] This conjunction was also associated with Isis, so it is not surprising that Cleopatra, like many Ptolemaic queens before her, considered herself the reincarnation of Isis. In 48 BC, when she ascended the throne, the heliacal rising of Sirius took place on 22 July according to the then-newly introduced Julian calendar. In Ptolemaic times Isis was closely identified with Hathor, goddess of beauty, love and healing, whose great temple at Dendera had just been founded by Cleopatra's predecessor, Ptolemy Auletes. Cleopatra herself was represented on the walls of the Dendera temple as the goddess Isis. It was at Dendera that special celebrations took place for the New Year's Day on the heliacal rising of Sirius (22 July in the Julian calendar), when the star rose in alignment with the small temple of Isis located at the southern end of the Dendera complex.

Much later, when Rome became the centre of the new Christian religion, many of the attributes of Isis were allocated to the Virgin Mary. Indeed, when Christianity became the official religion of the Roman empire, the cult of Isis had already spread far and wide, and many temples of Isis are known to have existed in Rome itself, as well as in Gaul (France) and even as far north as Oxford in England. Isis was the archetypal of the paragon of motherly devotion, and she slipped easily into the shoes of the Madonna. It is also likely, however, that in the primitive Christian Gnostic tradition, the combined goddess Isis-Hathor was identified with Mary Magdalene, the companion – perhaps even the lover, according to some accounts – of Jesus, whose ancient archetype was the dying-resurrecting man-god Osiris. It is perhaps not a coincidence, therefore, that the feast day of Mary Magdalene was also fixed on 22 July, the day of the heliacal rising of Sirius. This feast day was certainly established when the Julian calendar was still in use and, most probably, in Gnostic times. For it is known that the Gnostics had a special devotion for Mary Magdalene, and among the so-called Gnostic Texts found at Nag

Hamadi in 1946 was a complete Gospel of Mary Magdalene. Nag Hamadi, interestingly, is located only 40 kilometres from Dendera, where the goddess Isis-Hathor (whose feast day was determined by the heliacal rising of Sirius on 22 July) was venerated. As an aside, it is perhaps significant that when, in 1129, the Papal armies under the leadership of Arnold-Amalric attacked the Beziers stronghold of the Cathar 'heretics' – who are believed to have practised a primitive form of Christianity much resembling Gnosticism – they chose to storm the town on 22 July and rounded up the Cathar leaders in the church of Mary Magdalene where they had taken refuge.[8]

Recently the cult of Mary Magdalene has experienced a curious revival with the publication of Dan Brown's *The Da Vinci Code*. Dan Brown had popularised the controversial theory that Mary Magdalene was the favoured thirteenth apostle, and probably the secret wife of Christ, with whom he had a child and whose bloodline or 'holy blood' is none other than the true significance of the words Holy Grail, which in the defunct Cathar language can be transliterated as *sang real*, or 'holy blood'. In Dan Brown's book, much is made of Leonardo da Vinci's masterpiece, *The Last Supper*, in which, it is claimed, the young beardless person with long hair seated on the right hand of Christ is, in fact, Mary Magdalene. Other researchers have seen in Leonardo's more famous masterpiece, the *Mona Lisa*, a pun on 'Monad Iside', i.e. 'Isis the One and Only'. Whether all this has any historical truth is a matter for endless debate. What is more interesting to me, however, is that Isis and her star are still very much entrenched in the collective psyche of humanity. And if we couple this bizarre phenomenon with the fact that many of the Christian feasts are linked to the solar cycle – Christmas at the winter solstice, St John's Day at the summer solstice, Easter at the spring equinox, and so forth – and that this in turn is linked to the calendar whose origins lie in ancient Egypt and the rising of Sirius, then it could be argued that the cosmic order that so much affected and regulated the religious life of the ancient Egyptians is, through a circuitous route and curious twist of fate, still very much with us. The symbol of Sirius was the five-pointed star, which adorns the Nativity scenes and Christmas trees of millions of Christians around the world in late December. It is, at the very least, a strange irony that this very ancient archetypal star goddess is still lurking behind the veil of religious myth.

APPENDIX 5

The Death of the Living God

If the Divine Man grew old and became weaker, the Spirit within him also grew weaker...

Margaret Murray, *The Splendour that was Egypt*

She who reckons the Life-Period, Lady of Years, Lady of Fate...

G.A. Wainwright, 'Seshat and the Pharaoh'

Regicide

Many ancient people regarded their leaders or kings as having descended from a divine lineage, usually a pantheon of sky-gods. The king was thus seen as the direct link between the earthly and heavenly worlds. As such, the people felt duty bound not only to venerate him as a god but, paradoxically, to ensure that his godlike qualities were not despoiled by old age, which often entailed subjecting him to a ritual killing or 'regicide'.[1] This sacrificial death of the king was, no doubt, to be rewarded by a 'rebirth' among the divine ancestors in the sky. This gruesome custom probably originated in deep prehistory and was modelled on a mythology usually involving a man-god who had sacrificed himself by willingly accepting being put to death for the benefit and prosperity of his people. In Phrygia (modern western Turkey) this dying-resurrecting man-god was Attis; in Phoenicia (modern Syria) he was Adonis; in Greece he was Dionysos and in Persia (Iran) and Rome he was Mythras; in ancient Egypt he was

Osiris; and finally, in Christianity he was Jesus.[2] Archaic kings readily identified themselves with such 'dying and resurrecting' gods, and, in some extreme cases, willingly endured a sacrificial death in their prime for the salvation or affluence of their people. In his acclaimed book *The Golden Bough*, the distinguished anthropologist Sir James Fraser explains this macabre impulse:

> Now primitive people . . . sometimes believe that their safety and even that of the world is bound up with the life of one of these god-men or human incarnations of the divinity. Naturally, therefore, they take the utmost care of his life, out of a regard for their own. But no amount of care and precaution will prevent the man-god from growing old and feeble and at last dying. His worshippers have to lay their account with this sad necessity and to meet it as best as they can. The danger is a formidable one; for if the course of nature is dependent on the man-god's life, what catastrophe may not be expected from the gradual enfeeblement of his powers and their final extinction in death. There is only one way of averting these dangers. The man-god must be killed as soon as he shows symptoms that his powers are beginning to fail, and his soul must be transferred to a vigorous successor before it has been seriously impaired by the threatened decay . . .[3]

According to Fraser, the ritual killing of a king before the inevitable ageing process could weaken or cripple him and thus jeopardise the welfare of his kingdom was a common occurrence among ancient people. Many primitive tribes in Africa and Asia seem to have practised regicide in one form or another. Fraser draws attention to the primitive tribes of Cambodia, of the Congo, of Ethiopia, of the Shiluk of the White Nile and of the Dinka of Southern Sudan, as well as many others in central and southern Africa.[4] Fraser also gives particular attention to king-killing rituals practised in the ancient kingdom of Meroe near Egypt, where the rulers were once worshipped as Egyptian pharaohs: '. . . whenever the priests chose, they sent a messenger to the king, ordering him to die, and alleging an oracle of the gods as their authority for the command. This command the kings always obeyed . . .'[5]

Ritual king-killings were practised not only in Africa and Asia, but also in Europe. The ancient kings of Prussia, for example, willingly accepted being burnt alive on a sacrificial pier to comply with 'divine law'. The kings of Scandinavia agreed to be executed by the sword after a pre-fixed reign of nine years by the 'command of the gods'.[6] Also according to Fraser:

> . . . there are some grounds for believing that the reign of many ancient Greek kings was limited to eight years, or at least that at the end of every period of eight years a new consecration, a fresh outpouring of the divine grace, was regarded as necessary in order to enable them to discharge their civil and religious duties. Thus it was a rule of the Spartan constitution that every eight years the *ephors* should choose a clear and moonless night and sitting down observe the sky in silence. If during their vigil they saw a meteor or shooting star, they inferred that the king had sinned against the deity, and they suspended him from his functions until the Delphic or Olympic oracle should reinstate him in them. This custom, which has all the air of great antiquity, was not suffered to remain a dead letter even in the last period of the Spartan monarchy; for in the third century before our era a king, who had rendered himself obnoxious to the reforming party, was actually deposed on various trumped-up charges, among which allegation that the ominous sign had been seen in the sky took a prominent place.[7]

Fraser also speaks of a particular aspect of this ritual practised on the ancient Spartan kings, wherein, 'if the tenure of the regal office was formerly limited among the Spartans to eight years, we may naturally ask, why was that precise period selected as the measure of a king's reign? The reason is probably to be found in those astronomical considerations which determined the early Greek calendar . . .'[8] He was compelled to conclude that in some of these ancient cultures at least the kings were 'liable to deposition or death at the end of an astronomical cycle'.[9] This, of course, immediately brings to mind the rituals performed by the goddess Seshat (see Chapter Two) whose function, among others, was to decide on the length of the king's 'reign years' or 'life years'. It also brings to mind the very important royal festival practised in ancient Egypt known as the *heb-sed* (again see Chapter Two). The *heb-sed* festival is generally described by Egyptologists as a 'royal jubilee'. In reality it was much more than that. It was, in fact, a sort of pharaonic equivalent of a full medical check-up for the king in order to confirm to the people that he still retained his full sexual potency and physical and mental capacities. As G.A. Wainwright explains:

> nothing is more certain than that the pharaoh was divine . . . Kings of this type contained within themselves the power that produced prosperity . . . To do all this, a divine fertility-king must keep himself in good health and live a well-ordered life. For as he functions regularly and in good order, so will the universe remain stable and continue in its allotted course, for he is himself the universe. The service rendered by such kings has always been to ensure the fruitfulness of the earth, and consequent health of the people . . .[10]

The question that arises, therefore, is what happened when a king 'failed' the tests put to him at the *heb-sed*?

The first *heb-sed* festival for a king normally took place after the thirtieth year of his reign, but there is evidence that it also occurred at shorter periods and that originally it took place every seven years.[11] According to Wainwright, the *heb-sed* festival stemmed from 'the old sky and fertility-religion' and went back 'at least into prehistoric times'.[12] Most Egyptologists agree that the *heb-sed* is very old and was practised from the very early dynastic times all the way to the Late Period. Kings of the New Kingdom such as Amenhotep III and Rameses II appear to have performed their first *heb-sed* in the thirtieth year of their reign; but they also performed other *heb-seds* at shorter intervals. Unfortunately there are but few inscriptions that give details of the events that took place during this festival, and interpretations by scholars are usually based on pictorial scenes rather than textual ones. The best of these pictorial scenes are from the sun temple of Niuserra at Abu Ghurab (these, unfortunately, have been removed in modern times and are now displayed in various museums around the world).[13] We know of an important ritual performed at the *heb-sed* which required the king to run around the boundary walls of the ceremonial complex which, in some cases, could be over a mile. 'Thus we find,' wrote Wainwright:

[that the *heb-sed*] consisted essentially in a running ceremony, performed in archaic times before the king and from the First Dynasty onwards by the king himself . . . several of the old sky-gods figure in the ceremony . . . The ceremony clearly went back at least into Prehistoric times . . . Physical activity is essential in fertility-rites such as these clearly show. No doubt the king's agility here brought fertility to the fields, and induced the necessary activities in the skies in providing the water required . . . Thus we find that the Pharaohs were divine; controlled the activities of the sky; kept their people in health; hoed the ground; reaped the harvest; carried out a ceremony for the fertility of the fields, and concerned themselves with the opening of the dykes for the inundation . . . The Pharaohs were in fact fertility-kings, upon whose health and proper observance of the rites the health and wealth of the country depended . . .[14]

The rituals in *heb-sed* were by no means the only ones in which the king had to personally participate. His daily life was full of rituals to honour the gods and to ensure through them the welfare of his people and Egypt as a whole. If we are to believe the ancient Greek writer Diodorus, who visited Egypt in the first century BC, every daily activity of the pharaoh, from the moment he woke up to the moment he retired for the night, was ritualised 'according to a plan'.[15] In Diodorus' own words:

not only the order of priests but, in short, all the inhabitants of Egypt were less concerned for their wives and children and their other cherished possessions than for the safety of their kings . . . all their [the kings'] acts were regulated by prescriptions set forth in laws, not only their administrative acts, but also those that had to do with the way in which they spent their time from day to day, and with the food that they ate. And the hours of both the day and night were laid out according to a plan, and at the specific hours it was absolutely required of the king that he should do what the law stipulated and not what he thought best. For there was a set time not only for his holding audiences or rendering judgements, but even for his taking a walk, bathing, and sleeping with his wife, and, in a word, for every act of his life.[16]

The law that Diodorus is referring to which regulated every hour of the king's life was almost certainly Maat. And at one time the last duty imposed on kings by this cosmic law was, according to Wainright, to 'lay down their lives at the proper time for the good of their people'.[17] In full agreement with this conclusion, the mythologist Joseph Campell, in his book *The Mask of God: Primitive Mythology*, asserts that the kings of ancient Sudan and Napata, two regions that border the south of Egypt (and Napata was once annexed to Egypt), were allowed to rule for a limited period that was somehow 'computed' by astrologer-priests using the motion of the stars. And when apparently these astrologer-priests were asked how they calculated the life period, they explained that, 'Every night we keep watch on the stars, and we do not let them out of our sight. Every night we observe the moon, and we know from night to night, which stars are approaching the moon and which are moving away. It is by this that we know.'[18]

All this suggests that the ancient priests of these regions not only practised a sky religion whose 'law' was written in the stars, but also used the stars and the moon to determine the time of death of their kings. The combination of stars and moon is very much evident in the symbolism associated with the goddess Seshat, whose headdress, according to G.A. Wainright, was originally a reversed lunar crescent, the symbol for the month, cupping a seven-pointed star or flower.[19] Seshat was also the wife-companion of the moon god Thoth, who was regarded as the inventor of astronomy.[20] Interestingly, the Egyptologist Jane Sellers sensed that the lunar eclipses might somehow have played a part in the regicide rituals:

The possibility must be considered that total eclipses were considered a divine signal . . . In Egypt, it may have been that, with total eclipses, the living king who was the embodiment of Horus was then required to replace Osiris (that is 'become an Osiris') and a new Horus would come to the throne . . . The spectacular image of the sun being blotted out and then being 'reborn' had similar imagery of life after death, and such a spectacle could have been understood to mandate the living Horus, who was the Son-of-Re, to take his father's place now, and be himself replaced. It is a death and a rebirth, but one that has come to be, not the simplistic image of a stellar or solar deity, but rather a rebirth with a change of nature . . . The death of a Horus and the birth of a Horus; the death of Osiris and the birth of Osiris; these may have been believed to be ordained by events in the sky. Menes, first ruler of the unified Egypt, may have been brought to the throne by an eclipse, but another ruler may have been commanded to die. It is a death that must promise rebirth. A new king would become the new Horus, but the dead king would unite with the soul of Osiris, and become Osiris . . .[21]

Long-term predictions using astronomy are, however, usually made by using the stars. In Chapter Two we have seen how the seven-pointed star and the horns of Seshat's headdress may represent the seven stars of the Plough (Big Dipper). According to E.C. Krupp:

Seshat was portrayed with a seven-pointed star (although some have likened it to a seven-petaled flower) supported by a rod balanced upright upon her head. Like a canopy over her star hangs what may be a pair of upturned horns of a cow or bull. This emblem was also the hieroglyph for her name. Both the horns and the seven points of the star seem to have something to do with the Big Dipper. We already know that the Bull's Thigh, or Meskhetiu, was the Big Dipper, and the Dipper contains seven stars. It is certain that the Egyptians associated the number seven with the Big Dipper because several portrayals of Meskhetiu – at Dendera, Edfu, Esna and Philae – surround the picture of the bull's leg with seven stars.[22]

Seshat is principally known for her role in the 'Stretching of the Cord' ceremony, and according to Krupp the 'procedure required the observation of a certain star at a certain time and, probably, in a certain position . . . and orientation of the Big Dipper in its circular course around the pole'.[23] Could these stars have been used to cast a sort of 'horoscope' that determined the length of reign for the king?

Royal Substitute?

It is also possible that the king-killing ritual may have in time been replaced by the killing of a substitute such as a totem animal identified with the king. Bearing this in mind, we know that there existed from earliest times in Egypt such a totem for the king in the form of a bull known as the Apis. According to Egyptologist George Hart, the cult of the Apis began during the period of 'unification' which took place around 3100 BC.[24] The Apis bull was kept with great care and pomp in a temple at Memphis, and was regarded as the manifestation of Ptah, the creator god of that region. But when the Apis died (or perhaps was put to death), it was identified with Osiris whose constellation, Orion, was also in some cases the astral form of the departed king. It is thus quite possible that while alive, the Apis bull was also seen as the substitute for the living king who represented Horus, the son of Osiris. This seems to be confirmed by the fact that the 'mother' of the Apis bull was said to be the goddess Isis, mother of Horus and also wife of Osiris. According to George Hart:

> In the funerary cult this royal link with Apis continues . . . the bull was mummified on lion-headed alabaster tables some of which survived at Memphis. The funeral was an occasion of display and pomp, with men dragging to the tomb the sledge on which the embalmed and bejewelled bull had been placed in a couchant position. The burial place was in the northern quarters of the desert plateau of Saqqara . . . When Isis, mother of Apis, who had been brought to Memphis with her illustrious offspring, died she was given the honour of burial in the Saqqara necropolis in the vaults known as the Iseum, as yet not fully explored . . . Following concepts about the rank of the dead pharaoh in the Underworld, Apis, upon dying, becomes the god Osiris.[25]

Herodotus (fifth century BC) reported that the Apis was 'the calf of a cow which is incapable of conceiving another offspring; and the

Egyptians say that lightning descends upon the cow from heaven, and that from thence it brings forth the Apis. This calf, which is called Apis, has the following marks: it is black, and has a square spot of white on the forehead; and on the back the figure of an eagle.'[26] Several centuries later Plutarch (first century AD) wrote that 'the Apis, they say, is the animate image of Osiris, and he comes into being when a fructifying light thrusts forth from the moon and falls upon a cow in her breeding-season'.[27] Now the cow was a symbol of the goddess Isis, who also donned the moon disc between the cow horns on her headdress. The identification of the Apis to Osiris is also given by Diodorus (first century BC), who was probably an eye-witness to a funeral of the Apis bull:

> After the splendid funeral of Apis is over those priests who have charge of the business seek out another calf as like the former as they can possibly find, and when they have found one an end is put to all the mourning and lamentation, and such priests as are appointed for that purpose lead the young bull through the city of Nile and feed him forty days. Then they put him into a barge wherein is a golden cabin and so transport him as a god to Memphis ... For the adoration of the bull they give this reason: they say that the soul of Osiris passes into a bull and therefore whenever the bull is dedicated, to this very day the spirit of Osiris is infused into one bull after another for posterity.[28]

All Egyptologists agree that the living king was seen as the incarnation of Horus, son of Osiris and Isis, but when he died he became identified with Osiris. It thus follows that if the dead Apis is identified with Osiris, then the living Apis must also be regarded as the living Horus-king. This is made obvious by one of the titles for Apis, 'Son of Osiris', i.e. Horus.[29] Also, as George Hart explains:

> The pharaoh identifies closely with Apis–bull imagery (with its inherent notion of strength and fertility) being an ancient characteristic in the propaganda of the god-king, as can be seen from carved slate palettes and in one of the names used in the royal protocol 'victorious bull'. Celebrating his jubilee festival, a ceremony concerned with the

rejuvenation of the monarch's power, the pharaoh strides briskly alongside the galloping Apis bull. The ritual which took place at Memphis is vividly portrayed in a relief on a block from a dismantled chapel in the temple of Karnak at Thebes.[30]

Jane B. Sellers was also of the opinion that the sacrifice of the Apis bull may have had a connection with the *heb-sed* festival of the pharaoh and that it was used perhaps as a substitute for his regicide: '. . . If a substitute were needed (for the regicide) could the Apis have stood in the king's stead? Could this kind of "ritual regicide" explain the enigmatic occurrences of empty sarcophagi, or the strange custom of duplicating tombs for the rulers of early dynastic Egypt?'[31] Sellers' idea seems to have backing from several ancient authorities – Plutarch and Ammianus Marcellinus among them – who reported that the Apis bull was only allowed to live a certain number of years and was then put to death, usually by drowning.[32] The Roman historian Pliny reported that the Apis was put to death when it exceeded a number of years, and was killed by being drowned in the Nile.[33] This is clearly meant as a parallel to the death of Osiris, for we know from the Pyramid Texts that he too was drowned in the Nile, at a place called Nedyt, which is conspicuously near Memphis and Saqqara, the main cult centres of the Apis bull. Indeed, Saqqara, in fact, is where the Apis bulls were buried, in the stone sarcophagi of the huge subterranean maze. It is thus relevant that the region of Saqqara (the Memphite Necropolis) was known as 'the burial place of Osiris'.[34] There are, too, the so-called sun temples at Abu Ghorab, near Saqqara, to consider in the context of a possible sacrificial killing of the king or the Apis bull. These temples belong to kings of the Fifth Dynasty, and as we have already seen in Chapter Three, they contain reliefs showing scenes of the *heb-sed* festival.[35] Intriguingly, the sun temples included a 'slaughterhouse' as well as a huge sacrificial stone altar which may have existed for the purpose of ritual killings. According to Richard Wilkinson, the sun temples may have been oriented 'towards stars that would have risen above the predawn horizon around 2400 BC. If the latter is true, it may indicate that Userkaf's valley temple functioned as a kind of astronomical clock for sacrifices which were made at dawn.'[36] According to George Hart 'an average lifespan for Apis was fourteen years [twice seven?] . . . On the death of Apis Egypt mourned as if for the loss of the pharaoh himself.'[37]

All this evidence, when put together, provides us with a disturbing picture of a time when the king or a totem animal substitute may have been ritualistically put to death based on a 'law' or sky religion involving the stars and other celestial bodies. But if this is true, then who performed this sinister task of killing the king? Who were the royal executioners?

The Priests of Seth

According to Wainwright, the cult of Seshat was so ancient 'as to be already dying out in the Old Kingdom'.[38] This thus takes Seshat back to a time when the kings of Egypt were closely identified not only with Horus but also to Seth. In the Pyramid Texts the goddess Seshat was closely associated to Nephtys, the wife of Seth and the sister of Osiris and Isis. Indeed, Nephtys is given the title 'In Her name of Seshat, Lady of Builders'.[39] The complete text which concerns the resurrection of the Osiris-king reads:

> Horus has mustered the gods for you (Osiris-king), and they will never escape from you in the place where you have drowned. Nephtys has collected all your members for you in this her name of 'Seshat, Lady of Builders'. She has made them hale for you, you having been given to your mother Nut in her name of 'Sarcophagus'; she has embraced you in her name of 'Coffin', and you have been brought to her in her name of 'Tomb'. Horus has reassembled your members for you, and he will not let you perish; he has put you together, and nothing shall be disturbed in you. Horus has set you up, and there shall be no unsteadiness. O Osiris-king, lift up your heart, be proud, open your mouth, for Horus has protected you and he will not fail to protect you. O Osiris-king, you are a mighty god, and there is no god like you. Horus has given you his children that they may bear you up . . . Live, that you may go to and fro every day; be a spirit in your name of

'Horizon from which Re goes up'; be strong, be effective, be a soul, and have power forever and ever.[40]

The above passage presents us with a dramatic scene of the death of the 'Osiris' king and tells how his 'resurrection' was attended by his son or successor, the new king identified as Horus. The material components of the rebirth rites such as the pyramid tomb itself, and the sarcophagus and coffin, are symbols of the sky-goddess Nut. Mark Lehner has an interesting interpretation of this particular passage of the Pyramid Texts:

The king's tomb was also a cosmic womb, an idea articulated in the Pyramid Texts (616d–f): 'You are given to your mother, Nut, in her identity of the coffin; She has gathered you up, in her identity of the sarcophagus; You ascend to her in her identity of the tomb.' This suggests that the sloping pyramid passages descending to the burial chamber was seen in fact as 'ascending' to Nut in the Netherworld. The word for Netherworld was the Duat, often written with a star in a circle, a reference to Orion, the stellar expression of Osiris, in the Underworld. Osiris was the 'Lord of the Duat', which, like the celestial world (and the real Nile Valley) was both a water world and an earthly realm.

The lines which state that 'Horus has reassembled your members for you, and he will not let you perish; he has put you together, and nothing shall be disturbed in you. Horus has set you up, and there shall be no unsteadiness' are very suggestive of a mutilation ritual performed on the king's body perhaps in re-enactment of the mutilation of Osiris's body by Seth as reported in other narratives of this god's death.[41] Margaret Murray[42] was convinced that the myth of Osiris was constantly re-enacted by the pharaohs, and that was 'perhaps the most perfect example of that belief which is found in so many countries viz. that God is incarnated in man, which belief is usually accompanied by the rite of killing the Divine Man'.[43] According to Murray:

The chief centres of Osiris-worship were Abydos in the south and Busiris in the north; the difference in rituals shows that at Abydos the emphasis was laid on the death of the god, at Busiris on the resurrection. At Abydos there seems to have been a mystery play, showing forth the passion, death, burial, and resurrection of Osiris. In Ptolemaic times this was a puppet play, but under the pharaohs the performers were living actors and there is little doubt that in early times the men who took the parts of Osiris and Setekh [Seth] were actually sacrificed . . . in the beginning it was the ruler who suffered, later a substitute was put to death.[44] . . . Seth was one of the most important gods of Egypt . . . his worship seems to have been very primitive, and includes human sacrifice, probably the sacrifice of the king . . . Seth is closely connected with the sacrifice of the king. That strange priest, Kha-bau-Seker, who appears to have been the chief officiant in the shrine of Anubis, also held high office in the shrine of Seth; on both accounts I take him to be the executioner of the king or of the royal substitute. He belonged to the Third Dynasty . . . possibly . . . the priest of Seth was the appointed executioner to the divine king.[45]

Intriguingly, Murray discusses the role of Seshat in the 'Stretching of the Cord' ceremony, and adds that:

Another of her [Seshat's] function functions was to record the name of the king on the leaves of the Tree of Life,[46] so that his name might remain for evermore. But as her earliest known priest, the sinister Kha-bau-Seker of Memphis, was also the priest of Anubis and Seth and therefore connected with the death of the Incarnated God (the king), it is possible that Seshat was the deity who calculated the length of the king's life.[47]

One role for Seshat was that she be 'the deity who calculated the length of the king's life'; the other was helping the king in 'stretching the cord' to align his tomb towards the circumpolar stars and specifically the constellation of the bull's thigh (the Plough). This constellation, as we have seen in Chapter Three, is the 'Thigh of Seth'[48] and has seven bright stars. According to Wainwright, the pharaoh were originally allocated by Seshat reigns of seven years or increments thereof. It would be somewhat perverse not to see in the seven stars of the Plough some common denominator between the two roles of Seshat. Be that as it may, Murray's views that Seshat was the 'deity who calculated the length of the king's life' and consequently fixed the time of his death is also shared by Wainwright, who wrote that:

> . . . as religious ideas developed and anthropomorphic [human shaped] gods in heaven emerged, the priest or king becomes the incarnated god here on earth, where he acts for his heavenly prototype. But here a difficulty supervenes, for man, even the most divine, is but mortal. Hence the divinity within him would grow old and feeble as its human shrine became more decrepit and infirm. As this cannot be allowed, the holder should lay down his life whilst still in his prime, so as to pass on the power to his successor in its full vigour . . . The manner and period of the divine death vary greatly. Very often the king had to commit suicide at the appointed time . . . In Egypt it will be seen that Seth, the Storm-God, had been liable to death, and tradition states that the death had been by fire. But in historic times he, and the pharaoh his representative, were able to escape . . .[49]

Wainwright believed that many of these older sky gods 'were so ancient that they were lost during historic times', and that among the few that did survive were Horus, Seth and Seshat.[50] In Utterances 570–1 of the Pyramid Texts, the king claims that,

> I escape my day of death just as Seth escaped his day of death. I escape my half-month of death just as Seth escaped his half-month of death. I escape my month of death just as Seth escaped his month of death. I escape my year of death just as Seth escaped his year of death. Do not break up the ground, O you arms of mine which lift up the sky as Shu [the air-god]; my bones are iron and my limbs are the Imperishable Stars. I am a star which illumines the sky, I mount up to the god that I may be protected, for the sky will not be devoid of me and this earth will not be devoid of me for ever. I live beside you, you gods of the Lower Sky, the Imperishable Stars . . .[51]

I am the redness which came forth from Isis, I am the blood which issued from Nephtys. I am firmly bound up at the waist, and there is nothing which the gods can do for me, for I am the representative of Re, and I do not die. Hear, O Geb [earth-god], chief of the gods, and equip me with my shape; hear O Thoth, in who is the peace of the gods. Open, O Horus; stand guard, O Seth, that I may rise in the eastern side of the sky like Re who rises in the eastern side of the sky.[52]

Then in the Utterance 572, the goddess Isis greets the reborn king with these words:

'How lovely to see, how pleasing to behold!' says Isis, when you ascend to the sky, your powers upon you, your terror about you, your magic at your feet; you are helped by Atum just as he used to do, the gods who are in the sky are brought to you, the gods who are on earth assemble for you, they place their hand under you, they make a ladder (pyramid?) for you that you may ascend on it to the sky, the doors of the sky are open for you, the doors of the starry firmament are thrown open for you . . . Have they killed you or said that you shall die? You shall not die, but you shall live forever.[53]

The events described above which clearly take place among the circumpolar stars do so *at dawn and at the time of the heliacal rising of Sirius*. This stellar conjunction is further emphasised in Utterance 573, where the departed king addresses Horakhti (Horus of the Horizon) with these words:

May you wake [rise] in peace, O Purified, in peace! May you wake in peace, O Horus of the East, in peace! May you wake in peace, O Soul of the East, in peace! May you wake in peace, O Horakhti, in peace! . . . O my father [Osiris], take me with you to your mother Nut, that the doors of the sky may be opened for me and that the doors of the firmament may be thrown open for me. I am on my way to you that you may nourish me, command that I shall sit beside you, beside Him [Horakhti] who at the morning tide is on the horizon . . . give command to Him who has life, the son of Sothis [Horus-Sirius as the 'son' of

Canis Major], that he may speak on my behalf and establish my seat in the sky . . .[54]

From the above passages we can reconstruct a complete astronomical image of the sky at the time of the heliacal rising of Sirius in c. 2800 BC for the location of Heliopolis. Using an astronomical programme such as StarryNight Pro. or StarMap, we can see that this event took place about one hour before sunrise on the day of the summer solstice. At this time the constellations of Orion and Canis Major would have dominated the eastern horizon. We can also see that in the north the Plough/bull's thigh was standing upright with the 'hoof' star at about 4° 30′ east (to the right) of the northern meridian and about 16° above the horizon line. The first appearance of Sirius at dawn after the 70 days in the underworld was the signal for cosmic rebirth, and for the portals of the Duat to open to receive the departed king among the circumpolar stars. We can see why, perhaps, the priestess of Seshat took such great care to assist the king in aligning his pyramid or funerary complex towards this region of the sky and – as in the case of the Step Pyramid – to synchronise the observation with the rising of Sirius in the east. Perhaps it was at this moment that the 'reckoning of the life-years' for the new king was worked out by the priestess of Seshat and recorded on the famous notched palm branch. Seshat, it will be recalled, was also closely related to the *heb-sed* festival. Bearing this in mind, here is what Henri Frankfort, who was Professor of Pre-classical Antiquity at London University and Director of the Warburg Institute, wrote in his book *Kingship and the Gods*:

The Sed festival is usually called a jubilee, but it was not a mere commemoration of a king's accession. It was a true renewal of kingly potency, a rejuvenation of rulership *ex opere operato*. Sometimes it was celebrated thirty years after the accession, but several rulers celebrated it repeatedly and at shorter intervals. It is unlikely that the mere counting of years was the decisive factor, but we do not know on what grounds it was decided that the king's power ought to be renewed . . .

Also according to Frankfort, the *heb-sed* festival was performed at a very special time of year, which was

> ... the same as that reserved for the coronation, namely, the first day of the first month of the 'Season of Coming Forth' – the first of Tybi. The last five days of the preceding month, Khoiak, were dedicated to the Osiris mysteries; and it is remarkable that the Sed festival, in contrast to the coronation, does not refer to Osiris at all. But the difference is easily explained. At the (heb) Sed festival the king appears, not as newly ascending the throne, but as its occupant through a number of years. Consequently, it is not the succession – Horus following Osiris – which is the issue, but a renewal of all those beneficial relations between heaven and earth the throne controls.[55]

Could the priestess of Seshat and her observations of the seven stars of the Plough have been the basis of the computation of the king's reign and, in primitive times, the determination of the date of his ritual death?

Notes

Introduction

[1] Produced by Pioneer Production Ltd. in UK.

[2] Produced by the Dutch filmmaker Roel Oostra of Crescom Ltd.

[3] *Discussions in Egyptology*, Vol. 30, books review section.

[4] Anthony Aveni, *Starways to the Stars: Skywatching in Three Great Ancient Cultures*, Cassell, 1997, pp. 11–12.

Chapter One: The Star at the Head of the Sky

[1] Robert Bauval and Adrian Gilbert, *The Orion Mystery*, Heinemann, 1994.

[2] Stephen Quirke, *The Cult of Ra*, Thames & Hudson, 2001, p. 116.

[3] Was the original seated statue inclined? The levelled floor of the *serdab* suggests that it was not. But did it have to be inclined? The head is positioned behind the two peepholes, which are themselves inclined towards the lower northern sky, much like a seated astronomer would be positioned behind a set of binoculars that was inclined towards the lower northern sky. At any rate, the inclination is only about 15 to 17° to the horizontal, which requires a very small tilt of the head backwards to gaze at the same spot in the sky.

[4] Mark Lehner, *The Complete Pyramids*, Thames & Hudson, 1997, p. 84.

[5] Ian Shaw and Paul Nicholson, *The British Museum Dictionary of Ancient Egypt*, The British Museum Press, 2003, p. 87.

[6] Ibid., p. 153.

[7] Ibid., p. 134.

[8] Ibid.

9   *The Ancient Gods Speak*, ed. Donald B. Redford, Oxford University Press, 2002, p. 165.

10 Ibid.

11 See 'Osiris', in Shaw and Nicholson, op. cit., p. 213–14. *Khentiamentiu* was the ancient god of Abydos, a site sacred to Osiris and location of the Osireon at Abydos built by Seti I.

12 *The Ancient Gods Speak*, op. cit., p. 359.

13 The glyph *kh*, which is a sort of animal's belly (maybe a cow). This glyph is part of the Horus name of *Ntjr-y-(kh)-t* which may give it the full meaning of 'Most Divine of the Corporation' or 'the Corporation is Divine'.

14 A.M. Blackman, 'The Ka-House and the Serdab', *Journal of Egyptian Archaeology*, Vol. 3, 1916, pp. 250–4.

15 J.E. Manchip White, *Ancient Egypt, its Culture and History*, George Allen & Unwin Ltd., 1979, 2nd Ed., pp. 40–1.

16 Ibid., p. 41.

17 *The Orion Mystery*, op. cit.

18 Pyramid Texts, 1,277–9.

19 Alexander Badawy, 'The Periodic System of Building a Pyramid', *Journal of Egyptian Archaeology*, Vol. 63, 1977, p. 58.

20 Edwards, *The Pyramids of Egypt*, Penguin, 1982, p. 295.

21 Quirke, op. cit., p. 117.

22 The term 'Indestructibles' was used by I.E.S. Edwards in the BBC 2 documentary *The Great Pyramids: Gateway to the Stars*, first shown in February 1994.

23 James H. Breasted, *Development of Religion and Thought in Ancient Egypt*, University of Pennsylvania Press, 1972, p. 101.

24 R.T. Rundle Clark, *Myth and Symbol in Ancient Egypt*, Thames and Hudson, 1978, p. 58.

25 E.C. Krupp, *Echoes of the Ancient Skies*, Oxford University Press, 1994, p. 212. Also, according to Mark Lehner 'The "Imperishable Ones" are the circumpolar stars . . . Since these stars revolve around the celestial North Pole and neither rise or set, the long, narrow passages sloping up from the burial chamber in the northern sides of many pyramids were aimed like telescopes in their direction.' *The Complete Pyramids*, op. cit., p. 28.

26 Shaw and Nicholson, op. cit. p. 166.

27 Ibid., p. 153

28 R. H. Wilkinson, *The Complete Gods and Goddesses of Ancient Egypt*,

The American University in Cairo Press, 2003, p. 129.

29 Walter Scott (ed.), *Hermetica*, Shambhala, Boston, 1993, p. 485.

30 Blackman, op. cit., p. 254. This description and names given by Blackman would perfectly fit the Djoser Pyramid, with its so-called 'King's Apartments' under the Pyramid which are aligned (i.e. lead upwards and towards) with the *serdab* outside.

31 *The Orion Mystery*, op. cit.

32 Wilkinson, op. cit., p. 161.

33 Edwards, op. cit., pp. 267–8. Interestingly, the inscription also mentions the constellation of Orion, an indication of the connection between these stars and the soul of pharaoh.

34 Lehner, op. cit., p. 34.

35 A. Piankoff, *The Pyramid of Unas*, Bollingen Series 5, Princeton, 1968.

36 Christine Ziegler, *Les Pyramides D'Egypte*, Paris, 1999, p. 52.

37 Lehner, op. cit., p. 28.

38 Lehner, p. 90.

39 Alexander Gurshtein, 'The Evolution of the Zodiac in the Context of Ancient Oriental History', *Vista in Astronomy*, Vol. 41, Part 4, 1997, p. 509.

40 Josef Dorner, *Die Absteckung und astronomische Orientierung agyptischer Pyramiden*, University of Innsbruck, 1981 (Thesis +C14169207).

41 Wainwright, 'Seshat and the Pharaoh', *Journal of Egyptian Archaeology*, Vol. 26, 1941, pp. 30–40.

42 Wilkinson, op. cit., p. 166.

43 In his study of Egyptian myths and symbols, R.T. Rundle Clark makes no mention of Seshat (see Rundle Clark, op. cit.)

44 Wainwright, op. cit.

45 Krupp, op. cit., p. 212.

46 Wainwright, op. cit.

47 Anne-Sophie Bomhard, *The Egyptian Calendar: A Work for Eternity*, Periplus, 1998, p. 4.

48 E.A. Wallis Budge, *The Gods of the Egyptians*, Vol. I, Dover Publications, New York, 1969, p. 425.

49 This tradition of the superwoman/goddess is witnessed throughout Egyptian civilisation and right to its end, with Queen Cleopatra IV, who is said to have been proficient in nine languages and had studied astronomy, mathematics, architecture and medicine at the Great Library of Alexandria.

50 George Hart, *A Dictionary of Egyptian Gods and Goddesses*, Routledge & Kegan Paul, 1988, p. 193.

51 Edwards, op. cit., pp. 249–50.

52 R.W. Stoley 'Primitive Methods of Measuring Time with Special Reference to Egypt', *Journal of Egyptian Archaeology*, Vol. 17, 1931, p. 170.

53 Z. Zaba, *L'Orientation Astronomique Dans L'Ancienne Egypte et la Precession de l'Axe du Monde*, Prague, 1953, pp. 58–9.

54 Ibid.

55 Ibid.

56 Kate Spence, 'Ancient Egyptian Chronology and the Astronomical Orientation of Pyramids', *Nature*, Vol. 408, 2000, pp. 320–4.

57 *The Times*, *The Daily Telegraph*, *The Scientific American* and *New Scientist* were among the many newspapers and journals which, on 15 and 16 November 1999, announced Kate Spence's discovery.

58 Robert Bauval, 'A Brief Evaluation of Kate Spence's article in *Nature*, vol. 408, 16 November 2000, pp. 320–4' *Discussions in Egyptology*, Vol. 48, 2000, pp. 115–26.

59 In an interview with the science editor of *The Dallas Morning News* Spence stated that 'Khufu's Great Pyramid is the most accurately aligned pyramid of the bunch because it happened to be built around the time when a line drawn between Kochab and Mizar crossed the pole dead-on . . .'

60 Shaw and Nicholson, op. cit., p. 42.

61 All this has been fully discussed in my book *The Orion Mystery*, op. cit.

62 Ibid., Plate 15a.

63 Lehner, op. cit., p. 29.

64 *The Orion Mystery* tells the whole story.

65 Lehner, op. cit., p. 90. Lehner's angle of 13° for the *serdab* was recently quoted in a major television documentary featuring a plethora of eminent Egyptologists such as Dr Kate Spence (Cambridge University), Dr James Allen (Metropolitan Museum, New York), Dr Rosalie Davies (Manchester University) and Dr Zahi Hawass (Supreme Council of Antiquities in Egypt). The documentary was called *The Great Sphinx*, shown in the spring of 2002 and it was produced by the BBC for the Discovery Channel.

66 Jean-Phillippe Lauer, *Histoire Monumentale des Pyramides D'Egypte*, I, Le Caire, 1962.

67 Ibid. p. 3.

68 Edwards, *The Pyramids of Egypt*, 1993, Penguin ed., p. 41. Jacques Vandier, however, gives an angle of 17° to the vertical (see Jacques Vandier, *Manuel D'Archaéologie Egyptienne*, Tome I, Paris, 1952, pp. 936–7).

69 In July 2002 I had the opportunity to go to Egypt. I took with me a 15-inch Stanley spirit level as well as a Staedtler design protractor with a variomatic set-square that could be fixed on to the flat top of the spirit level. I also built another simple inclinometer using a large piece of cardboard on which were drawn angles ranging from 13° to 18°, and a plumb line attached to the focal point. I managed to get several readings from the west, east and north sides of the *serdab*. I also took readings from the slope of the lower course of the casing stones of the actual Step Pyramid that abuts against the back of the *serdab*. Judging from the readings we recorded, it was clear that the angle of inclination of the *serdab* was very close to 16°. This value is also quoted by Lauer and Edwards, I consider this value, therefore, conclusive.

70 For the year 2800 BC and an orientation of 4° 35′ east of north, StarryNight Pro. V. 4 gave 15° 37′ altitude; Skymap Pro7 gave 15° 33′. Both values are within the expected precision range to match the 16° incline of the *serdab*.

71 Edwards, op. cit., pp. 284, 286

Chapter Two: The Quest for Eternity

1 Anne-Sophie Bomhard, *The Egyptian Calendar: A Work for Eternity*, Periplus Publishing, London, 1998, p. 2.

2 I live about a mile from the Giza Necropolis. From my apartment I get a clear view of the Khufu and Khafra pyramids. The final draft of *The Egypt Code* was written here.

3 R.A. Schwaller de Lubicz, *The Temple of Karnak*, Inner Traditions, Rochester, Vermont, 2001, p. 1.

4 Jean Kerisel, *The Nile and its Masters: Past, Present, Future Source of Hope and Anger*, A.A. Balkema, Rotterdam, 2001, p. 37.

5 Allan Chapman, *Gods in the Sky: Astronomy from the Ancients to the Renaissance*, Channel 4 Books, London, 2002, pp. 32–3.

6 Henri Frankfort and John A. Wilson, *Before Philosophy*, Pelican Books, 1961, p. 51. Likewise, the British Egyptologist J.M. Plumley wrote that 'contrary to modern usage the Ancient Egyptians orientated themselves

to face southwards. At their back lay the Mediterranean and the rest of the ancient world. The west was for them the right, and the east the left.' *Ancient Cosmologies*, edited by Carmen Blacker and Michael Loewe, with contributions by J.M. Plumley et al., George Allen & Unwin Ltd., 1975, p. 19.

[7] *The Ancient Gods Speak*, op. cit., p. 254.

[8] Lehner, *The Complete Pyramids*, op. cit., p. 29.

[9] Chapman, op. cit., pp. 32–3.

[10] Lehner, op. cit., p. 28.

[11] Lucie Lamy, *Egyptian Mysteries*, Thames & Hudson, 1981, p. 48. I had proposed the same idea in 1989 that 'a major feature of the After-world often mentioned in the Pyramid Texts is the "Winding Waterway", which was, in all probability, seen as a celestial counterpart of the Nile' (Bauval, *Discussions in Egyptology*, Vol. 13, 1989).

[12] Herodotus, *The Histories*, Book II 18–24, p. 136.

[13] Richard H. Wilkinson, *The Complete Gods and Goddess of Ancient Egypt*, op. cit., p. 45.

[14] Bomhard, op. cit., in Preface.

[15] Pyramid Texts, 1, 704.

[16] W. M. Flinders Petrie, *Researches in Sinai*, John Murray, London, 1906, pp. 163–4.

[17] Leo Dupuydt, *Civil Calendar and Lunar Calendar in Ancient Egypt*, Uitgeverij Peeters en Department Oosterse Studies, Leuven, 1977, p. 9.

[18] Juan Belmonte, 'Some open questions on the Egyptian Calendar: an astronomer's view', *Trabajos de Egyptologia*, Issue 2, 2003, p. 10. Coincidence would have it that the vector of the proper motion of Sirius made it such that almost throughout the pharaonic era the star had a yearly cycle of exactly 365.25 days, thus requiring 1,460 years ($365 \div 0.25 = 1460$) for the civil calendar to return to the heliacal rising of Sirius.

[19] Censorinus, *Die Natali*, Chapter 18. See also Dupuydt, op. cit., p. 9.

[20] Recent research has suggested that the names of the months may have existed in earlier times, possibly even when the calendar was inaugurated, but no textual evidence has yet confirmed this. See Belmonte, op. cit., p. 7.

[21] Pyramid Texts, 1, 520.

[22] Pyramid Texts, line 1, 773.

[23] Pyramid Texts, 1, 944.

[24] Pyramid Texts, 1, 960–1.

[25] Dows Dunham & William K. Simpson, *The Mastaba of Queen*

Mersyankh III G7530–7540, Department of Egyptian and Ancient Near Eastern Art, Museum of Fine Arts, Boston, 1974, p. 8.

26 Five days added to the computed value of 267 days.

27 They may have got this name from Satis, the Egyptian star-goddess of the flood at Elephantine who was identified to Sirius. It was also called 'Sihor' by the Hebrews and 'Sirio' by the Romans.

28 R. Burnham Jr., *Burnham's Celestial Handbook*, Vol. I, Dover ed., 1978, p. 387. Sirius is the star that is brightest in the sky. The brightness of Sirius (which is a 'sun') in absolute terms is 23 times more so than our sun. It is also twice as massive as our sun, much hotter and its 9,400 Kelvin temperature making it look very white.

29 Burnham, op. cit., p. 387.

30 Stand in front of the Great Pyramid about an hour after sunset and look up towards the south.

31 The summer solstice may have originally marked the first day of the civil calendar. The idea was first proposed in 1894 by the astronomer Sir Norman Lockyer in *Dawn of Astronomy*. The German chronologist E. Meyer also proposed it in 1908. Recently the Spanish astronomer Juan Belmonte has revived this idea and further proposed that the summer solstice was the basis of the original calendar (Belmonte, op. cit.).

32 Otto Neugebauer & Richard Parker, *Egyptian Astronomical Texts*, Vol.1, 1964, pp. 38–43; pp. 70–3.

33 Scott, *Heremetica*, op. cit., Asclepius III

34 For a recent identification of Sah with Osiris and Orion see Kurt Locher (of the Berne Astronomical Institute) 'New Arguments for the celestial location of the decanal belt and for the origins of the Sah-hieroglyph', in *VI International Congress of Egyptology*, Torino, Vol. II, 1993, p. 279. See also S. Hetherington (ed.), *Encyclopaedia of Cosmology*, Garland Publishing Inc., New York 10993, p. 193.

35 Shaw & Nicholson, op. cit., p. 275.

36 Krupp, *Echoes of the Ancient Skies*, Oxford University Press, 1997, p. 22.

37 R.O. Faulkner, *The Ancient Egyptian Pyramid Texts*, Oxford University Press, 1970, p. 120.

38 Nathalie Beaux, 'Sirius Étoile et Jeune Horus', *Hommages à Jean Leclant*, Intitute Français D'Archéologie Orientale, Bibliotheque D'Etude 106/1, 1993, p. 64, n,14.

39 R.O. Faulkner, op. cit., p. 120.

40 According to Nataliè Beaux, in the Pyramid Texts Sirius is also sometimes

called the 'Morning Star' (see Beaux, op. cit.).

41 Beaux, op. cit., p. 64.

42 R. W. Sloley, 'Primitive Methods of Measuring Time, with Special Reference to Egypt', *Journal of Egyptian Archaeology*, Vol. 17, 1930, p. 167.

43 E.C. Krupp, op. cit., p. 23.

44 The chronologist Leo Dupuydt, however, has suggested that a better name for it would be the *Historical* Sothic Cycle because, strictly speaking, the value of 1,460 is not constant by changes slightly due to the proper motion of the star and the effects of precession (see Leo Dupuydt, 'On the Consistency of the Wandering Year as Backbone of Egyptian Chronology', *Journal of the American Research Centre in Egypt*, Vol. 32, 1995, pp. 45–6). For the varying length of the Sothic Cycle, see M.F. Ingham, in *Journal of Egyptian Archaeology*, Vol. 55, 1969, pp. 36–40.

45 Petrie, op. cit., p. 164.

46 The altitude of Sirius is taken as 1° and that of the sun -9°. Sirius would have had an azimuth of 109° 16'.

47 Marshall Clagett wrote 'If we work backward from 139 AD we would find the possible quadrennial dates of the beginnings of three Sothic Periods preceding the one beginning in that year: BC 1321–1318; 2781–2778; and 4241–4238. Meyer believed that the period beginning from 2781–2778 BC was too recent for the establishment of the calendar and so accepted the earlier period. He thought he had confirmed this when he had deduced from rather inconclusive considerations of the Gregorian dates for recent rising of the Nile that it was in the Sothic Period from 4241–4238 BC that the date of Sirius's appearance best conformed with the date of the Nile's rising. However, with the development and acceptance of the "short chronology" of Egyptian history which can be coordinated with the short chronology elsewhere in the Near East, the general opinion has switched to the third millennium for the establishment of the civil calendar since, at the beginning of the earlier period, Egyptian society was at an underdeveloped level of sophistication and was not a unified state' (Marshall Clagett, *Ancient Egyptian Science, Vol. II, Calendars, Clocks and Astronomy*, American Philosophical Society, 1995, pp. 30–1). See also Richard Parker, *The Calendars of Ancient Egypt*, Chicago University Press, 1950. For a recent discussion on this, see Paul Jordan, *Riddle of the Sphinx*, Sutton Publications, 1998, pp. 35–7.

48 David Ewing Duncan, *The Calendar*, Fourth Estate Publishers, London, 1999.

49 Chapman, op. cit., p. 59.

50 Manchip White, op. cit., p. 138.

51 E.C. Krupp, *Skywatchers, Shamans, and Kings*, Willey Popular Science, 1997, p. 223.

52 'O Atum-Khoprer (the rising sun), you rose high on the heights, you rose up as the benben stone in the Mansion of the Phoenix in Heliopolis.' Pyramid Texts Utterance 600.

53 Redford, *The Ancient Gods Speak*, op. cit., contribution by Spalinger, p. 125.

54 Tacitus also saw the phoenix as a solar symbol and further asserted that 'In the consulship of Paulus Fabius (AD 34) the miraculous bird known to the world by the name of the phoenix, after disappearing for a series of ages, revisited Egypt' (Thomas Bulfinch, *Bulfinch's Mythology: The Age of Fable*, Mentor Books, New York, 1962, p. 353).

55 Cornelius Tacitus, *The Annals of Tacitus,* trans. Alfred John Church and William Jackson Brodribb, Macmillan, 1877.

56 Stephen Quirke, *The Cult of Ra: Sun-Worship in Ancient Egypt*, Thames & Hudson, 2002, pp. 27–8.

57 Pliny the Elder, *Natural History,* Vol. III, trans. by H. Rackham, Harvard University Press, 1983, pp. 293, 295.

58 R.T. Rundle Clark, *Myth and Symbol in Ancient Egypt*, op. cit.,1959, p. 246.

59 I had met Dr John Brown at a conference in Glasgow in June 2004 and invited him on a tour of Egypt that I was conducting in November 2004 for the company Quest Travel of Cairo.

60 R.A. Krauss, *Sothis und Monddaten*, Hildesheim, 1985, p. 201. See also R. Weill, *Bases, Methodes et Resultats de la Chronologie Egyptienne*, Paris, 1926, pp. 133–5. Also Clagett, op. cit., p. 37, who argued that the length of the solar year was even known in predynastic times.

61 Redford, *The Ancient Gods Speak*, op. cit., p. 189.

62 Cyril Aldred, *Akhenaten, Pharaoh of Egypt: A New Study*, London, 1968, pp. 25, 67.

63 From a commentary by Germanicus on Aratus, translated by Nigidius Figulus. See Mommsen, *Chronologie*, p. 258. See Bomhard, op. cit. p. 9.

64 Norman Lockyear, *The Dawn of Astronomy*, Cassell & Co., London, 1894, p. 248.

65 Clagett, op. cit., p. 326. This is known as 'The Decree of Canopus', issued on the 9th year of the reign of Ptolemy III.

66 The Roman poet Lucan (AD 39–65), Cleopatra gave a feast at the palace in honour of Julius Caesar, where Caesar was first told of the Egyptian calendar by the Alexandrian scholar Acoreus. According to David Ewing Duncan, author of *The Calendar* (Fourth Estate Publishers, London, 1999), 'it was during this conversation that Caesar heard about Egypt's reliance on the sun for its year – measured by the annual rise of Sirius in the eastern sky and by the flooding of the Nile, which, the Alexandrian sage said, "does not arouse its water before the shining of the Dog-star (Sirius)".' This prompted Caesar to ask the court astronomer, Sosigenes, to create a new calendar for Rome. Sosigenes, without a doubt, based this calendar on the existing one of Egypt, with its 365 days, but this time finally added an extra day each 'leap year'. Even so, this new 'Julian Calendar' was still about 11 minutes in error to the true solar year, and was eventually readjusted in AD 1582 by Luigi Lilio under the orders of Pope Gregory XIII in Rome to produce the Gregorian calendar which we use today.

67 Bomhard, op. cit., p. 83.

68 The Gregorian reform of the Julian calendar was made in 1582. First 10 days were cancelled to bring the calendar into synch with the seasons. Then a formula was devised in order to make it adhere as closely as possible to the true solar (tropical) year. This entails considering that 3 leap years are cancelled over 400 years by declaring that the secular years are only bissextile if divisible by 400. But this is still not fine enough to match the true solar year, and will lead to a full day difference in 3,000 years.

69 The tropic year varies in length over time. Today it is 365.2422 days, but in 3000 BC it was 365.2425. Belmonte, op. cit., pp. 10 and 36.

70 Dr Malek reviewed my first book, *The Orion Mystery*, in 1994. See *Discussions in Egyptology*, Vol. 30.

71 Shaw and Nicholson, op. cit., p. 256.

72 Mark Lehner, op. cit., p. 84.

73 G.A. Wainwright, *The Sky Religion in Egypt*, Cambridge University Press, 1938, pp. 14–18.

74 G.A. Wainwright, 'Seshat and the Pharaoh', *Journal of Egyptian Archaeology*, Vol. 26, 1941, pp. 30–40.

75 Ibid. pp. 21–3.

76 Wainwright, *The Sky Religion*, op. cit., pp. 24–5.

77 Donald B. Redford, *Akhenaten the Heretic King*, The American

University in Cairo Press, 1989, p. 126.

78 H. Frankfort, *Kingship and the Gods*, Chicago, 1948, p. 86.
79 Redford, *Akhenaten*, op. cit., p. 127.
80 See Appendix 3.
81 Wilkinson, op. cit., p. 212.
82 Flinders Petrie, op. cit., Chapter XII, pp. 177–8.
83 E.A. Wallis Budge, *The Gods of The Egyptians*, Vol. 1, Dover Publications, New York, 1969, p. 425.
84 Wainwright, *The Sky Religion*, op. cit., p. 24–5.
85 E.C. Krupp, *Echoes of the Ancient Skies* op. cit., pp. 25–6.
86 Ali Radwan, 'Step Pyramids', *Treasures of the Pyramids*, ed. Zahi Hawass, White Star Publishers, 2004, p. 102.
87 Bomhard, op. cit., p. xi.
88 Wilkinson, op. cit., p. 76.
89 Rundle Clark, op. cit., p. 27.
90 Ibid., p. 263.
91 Patrick F. O'Mara, 'Was the Sed Festival Periodic in Early Egyptian History?', *Discussions in Egyptology*, Vol. 12, 1988, p. 55.
92 Nancy Hathaway, *Friendly Guide to the Universe*, New York, 1994.

Chapter Three: The Duat of Memphis

1 Miroslav Verner, *Abusir: Realm of Osiris*, The American University in Cairo Press, 2002, p. 11.
2 A Swiss Egyptologist, who I prefer not to name here, politely told me in a letter to concentrate on becoming 'a good engineer' and forget about the pyramids.
3 Verner, op. cit., p. 14.
4 J. Malek, 'Orion and the Giza Pyramids', *Discussions in Egyptology*, Vol. 30, 1994, pp. 101–14.
5 Lehner, *The Complete Pyramids*, op. cit., pp. 106–7.
6 Ibid., p. 120.
7 Ibid.
8 David G. Jeffreys, 'The topography of Heliopolis and Memphis: some cognitive aspects', in H. Guksch and D. Polz (eds.), *Stationen: Beitrage zur Kulturgeschichte Agyptens*, Rainer Stadelmann Gewimdet, Mainz, 1998, p. 70.
9 The bearing of the rising sun at summer solstice was near 28° north-of-east. Allowing for 2 degrees altitude for the full disc to be seen over a

mound or obelisk from Abu Ruwash, this brought the bearing to near 27° north-of-east.

10 The story is told in the Westcar Papyrus (Berlin Museum). Verner, op. cit., p. 70.

11 Malek and Baines, *The Cultural Atlas: Ancient Egypt*, op. cit., p. 154.

12 According to Miroslav Verner, the name Abusir derives from the Greek Busiris, which was taken from the ancient Egyptian Per Usir, meaning 'Realm of Osiris'. See Verner, op. cit.

13 Miroslav Verner attributes this discovery to Werner Kaiser (Verner, op. cit., p. 42).

14 Jeffreys, op. cit., pp. 63–71.

15 Ausim is some 20 kilometres north of the Giza pyramids.

16 Strabo, *Geographia*, Vol. XVII, I, 30.

17 George Goyon, '*Kerkasòre et L'ancien Observatoire D'Eudoxe*', *Bulletin de L'Institut Français D'Archeologie Orientale*, Tome 74, 1974, p. 142.

18 George Goyon, 'Nouvelles Observations Relatives à l'Orientation de la Pyramide de Kheops', *Revue D'Egyptologie*, Tome 22, Paris, 1970, p. 85.

19 Ibid., p. 89. See also Baines and Malek, *Altas of Ancient Egpyt*, op. cit., p. 15.

20 G.A. Wainwright, 'Iron in Egypt', *Journal of Egyptian Archaeology*, Vol. 18, 1933, pp. 6–11.

21 Shaw and Nicholson, op. cit., p. 42. Also Z. Zaba, *L'Orientation Astronomique dans L'Ancienne Egypte et la Precession de l'Axe du Monde*, Prague, 1953.

22 Zaba, op. cit.

23 Ibid., p. 60.

24 Wilkinson, op. cit., p. 206.

25 Ibid., p. 205.

26 Pyramid Texts, 351.

27 Shaw and Nicholson, op. cit., p. 162.

28 Ibid., pp. 96–7.

29 Ibid.

30 Herman Kees, *Ancient Egypt: A Cultural Topography*, Faber & Faber, London, 1961, p. 155.

31 James H. Breasted, *Development of Religion and Thought in Ancient Egypt*, University of Pennsylvania, 1972, p. 101.

32 R.O. Faulkner, 'The King and the Star Religion in the Pyramid Texts', *Journal of Near Eastern Studies*, Vol. 25, 1966, pp. 153–61.

33 I.E.S. Edwards, *The Pyramids of Egypt*, Penguin, 1982, p. 292.
34 Pyramid Texts utterance, 263.
35 Pyramid Texts, 360.
36 Pyramid Texts, 865.
37 Pyramid Texts, 351–353.
38 Lehner, *The Complete Pyramids*, op. cit., p. 28
39 Pyramid Texts, 819–821.
40 Pyramid Texts, 934–6.
41 One of the signs, Libra, is neither animal nor human.
42 Known also as the Seven Sisters.
43 E.A. Wallis-Budge, *The Gods of the Egyptians*, Vol. 2, Dover Publications, New York, 1969, p. 312.
44 George Goyon, 'Kerkasòre et L'ancien Obsevatoire D'Eudoxe', op. cit., p. 144.
45 Belmonte, op. cit., p. 32.
46 Virginia Lee Davis, 'Identifying Ancient Egyptian Constellations', *Archaeoastronomy* No. 9 (*JHA*, Vol. XVI, 1985).
47 Donald V. Etz, 'A New Look at the Constellation Figures in the Celestial Diagram', *Journal of the American Centre in Egypt*, Vol. XXXIV, 1997, pp. 143–61.
48 Selim Hassan, *The Sphinx, Its History in the Light of Recent Excavations*, Government Press, Cairo, 1949, p. 69.
49 I.E.S. Edwards, *The Pyramids of Egypt*, Penguin, 1961, p. 122.
50 Hassan, op. cit., p. 94.
51 Paul Jordan, *Riddles of the Sphinx*, Penguin, op. cit., p. 181.
52 Hassan, op. cit., p. 80.
53 Ibid., p. 127.
54 Lehner, *The Complete Pyramids*, op. cit., p. 127.
55 Hassan, op. cit., pp. 139–40.
56 Graham Hancock and I used this same logic in 1996 in our book *Keeper of Genesis* as part of our argument that the Sphinx represented Leo (Heinemann, 1996).
57 Christian Zivie-Coche, *SPHINX!*, Edition Noesis, Paris, 1994, p. 89.
58 Hassan, op. cit., p. 139–40. The association of Horakhti or Ra-Horakhti and the Sphinx is also made by Cyril Aldred *Akhenaten, King of Egypt*, op. cit., pp. 142, 237. See also Redford, *Akhenaten the Heretic King*, op. cit., p. 20.
59 Fakhry, Ahmed, *The Pyramids*, University of Chicago Press, 1969, p. 164.

60 Hassan, op. cit., pp. 55–6.

61 Zivie-Coche, op. cit., p. 89.

62 Zahi, Hawass, 'The Temples of the Rising Sun', in *Horus Magazine*, April 2001.

63 Redford, op. cit. p. 180.

64 Labib Habachi, *The Obelisks of Egypt*, The American University in Cairo Press, 1994, p. 5.

65 Ibid., p. 47.

66 Ibid., p. 90.

67 Ibid., p. 165.

68 Edwards, *The Pyramids of Egypt*, 1993, op. cit., pp. 284, 286.

69 Alexander Gurshtein, 'The Evolution of the Zodiac in the Context of Ancient History', *Vistas in Astronomy Journal*, Vol. 41, Part 4 (1997), p. 512.

70 Bauval and Gilbert, op. cit.

71 Lehner, op. cit., p. 29.

72 Nataliè Beaux, 'La douat dans les Textes des Pyramides', *Bulletin de l'Institut Français D'Archaéologie Orientale*, Vol. 94, 1994, pp. 1–6.

73 Hassan, op. cit., pp. 278–9.

74 Bauval and Gilbert, op. cit., pp. 262–3.

75 A South African author, Wayne Herschel, has also independently arrived at the same conclusion that the Pleiades represent the Abusir pyramid cluster. He published this in a book entitled *The Hidden Records* (by Hidden Records, 2005). Since Herschel's book was published before *The Egypt Code*, I acknowledge that this conclusion must be attributed originally to him.

76 Malek and Baines, op. cit., p. 154.

77 M. Verner, op. cit., p. 266.

78 Ronald A. Wells, 'The 5th Dynasty Sun Temples at Abu Ghorab as Old Kingdom Star Clocks: Examples of Applied Ancient Egyptian Astronomy', *Studien zur Altagyptischen Kultur* (SAK). Band 4, 1990, pp. 95–105.

79 Wilkinson, p. 121.

80 Lehner, op. cit., p. 151.

81 Ibid., p. 152.

82 Using geographical coordinates: Abusir to Heliopolis = 27,620 metres; Giza to Abusir = 11,420 metres; Letopolis to Heliopolis = 17,000.

83 The pyramid builders are thought to have used a unit of measurement

called the royal cubit which was equal to about 0.525 metres.

84 Bauval and Gilbert, op. cit., pp. 262–3.

85 E.C. Krupp, op. cit., p. 22.

Chapter Four: As Above, So Below

1 Pyramid Texts Utterance, 263.

2 Pyramid Texts, 360.

3 Pyramid Texts, 351–353.

4 Lady Duff Gordon, *Letters from Egypt 1862–1867*, Ed. Gordon Waterfield, Routledge & Keagan Paul, London, 1969, p. 180.

5 Scott, *Heremetica*, Asclepius III, op. cit.

6 Quoted in Lockyer, *The Dawn of Astronomy*, Cassell, 1894, pp. 231–2.

7 I used the words 'almost perfect' because, of course, the natural morphology of the Nilotic region and the contours of the Memphite necropolis imposed on the ancient surveyors constraints that forced them to deviate from an ideal plan. On the whole, however, the overall imagery of the celestial Duat is unmistakably seen defined on the land.

8 Arielle Kozloff, 'Star-gazing in Ancient Egypt', *Hommages à Jean Leclant*, Institut Français d'Archéologie Orientale, Bibliotheque D'Etude, Vol. 4, 1994.

9 Ibid.

10 In 1989, a few years before Kozloff's article appeared, I had arrived more or less at the same conclusion when I wrote that 'A major feature of the (celestial) After-world often mentioned in the Pyramid Texts is the "Winding Waterway", which was, in all probability, seen as a celestial counterpart of the Nile . . . The "winding" characteristic of this celestial-Nile perfectly describes the gyrations of the Milky Way about the earth, surely the only feature in the sky which can be regarded as a "winding waterway"', Bauval, *Discussions in Egyptology*, Vol. 13, 1989.

11 There is today a modern multi-storey building which somewhat serves the same purpose!

12 From Flinders Petrie's survey: Distance from the Khufu Pyramid to the Menkaura Pyramid measured from the SE/NW extend diagonals is 928.32m. The resulting geometry produces the angle 43° 50'. Others, such as the geometrician Robin Cook, have refined this angle to 43°20'.

13 Hertha von Deschend and Giorgio de Santillana, *Hamlet's Mill*, Nonpareil Books, 1992, p. 67.

14 E.A. Wallis-Budge, *The Gods of the Egyptians*, Dover, 1969, Vol. II, p.

312. See also Otto Neugebauer, *The Exact Sciences in Antiquity*, Dover Publications, New York, 1969. Also Otto Neugebauer, 'The History of Ancient Astronomy', *Journal of Near Eastern Studies*, Vol. IV, 1945, p. 24.

[15] Proclus, *Commentaries on the Timaeus of Plato*, Vol. I, 40B.

[16] Strabo, *Geography*, Vol. XVII, I, 29.

[17] Diodorus, *Bibliotheca Historia*, Vol. I, 98.

[18] Iambilicus, *Life of Pythagoras*, 12.

[19] Ibid., 4,19.

[20] See Proclus, op. cit., Vol. IV. See also Schwaller de Lubicz, *Sacred Science*, Inner Traditions, New York, 1982, p. 286. According to Hertha von Deschend (*Hamlet's Mill*, op. cit., p. 143): 'There is good reason to assume that he (Hipparchus) actually rediscovered this (the precession), that it had been known some thousand years previously, and that on it the Archaic Age based its long-range computation of time.'

[21] Z. Zaba, *L'Orientation Astronomique dans L'Ancienne Egypte et la Precession de l'Axe du Monde*, op. cit., p. 55.

[22] Schwaller de Lubicz, op. cit., pp. 279–80.

[23] Quoted by Schwaller de Lubicz, op. cit., p. 285.

[24] Lockyer, op. cit., p. 23.

[25] Alexander Gurshtein, 'The Great Pyramids of Egypt as Sanctuaries Commemorating the Origin of the Zodiac: An Analysis of Astronomical Evidence', *Physics-Doklady*, Vol. 41, No. 6, 1996, pp. 228–32. See also A. Gurshtein, 'On the Origins of the Zodiacal Constellations', *Vista in Astronomy*, Vol. 36, Part 2, 1993, pp. 171–91.

[26] Guilio Magli's paper is also on line at: http://xxx.sissa.it/abs/physics/0407108.

[27] Krupp, op. cit., p. 201.

[28] Ibid.

[29] A cataract is a change in level of the river. There are six main cataracts in all, the sixth being just north of Khartoum in the Sudan.

[30] Wilkinson, op. cit., p. 165.

[31] Ibid.

[33] Ron Wells, 'Sothis and the Satet Temple on Elephantine: A Direct Connection', Studien zur Altagyptischen Kultur (SAK). Band 12, 1985, p. 258.

[33] R. Wilkinson, op. cit., p. 212. The earliest phase of the Satet (Satis) temple was an early dynasty 'hut' built into the corner of the three boulders

enclosure. In the Third Dynasty this was enlarged and a forecourt was added. Further works took place in the Sixth Dynasty and various new temples were constructed on top of the ruins of the earlier one during the Eleventh and Twelfth Dynasties, especially by the pharaoh Sesostris I. In the New Kingdom the Eighteenth Dynasty queen-pharaoh Hatchepsut had the Satis temple completely rebuilt some two metres higher than the original three boulders. The Eighteenth Dynasty edifice was then extended to the east during the Ramesside period and again in the Twenty-sixth Dynasty. Finally a totally new temple was built over the ruins of the last one during the Ptolemaic period.

34 Wells, op. cit. p. 255.

35 Ibid., pp. 258–62. Wells also discovered that the temple had other alignments to Orion's belt as well as the Big Dipper (the thigh). According to Wells, 'it is evident that Orion also crossed the traverse axis of the temple . . . the axial positions were computed for the star called Alnilam (ε Orionis), the middle star of the "belt"'. Wells discovered that the designers of the temple seem to have intended to demarcate the two extreme variations of the Big Dipper constellation as it revolved around the north celestial pole. This is most intriguing, for we recall how other religious structures going back to the Old Kingdom were also linked to the star Sirius, Orion and the constellation of the Big Dipper, notably the Djoser complex at Saqqara and the Great Pyramid at Giza.

36 Extreme sceptics have argued that the succession of ancient surveyors were not aware that the older axis was not anymore directed to Sirius and simply oriented the new temple's axis without being conscious of the change. This may perhaps be possible had there been only one change in axis orientation. But the original axis was changed several times. Also, since the ancient surveyors must have known that the temple was dedicated to Satet, goddess of the flood, which in turn was linked to the heliacal rising of Sirius, this argument is simply untenable.

37 'The word Hwt ("Hat") . . . was used in the New Kingdom with the meaning "Temple". Jaroslav Cerny, 'The Temple as an abbreviated name for the Temple of Medinet Habu', *Journal of Egyptian Archaeology*, Vol. 26, 1940, p. 127.

38 Krupp op. cit., p. 258.

39 Malek and op. cit., p. 112.

40 Robert Bauval and Graham Hancock, *Keeper of Genesis*, Heinemann, 1996, pp. 208–214.

41 Heinrich Brugsch, 1891, *Thesaurus Inscriptionum Aegyptiacarum* p. 189 quoted by Lockyer, op. cit., pp. 204–5.

42 Auguste Mariette, *Denderah*, Vol. I, 1875, pp. 142 and 263.

43 Although we have shown that Horus was identified to Sirius in the Pyramid Texts (*c.* 2300 BC), from the Eighteenth Dynasty (*c.* 1500 BC) Sirius became identified to his mother the goddess Isis. See, 'Sirius, Etoile et Jeune Horus', op. cit., p. 64, n.14.

44 Krupp, op. cit., p. 257.

45 Ibid.

46 Ibid., p. 258.

47 Lockyer, op. cit., p. 193. Lockyer actually took *in situ* measurements and concluded that the alignment of the temple of Isis was 18° 30'; this was also roughly the average of the measurements obtained earlier by Lepsius and Mariette.

48 Lockyer, op. cit., p. 200.

49 Lockyer's calculations that the main temple was aligned to the star Dubhe (Alpha Ursa Major), the brightest star in the 'thigh' constellation, were based on very early dates which do not apply to the existing temple.

50 These drawings can be seen in Zaba, *L'Orientation Astronomique dans L'Ancienne Egypte et la Precession de l'Axe du Monde*, op. cit.

51 Mariette, *Dendera*, p. 206; see also Lockyer, *The Dawn of Astronomy* op. cit., p. 194.

52 Zaba, op. cit., p. 59.

53 Sylvie Cauville-Colin, 'Le Temple d'Isis à Dendera', *Bulletin de la Société Français D'Egyptologie* (BSFE), Vol. 123, March 1992, pp. 31–48.

54 John A. West, *Serpent in the Sky*, Quest Books, 1993, p. 103.

55 Wilkinson, op. cit., p. 37.

56 With the exception of the Great Sphinx, whose age is still an open question for researchers.

57 Henri Frankfort, *Kingship and the Gods*, University of Chicago Press, 1978, p. 4.

58 Jane B. Sellers, *The Death of Gods in Ancient Egypt*, Penguin, 1992, p. 94.

59 David O'Connor, 'The Interpretation of the Old Kingdom Pyramid Complex', H. Guksch & D. Polz (eds) *Stazionen: Beiträge Zur Kulturgeschicte Agyptens*, Rainer Stadelmann Gewidmet, Mainz, 1998.

Chapter Five: The Return of the Phoenix

1 Such terminology is still in use today. Thus when you travel from Cairo

to Luxor, you are said to be going from Lower Egypt to Upper Egypt.

2   Edwards, *The Pyramids of Egypt*, op. cit., p. 3.

3   Michael A. Hoffman, *Egypt Before the Pharaohs*, Ark, 1984, p. 289.

4   Verner, op. cit., p. 16.

5   Malek and Baines, op. cit., p. 31.

6   Frankfort, op. cit., p. 24.

7   Miriam Lichtheim, *Ancient Egyptian Literature*, Vol. 1, University of California Press, 1975, p. 52.

8   Ibid., p. 51.

9   Frankfort, op. cit., p. 24.

10 Lichtheim, op. cit., pp. 52–3.

11 Samuel Mercer, *The Religion of Ancient Egypt*, London, 1949, p. 331.

12 Lockyer, op. cit., p. 345.

13 Ron Wells, 'The Mythology of Nut and the Birth of Ra', *Studien zur Altagyptischen Kultur (SAK)*, Band 19, Vol. 19, 1992, pp. 303–21.

14 Dupuydt, *Civil and Lunar Calendars in Ancient Egypt*, op. cit., p. 62.

15 Ibid.

16 Lockyer, op. cit., Preface. On this matter Lockyer also wrote: 'My lectures, given in November, 1890, were printed in *Nature*, April–July, 1891, under the title "On some Points in the Early History of Astronomy", with the following note: "From shorthand notes of a course of lectures to working men delivered at the Museum of Practical Geology, Jermyn Street, in November, 1890. The notes were revised by me at Aswan during the month of January. I have found, since my return from Egypt in March, that part of the subject-matter of the lectures had been previously discussed by Professor Nissen, who has employed the same materials as myself. To him, therefore, so far as I at present know, belongs the credit of having first made the suggestion that ancient temples were oriented on an astronomical basis. His articles are to be found in the *Rheinisches Museum für Philologie*, 1885."'

17 At the Royal College of Science, South Kensington, now part of Imperial College.

18 Lockyer served as the editor of *Nature* until his death in 1920.

19 A astronomical observatory and radio station owned by the East Devon District Council and operated by The Norman Lockyer Observatory Society.

20 It would not be until 1981, nearly a century after Lockyer, that professional astronomers recognised archaeoastronomy as a 'truly

international' branch of science at the First Oxford International Conference in Archaeoastronomy (see Krupp, op. cit., Foreword).

21 There were two brothers, Heinrich and Emile Brugsch. As both were given the title of 'Bey', I cannot be sure which of the two brothers Lockyer met in 1891. Heinrich was 64 at that time, and Emile was 49. Emile was at the time assistant curator at the Cairo Museum. A decade earlier, in 1881, he had made a name for himself for having saved the haul of royal mummies found at Deir el Bahari in Upper Egypt by bringing them to Cairo. That same year Emile had also been part of the exploration team under Gaston Maspero who discovered the Pyramid Texts at Saqqara. Lockyer refers to various publications by 'Brugsch Bey', so I should think that it was Heinrich Brugsch that he met in Cairo.

22 Heinrich Brugsch, 'Astronomical and Astrological Inscriptions on Ancient Egyptian Monuments', trans. by George Chamberlain from *Thesaurus Inscriptionum Aegyptiacarum*, by Heinrich Brugsch, Vol. 1, 1883. The English translation was originally published as a series of 18 articles (from April 1978 to January 1980) in the monthly journal, the *Griffith Observer* (published by the Griffith Observatory in Los Angeles).

23 It was not until the formation of the *Services des Antiquitées* in Cairo in 1856 by Auguste Mariette that some form of official control was put into place to preserve ancient sites.

24 Lockyer, op. cit., pp. 98–106.

25 Today the axis of the Karnak temple would no longer be aligned precisely with the rising and setting sun at the two solstices because of the so-called *Milkovitch Factor*. In very simple terms the sun appears to oscillate to and fro from about 22° to about 24.4° in a period of about 40,000 years. Today the earth's axis has a declination (is tilted to the plain of the ecliptic) of 23°27′ but when Karnak was built it was nearly 24°.

26 Gerald Hawkins, *Beyond Stonehenge*, Arrow, 1977, p. 206.

27 Luc Gabolde, 'Brèves Communicotions', *Revue d'Egyptologie*, Vol. 50, 1999, p. 278.

28 I witnessed this effect on the 21st June 2003 (see plates).

29 Gerald Hawkins did not carry out actual astronomical observations at Karnak at the winter solstice, but rather obtained the orientation angle from survey maps at the Franco-Egyptian research centre at Luxor and, like Lockyer before him, calculated the position of the sunrise at the solstice rather than observe it. However, a few years later the astronomer

Ed Krupp confirmed Hawkins's values from actual observations. The observations were carried out at the east end of the Karnak temple from the so-called 'High Room of the Sun' located on the north-east corner (Krupp, op. cit., pp. 253–7).

30 Hawkins, op. cit., p. 205.

31 See Raymond Weill, *Bases, Methods et Resultants de la Chronologie Egyptienne*, Paris, 1926, pp. 121–2.

32 Marshall Clagett, *Ancient Egyptian Science, Vol. II, Calendars, Clocks and Astronomy*, American Philosophical Society, 1995, Fig. III. 6a.

33 Abdel Mohsen Bakir, 'The Cairo Calendar of Lucky and Unlucky Days (Journal d'Entrée, no. 86637)', *Annales du Service des Antiquités de L'Egypte*, Vol. 48, 1948, pp. 425–31.

34 Clagett, op. cit., p. 136, n. 25.

35 Ibid., p. 137.

36 Belmonte, op. cit., p. 36. The difference between my date of 2028 BC and Belmonte's date of 2004 BC is because he dates the inauguration of the civil calendar 2757 BC, which is the lower estimate in his calculations, rather than the accepted 2781 BC.

37 In the so-called 'golden Horus' name of Akhenaten (Aldred, *Akhenaten*, op. cit., p. 89).

38 Redford, *Akhenaten*, op. cit., p. 133.

39 Ibid., op. cit., p. 95.

40 Leo Dupuydt, 'On the consistency of the wandering year as backbone of Egyptian Chronology', *Journal of the American Research Centre in Egypt (JARCE)*, Vol. XXXII, 1995, pp. 45–6.

41 W.M. Flinders Petrie, *Researches in Sinai*, John Murray, London, 1906 p. 177: 'In the great festival of the renewal of a Sothic period in 139 AD, the signs of the months are prominent on the coins of Alexandria.' For the possible celebrations in the year 1321 BC see Dupuydt, 'On the consistency of the wandering year', op. cit., p. 46.

42 Gurshtein, 'The Great Pyramids of Egypt as Sanctuaries Commemorating the Origin of the Zodiac: An Analysis of Astronomical Evidence', op. cit., p. 229.

43 Gurshtein, 'The evolution of the Zodiac in the context of ancient oriental history', op. cit., pp. 515–16.

44 Belmonte, op. cit., p. 37.

45 Hassan, *Sphinx*, op. cit., pp. 184–5. See also Aldred, *Akhenaten*, op. cit., p. 142.

46 Redford, op. cit., p. 20.

47 According to Cyril Aldred: 'At the death of the sardonic old warrior Amenophis II (Amenhotep II), his son the youth Tuthmosis, Menkheperure, succeeded to the throne of Horus. He may have been preceded by an elder brother who served his father as co-regent but died before he could come into his own. Tuthmosis IV attributed his good fortune to the sponsorship of the supreme god of Lower Egypt, Re-Horakhti, who in a dream promised him the crown if he would clear away the sands that engulfed his giant image of the Sphinx at Giza . . . intervention at the highest level is seen in the undertaking of Tuthmosis IV to uncover the giant image of Re-Horakhti, the god of Lower Egypt, from the sand that engulfed his great sphinx at Giza' (Aldred, *Akhenaten, King of Egypt*, op. cit., p. 142).

48 The author Ahmed Osman is the originator of this hypothesis. See Ahmed Osman, *Moses and Akhenaten*, Bear & Company, Vermont, 2002.

49 Aldred, *Akhenaten,* op. cit., pp. 25, 67.

50 Rosalie David, *The Cult of the Sun*, J.M. Dent, London, 1980, p. 187. See also Alexandre Moret, *Alexander: Kings and Gods of Egyp*t, G.P. Putnam's Sons, New York, 1912, p. 52.

51 George Hart, *A Dictionary of Egyptian Gods and Goddess*, Routledge & Kegan Paul, 1988, p. 42.

52 Hermann Schlogl, 'Aten', in *The Ancient Gods Speak*, op. cit., p. 23.

53 Redford gives 1377 BC (*Akhenaten*, op. cit.), but Malek and J. Baines give 1353 BC, which seems to be generally accepted by most Egyptologists (*The Cultural Atlas of the World: Ancient Egypt*, op. cit.).

54 Redford, op. cit., p. 144.

Chapter Six: Lord of Jubilees

1 There is a scarab of Amenhotep III with this title, see William M. Flinders Petrie, *Historical Scarabs*, London, 1899, Pl. 40, no. 1263 (British Museum Catalogue BM 16912).

2 It was on this particular tour that I met Sandro Mainardi from Florence who kindly produced the graphics for this book.

3 B.J. Kemp and S. Garfi, *A Survey of the Ancient City of El-'Amarna*, The Egypt Exploration Society, London, 1993, p. 10.

4 Ibid.

5 The model was made by the architectural model-makers Tetra/Andy Ingham Associates in Clapham, south London. It was designed by

Michael Mallinson. Barry Kemp and Kate Spence served as consultants. The model can be seen on: http://www.mcdonald.cam.ac.uk/Projects/ Amarna/Model2004.htm/modelindex.htm. It was displayed at the Museum of Fine Arts in Boston in 1999.

6 Kemp and Garfi, op. cit., Map Sheets 4 and 5.

7 Aldred, *Akhenaten*, op. cit., p. 15.

8 Ibid., p. 47.

9 Redford, *Akhenaten*, op. cit., pp. 172–3.

10 Ibid., p. 180. Apparently the king also bore that title, David, op cit., p. 187. Also Moret, op. cit., p. 52.

11 Arthur Weigall, *Life and Times of Akhenaton, Pharoah of Egpyt*, G.P. Putnam's Sons, New York, 1923, p. 63.

12 It may be worth perhaps mentioning that also in the year 1360 BC, when Akhenaten moved the court to Tell el Amarna, Halley's Comet was making its reappearance in the eastern sky at dawn – perhaps seen as the cosmic phoenix returning to Heliopolis?

13 Redford, op. cit., p. 139.

14 Very rarely a small cobra was also included, (the so-called *uraeus*) at the bottom of the solar disc.

15 Wilkinson, op. cit., p. 212.

16 Redford, op. cit., p. 139. Redford translates *zep tepi* as 'First Occasion, i.e. the first moment of creation'.

17 Jocelyn Gohary, *Akhenaten's Sed-Festival at Karnak*, Kegan Paul International, London, 1992, pp. 29–30.

18 Gohary, op. cit., p. 29.

19 It means 'three' in Arabic, but could also be from the Italian word *tagliati* (cuttings), which makes more sense.

20 Francis Llewellyn Griffith, 'The Jubilee of Akhenaten', *Journal of Egyptian Archaeology*, Vol. 5, 1918, p. 62.

21 Gohary, *Akenaten's Sed-Festival at Karnak*, op. cit., p. 32.

22 See note 1 above.

23 Inscription on the First Boundary Stone, 13th Day, 4th Month, 2nd Season, 6th Year.

24 Griffith, op. cit., p. 62.

25 Hart, op. cit., p. 44.

26 Quirke, op. cit., p. 154.

27 Gohary, op. cit., pp. 2–3.

28 Redford, op. cit., p. 146.

29 Gohary, op. cit., p. 4.

30 Ibid.

31 This was during the Stars & Signs II Egypt Tour, which I organise with Quest Travel every year.

32 The Sphinx measures 15 metres in height. Another of Rameses' statues which lies on its back at Mit'Rahin (Memphis) would have been 18 metres high when upright.

33 The statue is also said to be a cryptograph of Rameses II's 'coronation name' *User-maat-re*.

34 Baines and Malek, op. cit., p. 184.

35 Hart, op. cit., p. 82.

36 H. te Velde, 'Some Remarks on the Mysterious Language of the Baboons', *Essays Dedicated to Prof. M.S.H.G. Heerma van Voss*, University of Amsterdam, Kampen 1988, p. 129.

37 J.M.A. Janssen, *Hieogliefen*, E.J. Brill Leiden, 1952, p. 7.

38 Jeane-Claude Goyon 'Textes Mythologiques II', *Bulletin de L'Institut Français d'Archéologie Orientale (BIFAO)*, Vol. 75, 1975, p. 376.

39 Jan K. van der Haagen, 'Au Grand Temple D' Abou Simbel: Le Secret des Pretres et des Astronomes', *Courier de l'Unesco*, October 1962.

40 Haagen, op. cit. It is interesting to note that an inscription carved on the cliff near the Abu Simbel temple reads *Rameses-ashahebsed*, which translates as 'Rameses-Rich-in-Jubilees'. Egyptologists attribute this to an official of the king's inner circle also called Rameses who was in charge of the construction of the temple (See T.G.H. James, *Ramesses the Great*, The American University Press in Cairo, 2002, p. 177).

41 There was something else worth mentioning in the astronomical alignment of the temple that caught the attention of the Belgian astronomer Professor M. Bonneval, a colleague of Haagen. The latter discovered that in *c.* 1260 BC, when construction work on the temple was probably started, another more frequent celestial spectacle would have been seen at night from late May to early December: the three bright stars of Orion's belt rising over the eastern cliffs in direct alignment with the axis of the temple. Haagen thus wrote: 'We know that Orion, or more precisely the three belt stars, played an important role for the Egyptians ... And it also is known from various texts that Orion (Sah in ancient Egyptian) was assimilated to Osiris, god of resurrection.' (Haagen, op. cit.)

42 Egypt's Supreme Council of Antiquities (SCA), however, was so convinced of Haagen's conclusions that when the Abu Simbel temple was

moved to a higher location in the mid–1960s it was aligned to the 22 October sunrise, the so-called 'Festival of the Sun'.

43 We have seen how the ancient Egyptians were particularly taken by the belief that there had been a 'First Time' from which the perpetual cycle of the sun-god had begun and which they calculated returned to its point of origin every 1,460 years. But in actual fact it takes 1,506 years for the civil calendar to re-coincide exactly. We have also seen how the point of origin was fixed at the summer solstice, which today falls on 21 June. It is my contention, therefore, that a 'super' jubilee was celebrated at those points of return, one of which would have been in *c.* 1275 BC. In that year, the 'jubilee date' of 1 Tybi would fall 120 days after the summer solstice, which is 19 October. The Great Temple of Rameses II at Abu Simbel may, indeed, be a memorial to such an event. Supporting this hypothesis is the name that was occasionally given to the jubilees, such as the *zep tepi heb-sed* and also the *zep tepi whmw heb-sed*, which respectively translate as 'the First Time Jubilee', and 'the First Time Return Jubilee'. (See Flinders Petrie, op. cit., p. 180. See also Patrick F. O'Mara, 'Was the Sed Festival Periodic in Early Egyptian History?', *Discussions in Egyptology*, Vol. 12, 1988, p. 55).

44 At this latitude the shift over 5,000 years would be practically unnoticeable to a naked-eye observer.

45 The Sphinx faces due east, but the causeway is oriented some 13 to 14° south-of-east. Calculations show that the sunrise would be at 13° south-of-east on 21 February and also on 19 October.

46 Colin Reader, 'Giza Before the Fourth Dynasty', *Journal of the Ancient Chronology Forum*, Vol. 9, pp. 5–21.

47 Malek and Baines, op. cit., p. 36.

48 Mark Lehner, 'Giza: A Contextual Approach to the Pyramids', *Archiv. Für Orientforschung*, Vol. 32, 1985, pp. 136–159.

49 Ibid.

50 Jeremy Naydler, *Shamanic Wisdom in the Pyramid Texts*, Inner Traditions Publishing, Rochester, Vermont, 2005, pp. 71–122.

51 Ibid., p. 99, Fig. 4.11.

52 Ibid., p. 103, Fig. 4.15.

53 Wilkinson, op. cit., p. 239.

54 Kemp and Garfi, op. cit., Map Sheets 4 and 5.

55 Roel Oostra's TV documentary is being made for the Dutch channel AVRO and the Italian channel RAI II.

Conclusion

1   Pyramid Texts, Utterance 600.
2   Due to precession, a star will also rise at a different position on the eastern horizon over a long period of time, and will return back to the original position every 26,000 years (but allowing a small difference due to the proper motion of the star).
3   Wilkinson, op cit., pp. 77–9.
4   E.A. Wallis Budge, *The Egyptian Heaven and Hell: The Book of What Is in the Duat*, Vol.1, Martin Hopkinson & Co., London, 1925, pp. 240, 258.

Appendix 1: Running the Heb Sed

1   G. Wainwright, *The Sky Religion in Egypt* (Cambridge, 1938), pp. 16–17.
2   Ibid., p. 4.
3   Jocelyn Gohary, *Akhenaten's Sed-Festival at Karnak* (London, 1992), p. 2. This is an excellent survey of the different theories about the *Sed*-festival, with a very complete biography on the subject.
4   The major works on the *Heb-Sed* are essential references to understanding its complexities. They are: C.M. Firth and J.E. Quibell, *The Step Pyramid* (2 vols.) (Cairo 1935); F.W. von Bissing and H. Kees, *Das Re-Heiligtum des Konigs Newoser-Re II and III* (Leipzig, 1923 and 1928); and E. Naville, *The Festival Hall of Osorkon II in the Great Temple of Bubastis* (London, 1892).
5   H. Frankfort, *Kingship and the Gods* (Chicago, 1948), p. 80.
6   Ibid., p. 84.
7   Ibid., p. 85.
8   Firth and Quibell, op. cit., Vol. I, p. 11. Frankfort, op. cit., p. 80, states just the reverse.
9   Alan Gardiner, 'Horus the Behdetite', *Journal of Egyptian Archaeology*, Vol. 30, 1944, p. 27.
10 Ibid., p. 28, note 1.
11 Firth and Quibell, op. cit., Vol. I, p. iii.
12 Ibid., Vol. I, p. 23.
13 Barry J. Kemp, *Ancient Egypt, Anatomy of a Civilization* (London, 1991), p. 100. This is an excellent dicussion of the ideal type in Egyptian architecture.
14 E. Uphill, 'The Egyptian Sed-festival Rites', *Journal of Near Eastern Studies*, Vol. 24, 1965.

[15] J. Wilson, 'Illuminating the Thrones at the Egyptian Jubilee', *Journal of the American Oriental Society*, Vol. 56, 1936, pp. 293 ff.

[16] Kemp, op. cit., p. 97.

[17] Firth and Quibell, op. cit., Vol. I, p. 69.

[18] Ibid., Vol. II, pl. 15.

[19] Wilson, op. cit., p. 378.

[20] Ibid., p. 377.

[21] Ibid., p. 379.

[22] Frankfort, op. cit., p. 92.

[23] Ibid, pp. 364–5, n. 49.

[24] A.M. Roth, 'The Pss-Kf and the "Opening of the Mouth" Ceremony: A Ritual of Birth and Rebirth', *Journal of Egyptian Archaeology*, Vol. 78, 1992, pp. 113–47.

[25] Ibid., p. 124.

[26] W.J. Murnane, 'Servant, Seer, Saint, Son of Hapu; Amenhotep, Called Huy', *KTM*, Vol. 2:2, Summer 1991, p. 11.

[27] Ibid., p. 13.

[28] W.R. Johnson, 'The Dazzling Sun Disk: Iconography Evidence that Amenhotep III reigned as the Aten Personified', *KMT*, Vol. 2:2, Summer 1991, p. 22.

[29] Ibid., p. 60.

[30] W.E.A. Budge, *The Book of Opening the Mouth*, London, 1909, p. 31.

[31] Firth and Quibell, Vol. I, p. 58.

[32] A.J. Spencer, 'Two Enigmatic Hieroglyphs and Their Relation to the Sed-festival', *Journal of Egyptian Archaeology*, Vol. 64, 1978, p. 55.

[33] Raymond O. Faulkner, 'The King and the Star-Religion in the Pyramid Texts', *Journal of Near Eastern Studies*, Vol. 25, 1966, p. 160.

[34] Alan Gardiner, 'Review of J. Fraser's *The Golden Bough*', *Journal of Egyptian Archaeology*, Vol. 2, 1915, pp. 121–6.

[35] Frankfort, op. cit., p. 86.

[36] A. Piankoff, *The Pyramid of Unas* (Princeton, 1969), pp. 4–5.

Appendix 4: The Cosmic Order, the Egyptian Calendar and Christianity

[1] Ahmed Osman, *Moses and Akhenaten*, Bear Publications Inc. New York, 2004. See also Timothy Freke and Peter Gandy, *The Laughing Jesus*, Harmony Books Inc, New York, 2005.

[2] Timothy Freke and Peter Gandy, *The Jesus Mysteries: Was the original*

Jesus a pagan god?, Harmony Books Inc., New York, 1999.

3   Richard A. Parker, *The Calendar of Ancient Egypt*, Chicago, 1950, p. 56.

4   Belmonte, op. cit., p. 9.

5   Duncan, op. cit., 1999.

6   Calculations for the Gregorian calendar were based on the assumption that the year was 365.2425 days, which is the same as 365 97/400. The rule is that 1 day is added every 4 years as in the Julian calendar, but that leap years are omitted in years that are divisible by 100 but not by 400. In fact, however, the exact solar/tropical year has 365.2422 days, a little less than the assumed value for the Gregorian calendar. This means that every 3,300 years the Gregorian calendar will shift one day in relation to the true solar/tropical year.

7   Anthony J. Spalinger, *Revolutions in Time: Studies in Ancient Egyptian Calendrics*, Van Siclen Books, 1994, p. 51

8   Robert Bauval and Graham Hancock, *Talisman*, Penguin, 2005, p. 119.

Appendix 5: The Death of the Living God

1   This term means the ritual killing of a king. (Margaret Murray, *The Splendour that was Egypt*, Sidgwick and Jackson, 1954, pp. 164–5. See also G.A. Wainwright, *The Sky-Religion in Egypt*, op. cit.).

2   Timothy Freke and Peter Gandi, *The Jesus Mysteries*, Harmony Books Inc., New York, 1999.

3   Sir James Fraser. *The Golden Bough*, 1922, Chapter 24, 'The Killing of the Divine King', pp. 264–82.

4   Ibid., pp. 266–75.

5   Ibid., p. 266.

6   Ibid., p. 274.

7   Ibid., p. 279.

8   Ibid.

9   Ibid., p. 280.

10   Wainwright, op. cit., pp. 14–18.

11   G.A. Wainwright, 'Seshat and the Pharaohs', op. cit., pp. 30–40.

12   Ibid., pp. 21–3.

13   E. Uphill, 'The Egyptian Sed Festival Rites', *Journal of Near Eastern Studies*, Vol. 24, 1965, pp. 365–83. For illustrations see Mirolav Verner, *Abusir, The Realm of Osiris*, The American University in Cairo Press, New York, 2002, p. 83.

14   Wainwright, *The Sky Religion*, op. cit., pp. 24–5.

15 The so-called Sun-King of France Louis XIV apparently at least during one stage of his life was woken up at sunrise.

16 Diodorus Siculus, *Bibliotheca Historica*, Vol. I, pp. 70, 71. Wainwright, op. cit., pp. 25–6.

17 Wainwright, op. cit., p. 26.

18 Joseph Campbell, *Primitive Mythology*, Penguin, 1959, pp. 151–66. Diodorus, *Biblioteca Historica*, Vol. 3, pp. 5–6.

19 Wainwright, 'Seshat and the Pharaohs', op. cit., p. 31.

20 George Hart, *A Dictionary of Egyptian Gods and Goddesses*, Routledge & Kegan Paul, London, 1986, p. 214.

21 Jane B. Sellers, *The Death of Gods in Ancient Egypt*, Penguin, 1992, pp. 285–6.

22 Krupp, op. cit., pp. 25–6.

23 Ibid., p. 6.

24 Hart, op. cit., p. 28.

25 Ibid., pp. 29–30.

26 Herodotus, *Histories* Vol. III, p. 28.

27 Plutarch, *De Iside et Osiride*, Chapter 43.

28 Quoted in Lewis Spence, *Myths & Legends: Egypt*, Dover Publications, New York, 1990, p. 285.

29 Wallis Budge, *The Gods of the Egyptians*, Vol. II, Dover Publications, New York 1969, p. 350.

30 Ibid., p. 29.

31 Sellers, op. cit. p. 292. Many of the sarcophagi of early royal tombs were found 'empty' viz. those of Djoser, Hetepheres I and other Old Kingdom royals. Also early rulers were 'buried' in two places, one being Abydos in the south, and the other being Saqqara in the north, one of the tombs being a 'cenotaph' or symbolic tomb.

32 Wallis Budge, op. cit., p. 349.

33 Ibid., p. 347.

34 Miriam Lichtheim, *Ancient Egyptian Literature*, Vol. I, University of California Press, 1975, p. 53.

35 Wilkinson, op. cit., p. 120–1.

36 Ibid., p. 121.

37 Hart, op. cit., p. 29.

38 Wainwright, op. cit., pp. 30–40.

39 Pyramid Texts, 616.

40 Pyramid Texts, 615–21.

41 E.A. Wallis Budge, *Egyptian Religion*, Barnes and Noble Books, New York, 1994, pp. 101–2.

42 Murray, op. cit.

43 Ibid., p. 164.

44 Ibid. pp. 168–9.

45 Ibid., p. 171, 173. Murray spells Seth as 'Setekh'.

46 A well-preserved scene showing Seshat and Thoth recording the life period in the Tree of Life can be seen at the Temple of Edfu on the upper part of the ceiling of one of the rooms in the north-east part of the temple.

47 Murray, op. cit., p. 179.

48 Wallis Budge, *The Gods of the Egyptians*, Vol. II, op. cit., p. 250.

49 Wainwright, *The Sky Religion*, op. cit., p. 4.

50 Ibid., p. 9.

51 Pyramid Texts, 1,453–6.

52 Pyramid Texts, 1,464–5.

53 Pyramid Texts, 1,472–7.

54 Pyramid Texts, 1,480–2.

55 Henri Frankfort, *Kingship and the Gods*, University of Chicago Press, 1978, ed., p. 79.

Index